D1283822

Charles Dickens: Radical Moralist

Oliver Asking for More.
From *Oliver Twist,* drawn by Cruikshank.

Charles Dickens: Radical Moralist

by Joseph Gold

University of Minnesota Press,
Minneapolis

Printed and bound in Canada

Published in the United Kingdom and India by the Oxford University Press, London and Delhi.

International Standard Book Number: 0-8166-0666-8
Library of Congress Catalog Card Number: 72-80266

In Memoriam: Frederick J. Hoffman.
Gentleman, Scholar, Teacher and Friend.

Contents

Preface

Wherever there is a large body of criticism centred on a single author, and there is now an awesome accumulation of writing about Dickens, the critic who would add to it is in a particularly difficult position. He is anxious to use his precious space to say all he can about his subject, yet he is at the same time compelled to acknowledge his debt to and indicate his awareness of other scholarship. Very often others have said better what needs to be said again for the author's present purposes. Moreover, the best commentaries of the past become the assumptions of the present. Hillis Miller deals with this problem by virtually omitting all reference to other criticism in order "to achieve a maximum of concentration upon Dickens himself."[1] Earle Davis, on the other hand, spends much time in noticing the work of others.[2] I have tried to find my way between these extremes by reference to other criticism, not only where it seemed pertinent or exemplifying but where a point was made more clearly or aptly than I could make it. Among all of the valuable writing that any Dickens scholar must survey, I wish to acknowledge a particular debt to the work of Humphry House, George Orwell, Hillis Miller, Edgar Johnson, Steven Marcus,

George Ford, and Monroe Engel. I am grateful to Lauriat Lane Jr. for his advice, information and conversation. Finally, among those scholars to whom I am deeply indebted, it is a pleasure to acknowledge Lionel Stevenson, who has read the manuscript with great care and made innumerable suggestions for its improvement.

This book has been published with the help of a grant from the Humanities Research Council of Canada, using funds provided by the Canada Council. It could not have been completed without a great deal of hardship and difficulty had it not been generously supported by grants from the University of Manitoba as well. To be able to publish in Canada is for me the best gift of all. I hope all these institutions will regard the book itself as a "thank you."

My wife, Sandra, has acted throughout as typist, critic, and librarian. It is impossible to thank her adequately, or to indicate to anyone else how deeply I have been dependent on her literary insight, her intelligence and her encouragement. Thanks are also due to my students in graduate seminars on Dickens, both at the University of Manitoba and the University of Waterloo, Ontario, for their interest, intelligence and forbearance. I can only hope they have found the exercise to be even half as valuable as I did. In particular I should mention Terence Angus, who gave me special insights to *Dombey and Son*, and Judith Miller who assisted me in developing the *Hamlet* analogy in *Nicholas Nickleby*. I am grateful for the patient assistance rendered to me in the course of research by the librarians at the Pierpont Morgan, the New York Public, the Victoria and Albert, the British Museum, and the University of Manitoba libraries.

I have used the New Oxford Illustrated Dickens throughout as the most readily available complete reprint and all page references to Dickens' novels are to that edition and follow quotations in the text, the title of the novel being given only when it is not the principal subject of the chapter. I have omitted a bibliography because of the availability of *The Stature of Dickens*,[3] my recent centenary listing of Dickens criticism. Part of the chapter on *Oliver Twist* first appeared as an article in *Mosaic*.

The epigraphs that appear before every chapter are designed to broaden very widely the context in which Dickens is usually examined. My own conviction is that we must see Dickens in the mainstream of a literary and intellectual tradition of English art and thought. The persistent quotations from William Blake indicate not only certain complex similarities in his and Dickens' moral or "religious" views, but also that I find Blake's writing more useful as precise and concentrated metaphoric commentary on art, than any other source and the pieces quoted serve to pinpoint some seminal thought in the work to be discussed. This design, of drawing Blake clearly, if indirectly, into my discussion, was conceived before I was aware of, and could thereby take security from, the important new book by F. R. and Q. D. Leavis, with its chapter "Dickens and Blake: *Little Dorrit*," which I have subsequently read, as I have the rest, with great interest.[4]

[1]*Charles Dickens: The World of his Novels* (Cambridge, Mass.: Harvard Univ. Press, 1965).

[2]*The Flint and the Flame: The Artistry of Charles Dickens* (Columbia: Univ. of Missouri Press, 1963).

[3]*The Stature of Dickens* (Toronto: Manitoba and Toronto University Presses, 1970).

[4]*Dickens the Novelist* (London: Chatto & Windus, 1970).

It's coming yet, for a' that
That man to man the world o'er
Shall brothers be for a' that.

ROBERT BURNS

•

I will not cease from Mental Fight,
Nor shall my Sword sleep in my hand
Till we have built Jerusalem
In England's green and pleasant land.

WILLIAM BLAKE

•

I see a beautiful city and a brilliant people rising from this abyss . . .

CHARLES DICKENS

INTRODUCTION

This book began to take firm shape for me when, having formed an initial impression of Dickens' work, I then read certain comments by Humphry House and George Orwell, in what still seem to me the best essays ever written on Dickens.[1] These critics took two popular assumptions and confronted them at a new level of enquiry. It is with these same assumptions that I also am primarily concerned and to which I think Dickens criticism must return. They are "Dickens is a reformer" and "Dickens is a moralist." Two questions inevitably and usefully arise: "What sort of reformer?" and "What sort of morality?" This work is an attempt to look for an answer to these questions. Naturally, other questions arise. How does Dickens' technique serve his moral purposes? What change or growth is there in the literary career? What is the relationship between Dickens the psychologist and Dickens the moralist and reformer? This study places heavy emphasis on the psychology in the fiction, and it is in the psychological investigation of character and its relation to the novel-structure that I have tried to add a further dimension to the consideration of Dickens as a reformer and a moralist. Several medical and psychiatric authorities have been awed and fascinated by Dickens' knowledge of human psychology and his skill in portraying aspects of its workings.[2] Humphry House himself was well aware that Dickens is capable of profound psychological insight: "Whatever language this is [the passage on Carker's flight in *Dombey*] it is not the language of melodrama; it is a tremendous analysis of the psychological effects of guilt, shame and thwarted vanity."[3]

I intend to show that one of Dickens' principal concerns and talents was the exploration of the psychology of behaviour and why this is so. How can we relate this talent for the presentation of states of mind to the moral purposes of the fiction? Humphry House once again crystallizes the critical problem: "One of the problems that face the critic of Dickens is to explain how this intimate understanding of morbid and near-morbid psychology links on to his apparent optimism, and above all to his humour."[4] I hope to show that the answer to this question is central to an understanding of Dickens' fiction. It lies in discovering, through the novels themselves, how the novelist's moral vision can lead first to a satiric and radical anatomy of society in general terms, and then to an analysis of the individual values and states of mind that make up the "fallen" society.

Dickens' canon can be divided along roughly chronological lines into major phases of preoccupation. The first, which I would call Anatomy of Society, describes those earlier novels that centre mainly on the attempt of character to be happily integrated into a hostile and destructive society. The emphasis here is on a society that ought to be radically altered so as to permit the integration of the individual and an end to injustice and cruelty. The second phase could be described as Autonomy of Self, to indicate how the later novels concentrate on the individual character and on the search for freedom and for answers within himself, regardless of how society swirls around him. Society becomes more and more an abstraction and self becomes more and more a concrete reality in Dickens' work. The two divisions are obviously crude yet they serve to give the direction of my reading of the subject.

In other words the vision of a world built on love and wisdom, on uncorrupted or at least redeemed perception, is also a vision of whole, redeemed individuals. Tortured minds and distorted perceptions breed a sick society. The optimism and humour of which House speaks are the signs of the moral visionary; the "intimate understanding of morbid and near-morbid psychology" is the sign of the radical reformer who sees that it is individual corruption and fragmentation that lie as the obstacle before the attainment of his vision. George Santayana, with one eye on Dickens and the other on the torments of his own culture, says: "But for the excellence of the typical single life, no nation deserves to be remembered more than the sands of the sea; and America will not be a success, if every American is a failure."[5] Another critic recently put it this way:

> If a radical is one who goes to the root of things, then Dickens is a radical, and that preoccupation with the condition of man's heart that is sometimes held to be an indication of his political unreality is in fact the proof of his radicalism.[6]

The happy endings of Dickens' novels turn out to be not so

happy, or at least ambivalent, on closer inspection. Dickens seems in every case to be clearly indicating his sophisticated awareness that we have a choice as to the kind of endings we will write for every story, his or our own. What he did explicitly for *Great Expectations* seems implicitly done elsewhere. Pickwick creates his own garden society, but "Messrs. Dodson and Fogg, continue in business, from which they realize a large income, and in which they are universally considered among the sharpest of the sharp." (*Pickwick Papers,* p. 800) Oliver finds a world of love and family harmony, again in a country setting, but Dick has died and Nancy and Fagin have been "butchered." As Amy Dorrit and Arthur become "inseparable and blessed" they move still through a world in which the "arrogant and the froward and the vain, fretted, and chafed, and made their usual uproar." (*Little Dorrit,* p. 826) Every novel has this dual quality, this double-vision ending, and it is here that one may see just how Dickens blended the humourist, the moralist and the social, radical reformer-psychologist. By examining how others have used some of these terms, I can indicate the dimensions of my discussion.

Orwell has pointed out that Dickens was not a reformer in any conventional sense:

> Whatever else Dickens may have been, he was not a hole-and-corner soul-saver, the kind who thinks that the world will be perfect if you amend a few by-laws and abolish a few anomalies.[7]

Humphry House suggests something very similar:

> In dealing with these problems he accepted none of the current curative nostrums without criticism, nor did he substitute any alternative plan of his own. He was not a Benthamite or Philosophical Radical or Chartist or Owenite or Christian Socialist or Young Englander, nor did he start a Dickens party.[8]

He was rather a moralist. "The truth is that Dickens' criticism of society is almost exclusively moral."[9] If Dickens was not a conventional reformer, what sort was he? "Even if Dickens was a bourgeois, he was certainly a subversive writer, a radical, one might truthfully say a rebel."[10] This view of Dickens as a radical was expressed earlier by Trollope: "I never heard any man call Dickens a radical; but if any man ever was so, he was a radical at heart. . . ."[11] Can a moralist be a radical, a subversive, as Orwell suggests?

> But it is not at all certain that a merely moral criticism of society may not be just as "revolutionary" . . . as the politico-economic criticism which is fashionable at this moment. Blake was not a politician, but there is more understanding of the nature of capitalist society in a poem like "I wander through each chartered street" than in three-quarters of Socialist literature.[12]

Not only did Orwell see that the moralist and the radical meet in Dickens but he also managed a penetrating glimpse into the method by which reform could be envisioned by the moralist. "It seems that in every attack Dickens makes upon society he is always pointing to a change of spirit rather than a change of structure."[13] House, too, understands that the moralist-radical might be a visionary closer in some ways to Blake than to Marx. "He [Dickens] made . . . a complete world with a life and vigour and idiom of its own, quite unlike any other world there has ever been."[14] Orwell shows that it is possible to reduce this vision to a single incredibly facile proposition. "His whole 'message' is one that at first glance looks like an enormous platitude: If men would behave decently the world would be decent."[15] What follows in this book might be regarded as a second glance at the implications of such a thesis. I would suggest, moreover, that the resurgent and persistent popularity of Dickens, the way his work has proved adaptable to the popular theatre of two centuries, stems in part precisely from this quality of visionary aspiration for a humanly redeemed world, for a fairy-tale land of joy and protection, where beasts are transformed by a kiss and the frozen princess is awakened and thawed by love. The universal sympathy and pleasure evoked by Dickens' world may depend most on this persistent and profound human desire for personal and social harmony. It is a compulsion that senses that alterations in social structure are a pathetic embodiment of the kind of transformation really wanted; a desire which, for this very reason, puts a high value on the image of more humane social structures. Images of a protected and happier world are the reminder and the reinforcement of a desire for a more profound and total redemption.

Orwell's word "decent" reveals how much remains to be done in Dickens criticism. This study proposes that such a search makes necessary the analysis of evil that gives the novels so much of their extraordinary and memorable force and colour. To my mind no other body of prose (or poetry for that matter, with the inevitable exception of Shakespeare) presents such a searching and vivid and indeed entertaining examination of modes of evil and error or of the psychology of those who are distorted by destructive passions or mistaken values. It is my intention to convince the reader that Dickens' work was, in its fundamental disposition, all of a piece, that it constitutes a unity of vision. It will, I hope, become clear as one moves through these essays that Dickens became through his career increasingly and more deeply concerned with questions implicit in the early works. There are no changes in the author's convictions from Pickwick to Boffin. But there is no John Rokesmith in the early novel, nor could there be, for while Dickens saw perfectly from the start what good and evil looked like, in all their guises, he did not explore their underlying psychology until much later. The question of identity, of self-definition and of truth or distortion in individual personality, increasingly becomes the preoccupation. The necessity for self-awareness, not "in the letter" as it is possessed by Ralph Nickleby, but in the spirit as it is acquired by later characters, becomes more and more the central moral force of Dickens' fiction. Self-deceit, illusion and delusion, rationalization and wish-fulfillment are explored in the Dickens canon with ever-increasing perception and persistence. We are shown self-questioning, the analysis of motivation, the search for the self, the questioning of the past. Only through these means, Dickens comes to say, can the individual reconcile himself to his humanity and thus overcome his weakest impulses and compulsions, and subsequently the evils of his society. The world of automatic response in *Oliver Twist* and of acting and pretension in *Nicholas Nickleby* becomes a world of more intense individual concern and interaction in *Great Expectations* and *Little Dorrit* and *Our Mutual Friend*. Thus it is that the great last novels are more complex and earnest and difficult and "dark." They penetrate more deeply to seek answers to questions inherent from the start. In the search for these answers it seems to happen that Dickens discovers the object of his search to be not social evil at all, but the everlasting existential questions that great art always leads to. It is impossible not to regard Dick's death, at the end of *Oliver Twist,* as connected with social causes, with the workhouse world and inhumane treatment. Increasingly, however, we become aware of a deepening tragic tone. The situations become cosmic and human rather than social. Steerforth dies, Ham dies, Estella suffers, Pip learns, Mrs. Clennam festers, Wrayburn is nearly murdered, not because of bad institutions or inhumane laws. These are personal events bred from the nature of humanity itself. It is in the struggle to understand and portray these complexities that the canon grows richer and more profound. Given that one is born and is human and will die; given that one has a past, parents, class and personality; given that we are driven, deluded, tossed by emotions and desires, how can we move to some personal peace and redemption, to love, to forgiveness, to reconciliation with our humanity?

The moralist must believe that such a peace is possible; that if we have a bad and a good self, a bad and a good angel, as do many of Dickens' characters, a meaningful struggle between them can happen and a victory be achieved. The moralist starts from faith, from a hard foundation of belief that what we do and what we are matters and can be changed. Dickens, as moralist, moves with increasing penetration to the expansion of how this may be done. The novelist ultimately has only models, the philosopher, abstractions. The novelist shows us what moral redemption might look like as perceived by his vision. There is not, in fiction, a moral method to be followed. It is not a theology. Yet more and more Dickens strives to present such a method. His moral vision becomes clearer and more forceful with every work and his desire to be explicit becomes more evident, but this path to goodness, this pilgrims' way, remains elusive. Rokesmith's interior monologue and self-analysis is not, finally, as powerful as the novel's metaphor of drowning and rebirth, the explicit affirmation that change and love and vision are possible. It is the affirmation itself that finally grasps the reader's mind and heart. What never changes in Dickens is the conviction of the value of human love; the methods of expressing that conviction become ever more complex. The following chapters are one attempt to trace that moral quest.

No single book, or library of books, can begin to touch the vastness of Dickens' novels, the hundreds of characters, places, plots, descriptions, observations; the style, the language, the diction, the structure, the mode, the mood; the history, the sociology, the psychology; the influences, the sources, the allusions, the borrowings, the echoes. Each work of criticism must inevitably, furthermore, distort its subject. Dickens was not a philosopher or historian. When we abstract we no longer have Dickens, for his "message," or more properly, his vision, is its embodiment in fiction. Rather we should regard the critic as throwing some tinted illumination on the work which, while it does not itself change, may thereafter appear to the reader in a new and interesting light.

Erich Fromm has said that loving is an art, the most important art of all, and that this art takes its meaning, like all arts, from its being practised, from being a process, yielding rewards in the very act of loving and being in process. I would suggest that loving is part of an even more demanding art, the art of being human. Fielding means something similar when he says: "Life may as properly be called an art as any other; and the great incidents in it are no more to be considered as mere accidents than the several members of a fine statue or a noble poem."[16] To explore the sources and nature of one's humanity, to seek the fringes of one's own human possibilities, to examine the quality of all aspects of one's relations to man and nature, to sound the depths of one's own core of being, these are the characteristics of the art of being human. I would like to show that Dickens is the celebrant of this art. He was the writer who consciously directed the power of his imagination to the creation of a mythology of society. Dickens devoted his creative life to the exploration of social experience, from the fully human being to the fragmented and partially human creature. His novels constitute an unparalleled presentation.

Perhaps we need Dickens today more than ever, for his writing produces that sense of liberating courage, that vision of human complexity and possibility that restores our faith in our own humanity. Whatever else his work may be, however we may disagree on particulars, it is unmistakably a celebration. In this sense, as well as in many others, Dickens is joyously existential in his vision. It is because of Dickens' incredible energy, his manifest engagement with the people and action of his novels and his vision of individual possibility, which when realized or even glimpsed can alone produce a society of a different quality, that I am led to think of his work as a comic quest. It is comic in its faith in the redeemed society peopled by whole human beings; it is a quest characterized by a mocking castigation *en route* of a frenetic society and the fragmented individuals who sustain it. A comic quest is a journey of the imagination undertaken by one who believes that

> There are dark shadows on the earth, but its lights are stronger in the contrast. Some men, like bats or owls, have better eyes for the darkness than for the light. We, who have no such optical powers, are better pleased to take our last parting look at the visionary companions of many solitary hours, when the brief sunshine of the world is blazing full upon them. (*Pickwick Papers,* p. 799)

This "brief sunshine of the world" has, by the last complete novel, become the illumination of the individual face and soul, redeemed by love and brought to life by giving up all the illusions of "Society."

> "Now my wife is something nearer to my heart, Mortimer, than Tippins [Society] is, and I owe her a little more than I owe to Tippins, and I am rather prouder of her than I ever was of Tippins. Therefore, I will fight it out to the last gasp, with her and for her, here in the open field. . . ." The glow that shone upon him as he spoke the words so irradiated his features, that he looked, for the time, as though he had never been mutilated. (*Our Mutual Friend,* p. 813)

This study is an attempt to trace the fictional journey, the quest, from Dickens' perception of the "brief sunshine of the world" to the individual's irradiated face, to a love that can transform the living dead "as though he had never been mutilated." It is every man's quest for meaning. Dickens explores evil without compromise, but he provides us with images of courage and faith. He shows us that more often than not life is neither easy, pretty nor happy, but he also convinces us that it is endlessly entertaining and even, by the end of the canon, meaningful. We can, he says, redeem ourselves by this perception.

Our experience of our own world is not only more than enough, it is all that there is. When we have seen this and have shed all the illusions that distract us from this perception, we are reconciled to our own imaginations and the materials to be perceived. We lose our sense of alienation. We are living instead of thinking about living, and our world becomes infinitely fascinating. It is while we are fascinated, while we are moved by compassion, while we are part of what we see, that we are redeemed. We have left the world of time and entered eternity now. Dickens shows us that the world may be perceived as he perceives it in his fiction. This is the fact of his fiction, one supposes of all great art. Its existence proves its point. We are converted into believers willy-nilly. Dickens could have done this without creating any characters in his fiction who also come to this perception. Had this been the case he would have been a great compassionate satirist, with a kind of Chaucerian detachment, creating a world in which no one perceives what the creator perceives. But the moralist in Dickens would not permit him to remain so detached and he adds to his fiction a whole range of characters who become in their turn joyful, compassionate creators of worlds. Once we have seen the mythological force of this fiction we may lose our fear of identification with these characters, from Pickwick and the Cheerybles to Amy Dorrit and the Golden Dustman. These characters are the artists of being human; they create whole worlds. It is our inadequacy, not their unreality, that makes us so shy of their love and compassion. Strangely enough it is the "good" people in Dickens who have most frequently run foul of the critics. Even Santayana, one of the most sympathetic readers, confesses to this inadequacy, but he is humble and wise enough to see it as his failure and not the author's:

> I must confess, though the fault is mine and not his, that sometimes his absoluteness is too much for me. When I come to the death of little Nell, or to What the Waves were always Saying, or even to the incorrigible perversities of the pretty Dora, I skip. I can't take my liquor neat in such draughts, and my inner man says to Dickens, Please don't. But then I am a coward in so many ways! There are so many things in this world that I skip, as I skip the undiluted Dickens![17]

Many people have the same difficulty with children and the child's perception as do many readers with the loving, compassionate or playful characters of Dickens' novels, and for similar reasons. Indeed, Dickens himself knew this and provided children a central rôle in his fiction, not simply because their perception was valuable to the moralist in him, but because he wanted to expose and explore the inadequacies of those who are alienated from or threatened by children. Blake found the image of the child and the child in adult society equally valuable for his mythology. The moralist as artist is someone who believes in and reveals to us our own possibilities for living more meaningfully. The reformer is someone who wants to see a different society appear by some means or other. When these two figures meet in one, as they did in Dickens, they produce a visionary who sees that society is after all the product of our perception of it. Enlighten our perception, free our imagination, and the society we know must disappear, dissolve and be replaced by a world of grace: this is what the fiction comes to say. Dickens is not concerned with the philosophical question of whether such a world is possible. He makes it happen in his art. There are few artists who leave one with the astonished sense that until we saw with their eyes, until they held their world up for us, we never realized how interesting, how fantastic and finally how ordered, our own had been all along.

In view of my debt to Orwell as acknowledged above, it is appropriate that he should have the last word on the face behind the masks we are about to consider:

> It is the face of a man of about forty, with a small beard and a high colour. He is laughing, with a touch of anger in his laughter, but no triumph, no malignity. It is the face of a man who is always fighting against something, but who fights in the open and is not frightened, the face of a man who is *generously angry*—in other words, of a nineteenth-century liberal, a free intelligence, a type hated with equal hatred by all the smelly little orthodoxies which are now contending for our souls.[18]

[1]Humphry House, *The Dickens World* (London: Oxford Univ. Press, 1941) and *All in Due Time* (London: Hart-Davis, 1955), and George Orwell, "Charles Dickens," in his *Critical Essays* (London: Secker & Warburg, 1946).

[2]Richard A. Hunter and Ida Macalpine, "A Note on Dickens's Psychiatric Reading," *Dickensian* 53 (Jan. 1957): 49-51; James A. Brussel, "Charles Dickens: Child Psychologist and Sociologist," *Psychiatric Quarterly Supplement* 12, Supplement 1 (1938): 163-74; Sir Russell Brain, "Dickensian Diagnoses," *British Medical Journal* (Dec. 24, 1955): 1553-6.

[3]*All in Due Time*, p. 186.

[4]*All in Due Time*, p. 187.

[5]"Dickens," in *The Dickens Critics,* ed. George H. Ford and Lauriat Lane, Jr. (Ithaca, N.Y.: Cornell Univ. Press, 1961), p. 142.

[6]Monroe Engel, *The Maturity of Dickens* (Cambridge, Mass.: Harvard Univ. Press, 1959), p. 70.

[7]Orwell, "Charles Dickens," p. 9.

[8]*The Dickens World,* p. 50.

[9]Orwell, "Charles Dickens, " p. 9.

[10]Orwell, "Charles Dickens," p. 8.

[11]"Charles Dickens," *St. Paul's Magazine* (July 1870): 374.

[12]Orwell, "Charles Dickens," p. 21.

[13]Orwell, "Charles Dickens," p. 21.

[14]*The Dickens World,* p. 224.

[15]Orwell, "Charles Dickens," p. 10.

[16]Henry Fielding, *Amelia,* Vol. 1 (London: Dent, 1962), p. 4.

[17]"Dickens," *The Dickens Critics,* p. 145.

[18]Orwell, "Charles Dickens," p. 56.

"THE FIRST RAY OF LIGHT" THE PICKWICK PAPERS

He that has light within his own clear breast
May sit in the center, and enjoy bright day,
But he that hides a dark soul and foul thoughts
Himself is his own dungeon.

JOHN MILTON

•

"The Mischief is just the same whether a Man does it Ignorantly or Knowingly."

WILLIAM BLAKE

•

"I wonder what these ghosts of mail coaches carry in their bags," said the landlord, who had listened to the whole story with profound attention.

"The dead letters, of course," said the Bagman.

"Oh, oh! To be sure," rejoined the landlord. "I never thought of that."

THE PICKWICK PAPERS

•

Given the depths of Dickens' resourcefulness in choosing names for his characters, it must be of some interest to the reader to note that both Pickwick and his servant have the name Samuel. The reason for this is that they are parts of a whole and together make a unity. If Mr. Pickwick must discover not only the evil of the world, but his own relation to it, it is not surprising that he must acquire his other half, Sam Weller. Pickwick brings to the partnership a resilient faith in human goodness, an unremitting interest in people that provides a motive for action. Weller contributes a worldly wisdom that ensures survival for virtue. They are mutually supportive, they become inseparable. Apart, the one is likely to be crushed by villainy, the other doomed to remain a menial clown. Together they constitute meaning in action, a kind of composite, unassailable virtue.

> "Can such things be!" exclaimed the astonished Mr. Pickwick.
> "Lord bless your heart, sir," said Sam, "why where was you half baptized?" (p. 166)

Innocence has become, in modern critical parlance, the supreme virtue among the values discoverable in literature, yet in *The Posthumous Papers of the Pickwick Club* it is made clear that to be only half-baptized is to be excluded from the community of fallen humanity and therefore to be unable to share in its range of experience, social and psychological. Baptism by experience, by suffering leading to self-discovery, is the underlying and unifying theme of the novel. It is not baptism into a church, but into the larger community of man into which "the church" has been expanded in Dickens' work. Herein lies the clue to Dickens' angry anti-sectarianism. The Fleet becomes a symbol for the condition of humanity and Pickwick's volunteering to go to prison is his adult baptism into the human community. He is, of course, a member of this larger club, willy-nilly. What is required is his recognition and acceptance of his participation. Winkle's sportsmanship, Snodgrass' poetizing, Tupman's gallantry and Pickwick's scientism, are all rôles, playful enough, but fragmenting and separating them. Their descent from Olympus is to be, in one form or another, a model for all of Dickens' fiction. Freedom in *Pickwick Papers* is enlightened perception. Pickwick becomes free by learning the truth about himself and his world, by knowing enough to make meaningful choices, by acquiring free will, being active, rather than being impelled by ignorant instinct, that is, being passive. Paradoxically, this freedom involves being imprisoned, an idea to be later fully developed in *Little Dorrit*. The primary moral impulse in all the fiction is the attempt to represent a search for human personal freedom within the limits of human suffering and mortality. Dickens propels his heroes on a journey towards reconciliation with nature, including human nature. It is perhaps worth noting that in 1836 Darwin returned from his voyage on the Beagle, and Dickens' formative years were spent amidst one of the most significant philosophic and social debates of English history, the debate on natural law and its effects on human free will, theology, and the relations of God and man.[1] It is a debate continued to this day. The issues of this debate inform all of Dickens' fiction, and it may be this fact, in part, that accounts for the extraordinary sense of relevance felt by today's reader of these novels. Dickens attempts in his first novel to show what sort of Grace is possible in the 1830's. Pickwick leaves prison by overcoming his pride, and he does this by recognition of what he shares with his fellow prisoners. His isolation in a prison apartment is not satisfactory. His imprisonment has not defeated Dodson & Fogg. He pays their damages while retaining his righteous indignation. He names them robbers, and having thus identified them accurately he and they go their separate ways. They remain in the world, however, and their robbery will continue. What their evil must not be allowed to do is contaminate Pickwick or sour him. It is a theme fully developed in Jarndyce of *Bleak House*, a later Pickwick.

There are three kinds of law that to one degree or another appear in *Pickwick*. One is the obvious social law of the courts, the existence of which suggests the presence of the second kind, natural law, which incorporates the evil that is part of man's nature, an inescapable feature of imperfectible man, and a central interest for Dickens the moralist. The third kind of law is the theological attempt to control evil. The history of the Judeo-Christian tradition may broadly be divided into two attempts to cope with the fact of evil. There is first Mosaic Law, an attempt to control evil by a process of elimination, of excluding enough major sins to leave the vessel more or less clean. Secondly there is Grace through Divine intervention, the provision of intercessors who by perfect example mediate between God and Man. The perfect intermediary, Christ, is half-god and half-man, able to interpret one to the other. For Dickens, as for many of his contemporaries, neither of these orthodoxies was satisfactory, yet the moral life must still be insisted upon. Neither law nor theology nor orthodox faith, neither ritual nor sacrament, church nor state, would answer. It is out of this need that the full flowering of humanism is found in Dickens. Partaking on the one hand of the rigour and discipline of Old Testament law, and on the other of the humanist perfection and charity embodied in Christ, it is wholly neither. Dickens' morality adds an element of ancient Stoic accord and a highly modern psychological exploration of self, to the image of a tenuous Grace. Redemption is to be achieved, not later but now, and not by casting off the world, but by compassionate acceptance of it. Evil is part of the human composition, a force not in "them" but in us. Pretension, hypocrisy and rationalization are dangerous because they deceive us as to our own nature. We take ourselves in first. Hillis Miller says that "Pickwick must, in a way, be his own God."[2] It would be nearer to the truth to say that he must be his own man. God is undoubtedly at work and Dickens' writing is imbued with a sense of universal order, an order too large to be perceived by most of his characters, but whose presence is felt strongly by the author. The struggle of all Dickens' heroes is an attempt to apprehend a great Divine system and their relation to it. It is a striving in one form or another to see in all things a meaning that is agonizingly elusive, but Dickens' insistence that the meaning is there cannot be escaped. The attempt to give a shape to human affairs is the dynamic of Dickens' art which becomes a private theology much as Blake's poetry is a private mythology.

Quite suddenly we are told in *The Pickwick Papers* that there is a Moses Pickwick, a conjunction of names that deeply affects Sam Weller. A Pickwick ought rightly to be a Samuel. Now Samuel was the anointer of kings, forerunner of the house of David who had his fulfillment in Christ. Mr. Pickwick does not share his servant's indignation and enters the coach of his namesake as willingly as he later enters prison, to emerge a wiser man. It is tempting here to conclude that, the name Boz being a playful corruption of Moses, Dickens is saying something extremely sophisticated, and subtle, about himself.[3] For my own part I see this inserted joke about the coachman, Moses Pickwick, as a commentary, albeit recondite and cursory, on the necessity to reconcile law and grace. Even if one concludes, most obviously, that Sam Weller is being merely anti-semitic, this is still, nevertheless, also anti-Mosaic, in the Christian context of the novel, and it is important to remember that before *Pickwick Papers* was concluded, Dickens had begun work on *Oliver Twist,* which explores this Mosaic versus Grace dialectic thoroughly. Nor is the Mosaic law without its contemporary parallel for Dickens. His reaction to the wave of evangelicalism, the new Puritan spirit typified in Sunday observance and a hostility to children and their "carnal" nature, is everywhere evidenced in his fiction from *Sketches* to the end. At first glance Dickens' morality looks like the goodness-of-heart Christian liberalism that so many critics have found it to be, but in reality his is a much more penetrating analysis of human dilemmas. Evil, Dickens is saying, and inhumane institutions, are the result of too much concentration on human sin. By persuading people of their badness, a cycle of sin and suffering is generated that nothing short of personal revolution will change. This is the explanation of the ending of *Pickwick.*

> Let us leave our old friend in one of those moments of unmixed happiness, of which, if we seek them, there are ever some, to cheer our transitory existence here. There are dark shadows on the earth, but its lights are stronger in the contrast. Some men, like bats or owls, have better eyes for the darkness than for the light. We, who have no such optical powers, are better pleased to take our last parting look at the visionary companions of many solitary hours, when the brief sunshine of the world is blazing full upon them. (p. 799)

Dickens' career is an artistic struggle to realize in fiction the images of personal redemption, the only hope for a more humane society. The novels are never celebrations of mindless goodness. They are explorations of the uses to be made of the good that is part of the human make-up.

Critical writing abounds with influences on *Pickwick* traced from the eighteenth century. Without wishing to add to this list, I believe it is fruitful to consider what happens in *Tom Jones.* Tom sets out to find Sophia, that is, both wisdom and a wife. Like Pickwick, he is "half-baptized" in his knowledge of his origins, of the evil of Blifil and of the goodness of Allworthy. He, too, completes his baptism and finally achieves his goal. Sophia is won and in his ideal marriage he unites law and liberation, order and joy. Marriage as a symbolic union of human beings with each other, with themselves and with God becomes the most important image of human reconciliation in Dickens' novels. Marriage is, ideally, a voluntary submission to the laws of God and society and these include a recognition of one's own nature. Wherever marriage falls short of this ideal it is castigated by Dickens. When it achieves this ideal union it represents a joyous fulfillment, a final liberation in idyllic captivity, as it does for Rose and Harry, Nicholas and Madeline, Arthur and Amy, and Rokesmith and Bella. Let us at this point indulge in a little harmless critical fantasy. It is both amusing and possible to think of Dickens, in his last complete novel, as projecting versions of himself into the fiction. After all, we have had his mother and his father and his sister-in-law and his wife in the fiction—upon this all critics seem agreed—why not the inimitable himself? He is Boffin, the golden dustman, who grew from rags to riches and by manipulating the characters and events of the story made all come right in the end. He is Wegg, who declines and falls and drops into poetry; who gives, in a sense, public readings and is a humbug, like the rest of us, looking for treasure that isn't there. He is Mr. Venus, the articulator of human bones, perfect aphorism for the artist, painstakingly putting together the bits and pieces to produce a human form. It is Mr. Venus, we remember, whom the ailing Dickens at the end of his career, causes to reply to Wegg's "never say die," that it is not saying it that he objects to so much as doing it. It is a coincident point of biography and fiction that the sensitive reader must find extraordinarily moving. We are still, for the sake of argument, in the realm of fantasy, and while there, we can find in *Pickwick* some career-opening parallel to the finale of *Our Mutual Friend.* The first sentence of the first novel begins, "The first ray of light which illumines the gloom . . . ," which seems to be a provokingly loud announcement of the young genius embarking on an illustrious career. This impression is not dispelled by the actual framework of the plot, in which Pickwick is to set forth on the Earth, like an Olympian god on a voyage of discovery, such a voyage as Dickens himself is about to undertake in a number of dimensions. Like Pickwick, Dickens has so far confined himself to researches in, so to speak, "Hornsey, Highgate, Brixton and Camberwell," (*Sketches by Boz*), which is all well and good, but not to be compared to the "benefits which must inevitably result from carrying the speculations of that learned man into a wider field . . . ." (p. 1) If all this is fantasy, it can nevertheless be critically valuable, for by making this kind of whimsical concession to the novel's opening we are led to an awareness of its highly self-conscious themes, themes which are to remain central to Dickens' fiction for the rest of his life.

Steven Marcus uses the term "unconscious" in speaking of the novel's achievement,[4] and A. O. J. Cockshutt, in the most patronizing book on Dickens that I know of, says of Dickens that, "When he was thinking, he unconsciously assumed that religion was irrelevant."[5] W. H. Auden, in his celebrated essay "Dingley Dell and The Fleet," comes nearest to granting significance to the novel, though he, too, believes that it happened unconsciously: "The conclusion I have come to is that the real theme of *Pickwick Papers*—I am not saying Dickens was consciously aware of it and, indeed, I am pretty certain he was not—is the Fall of Man."[6]

The one overriding claim made for Dickens' art in these pages is his consciousness as an artist. This is to say that not only were his purposes clear to the author, but that his control of language and thought and subject and structure in the novels was as complete as it is in only the finest of writing. I am not saying that Dickens' judgement was always perfect, as hindsight may show. In a game, a competitor may execute perfectly a carefully selected play, yet find at the end of the game that he should have chosen some other move in order to win. Certainly Dickens' judgement becomes more unerring as his career proceeds. The range of devices, the precision of language, the manipulation of plot and a hundred other skills are more evident in the later work. What I am saying is that, all along, Dickens does have a full control of the materials available to him. This book assumes that a full understanding of the novels depends upon granting Dickens a profound, controlling intelligence.

It is curious how many elements of the religious can be found in *Pickwick*. G. K. Chesterton speaks of "a sense as of the gods gone wandering in England,"[7] and W. H. Auden reads the novel as an allegory of Genesis.[8] The celebration of Christmas at Dingley Dell is perhaps the best remembered of all the events of the novel and as much as anything else has given rise to the *philosophie de Noël* attributed to Dickens, that leads to Maurois calling him "a blend of Pickwick and Marcus Aurelius, a Christmas-tree Epictetus."[9] We are told in the novel that "Muggleton is an ancient and loyal borough, mingling a zealous advocacy of Christian principles with a devoted attachment to commercial rights." (p. 87) There is also the major theme of Stiggins' running battle with the elder

Mr. Weller. Dickens makes his own position clear when he emphasizes what the "shepherd" did not say.

> Mr. Stiggins did not desire his hearers to be upon their guard against those false prophets and wretched mockers of religion, who, without sense to expound its first doctrines, or hearts to feel its first principles, are more dangerous members of society than the common criminal. . . . (p. 637)

Mr. Pickwick, setting out to discover the nature of the world, does indeed go on a quest.

> The true dramatic center of *Pickwick Papers* is not the unraveling of any plot, nor is it the change of Pickwick or of any other character. It is Pickwick's gradual discovery of the real nature of the world.[10]

And that means his discovery of himself. In his last speech of the novel, Pickwick voices the hope that he has gained "enlargement of my mind, and the improvement of my understanding." (p. 797) The author knows the evils of the world that Pickwick discovers. It is for Pickwick to learn that he is an integral part of that world, to discover his relationship to it. From the beginning Pickwick regards himself as apart from the world he inhabits. In his belief that the world can be observed and recorded as by a god, he overlooks his own humanity. Not only his gullibility, but his passion, his self-righteousness, his share of the humbug, must be encountered. Not only is Pickwick's scientific "objectivity" satirized, but there is a persistent ridicule of the absurd self-deception in Pickwick's conception of himself as detached observer. We begin with this at once, in the case of the cabman's ancient horse, and it continues until Pickwick, with his modern lantern, becomes someone else's datum. The comedy of all this lies in the observer's failure to account for his own perception in determining the outcome of his "experiment," and reveals on Dickens' part a highly sophisticated and modern view of the dangers of "fact." More importantly it is the basis for Dickens' moral point—that Pickwick cannot know the world until he knows himself as part of it.

In discussing this I am touching the very centre of the novel's plot, which coincides exactly with its moral climax. There is, in other words, a distinct relationship between the Pickwick who observes cab horses, who collects bogus runic inscriptions, and the Pickwick who is sued for breach of promise. From his scrape with the cabman, his desertion by Jingle, through all the mishaps and their consequences so liberally sprinkled through the novel, down to Pickwick's discovery of his relation to law, courts and prisons, we find a carefully documented portrait of Pickwick's failure to know himself. The "science" of human affairs, of society, is shown to begin with self-knowledge, if it can have any validity at all. What is Pickwick but an amateur sociologist, guilty of the same errors as his fashionable and equally absurd successors of our own day? His is the failure to take account of human nature, and his attempt to make the data fit his preconceptions and desires would, in a less comic novel, lead to a good deal of cruelty and suffering. Here it leads to both a comic misunderstanding and to self-awareness. But even here one cannot escape the sense that the trial of Bardell versus Pickwick, and its almost surreal courtroom comedy, has a kind of poetic truth to its condemnation of Pickwick. Funny though it is, innocent though he is, is there not something heartless, or potentially heartless, in Pickwick's complete failure to have seen Mrs. Bardell at all? It is an error of which Boffin, the comprehensively sensitive latter-day Pickwick, is incapable. So what we have here is precisely the plot form requested by Seymour as a vehicle for his illustrations, with all its scrapes and mistakes and bathos as originally conceived, but with the addition of a highly controlled moral quest for self-knowledge underlying all. The climax of Pickwick's knowledge-gathering is the trial for breach of promise, a charge of which Mr. Pickwick is innocent. Ironically, while the prosecution tries to present the defendant as a vicious, designing Lothario, it is precisely because of his naiveté, ignorance, and blindness that he finds himself in court at all. That Mr. Pickwick could be a desirable male and an eligible bachelor never crosses his mind. Compare him for instance with Tony Weller, who is well aware of his own attractions and is forced to spend much time in defending himself against designing widows. Pickwick, however, frequently participates in embarrassing encounters with the fair sex, and it is his total ignorance of Mrs. Bardell that leads to his indiscreet double-meaning, when he proposes to his landlady that he is about to take a man, and is supposed to be announcing his intention to take a wife. His fault is not very different from Mr. Winkle's with Mrs. Pott, and the hapless Winkle comes close to landing himself in an equally dangerous situation. Dickens makes his point quite clear when he has Mr. Pickwick, in a very superior manner, make a speech to his friends on their sexual indiscretion:

> "Is it not a wonderful circumstance," said Mr. Pickwick, "that we seem destined to enter no man's house without involving him in some degree of trouble? Does it not, I ask, bespeak the indiscretion, or worse than that, the blackness of heart—that I should say so!—of my followers, that, beneath whatever roof they locate, they disturb the peace of mind and happiness of some confiding female? Is it not, I say—" (p. 243),

at which point a messenger arrives with notice of Mrs. Bardell's suit. Be it "blackness of heart" or not, the weaknesses of nature that are everywhere here documented are shared by all, including the angel in gaiters. Pickwick is not a god, after all, and it is his own humanity and his human brotherhood that he must learn. Paradoxically it is the subjective observer who becomes the good "scientist." This is exactly illustrated by the Pickwick who finally walks the Fleet and is able to see those who are imprisoned like himself. Now he can exercise his compassion for Jingle, whom he has pursued so relentlessly. Pickwick gains stature by losing distance. That he and Jingle find themselves in the same prison, is not a mere trick for neatly wrapping up the plot.

This idea of a humanized redemption through perception and behaviour, of moral grace through compassion and understanding, informs the entire novel, including most of its diversionary tales, for instance in the story of Gabriel Grubb, which is a forerunner of *A Christmas Carol.* There is a cynical rejection of any knowledge of our link with an afterlife, and the frequent supernaturalism that does occur, takes the form of comic tales that comment precisely on some moral failure in life. Sam's cobbler room-mate in the Fleet tells of a relation who "went off" and in answer to Sam's question, "where?" says,

> "How should I know where he went?" said the cobbler, speaking through his nose in an intense enjoyment of his pipe. "He went off dead." (p. 620)

The pleasure the speaker takes in his pipe is a Dickensian pleasure, that is, one of those pleasures which signify a human reconciliation to one's mortal lot. The effect of mentioning such an enjoyment here is to reinforce the cobbler's wisdom in confining his speculation to what he knows. Tony Weller's conversation is always in the same spirit and is the antithesis of Stiggins', whose pleasures are surreptitious and rationalized by nonsensical abstraction drawn from religious cant. Stiggins cannot indulge himself without some pietistic rhetoric that anticipates the later Chadband. The death of Tony Weller's wife brings to the fore this moral antithesis between Weller's outlook and Stiggins'. We are told of the dying woman's enlightenment,

> "I begin to see now," she says, "ven it's too late, that if a married 'ooman vishes to be religious, she should begin vith dischargin' her dooties at home, and makin' them as is about her cheerful and happy, and that vile she goes to church, or chapel, or wot not, at all proper times, she should be wery careful not to con-wert this sort o' thing into a excuse for idleness or self-indulgence." (p. 733)

Shortly after, Dickens constructs the following revealing dialogue:

> "Vell," said Sam, venturing to offer a little homely consolation, after the lapse of three or four minutes, consumed by the old gentleman in slowly shaking his head from side to side, and solemnly smoking; "vell, gov'ner, ve must all come to it, one day or another."
>
> "So we must, Sammy," said Mr. Weller the elder.
>
> "There's a Providence in it all," said Sam.
>
> "O' course there is," replied his father with a nod of grave approval. "Wot 'ud become of the undertakers vithout it, Sammy?"
>
> Lost in the immense field of conjecture opened by this reflection, the elder Mr. Weller laid his pipe on the table, and stirred the fire with a meditative visage. (p. 733)

It is indeed an "immense field of conjecture," for Dickens' comic genius has the father characteristically misunderstand his son's "Providence" and take the term literally, as provide-ence. In rejecting this "religious" consolation, and converting it to a more prosaic one by his own brand of comprehension, Tony recalls the shepherds and confirms his wife's discovery, that the only true consolation for death is in the well-lived life. Put on his guard by his acquaintance with false religion, the elder Weller will accept no false and conventional consolation. The link between this and Mr. Venus's comment that since he must die he "can't afford to waste time groping for nothing in cinders," suggests just how thorough is the unity of Dickens' work.

However powerful is the influence of Fielding and Smollet, Sterne and Richardson on Dickens' work, the eighteenth-century insistence on a classical order and symmetry is over. By the time of Pickwick, a more urgent moral necessity has become evident. The social cracks cannot be papered over, the end of biblical literalism requires a new moral imperative. The story the bagman's uncle tells of a journey of kidnap and rescue and romance, beginning in a graveyard for mail coaches of a bygone era, reads like a parody of *Clarissa Harlowe*. What is carried in these ghostly mail coaches of yesterday, asks a listener. "Dead letters, of course." We should remember that Richardson's novel is written entirely in the epistolary form. Dead letters are those for which no address can be found, and this comic tale should be read as Dickens' announcement that his audience is no longer to receive those amusing but ghostly romances of a past time. But dead letters are also laws that are no longer honoured, the laws of the prophets and churches of an earlier age. New prophets and new laws are called for, and Dickens, in the first flush of a genius arrived, in the sparking of the rocket that was to light the cultural sky of the English-speaking world for more than thirty years, offers his nineteenth-century readers "the first ray of light," the new images of grace and redemption, of human goodness humanly arrived at, that were to grip the minds of millions of readers for a century. The almost incredible power that Dickens exercised over audiences, vast in range and class and number, was not achieved merely because his work was brilliant fun or vivid narrative. That power derived from moral images that it was possible to accept. In Dickens' time there was an audience thirsting for hope, desperate for images of moral redemption, anxious to *see* how they and their world might be better than they seemed to be. There were millions who wanted, not a debate between Huxley and Newman, but gripping parables about the struggle between goodness and evil in which they were actually engaged, even engulfed. Dickens was truly the voice of the nineteenth century.

THE PICKWICK PAPERS

[1]For an excellent but brief discussion of the religious background to the early nineteenth century see Robert M. Young, "The Impact of Darwin on Conventional Thought," in *The Victorian Crisis of Faith,* ed. Anthony Symondson (London: S.P.C.K., 1970).

[2]*Charles Dickens: The World of His Novels,* p. 32.

[3]I am indebted for this observation to a remarkable paper, to my knowledge unpublished as yet, given by Steven Marcus at the Edmonton Dickens' Centennial Conference in 1970.

[4]*Dickens: From PICKWICK to DOMBEY* (New York: Basic Books, 1965), p. 18.

[5]*The Imagination of Charles Dickens* (London: Methuen, 1961), p. 13.

[6]In *Dickens; A Collection of Critical Essays,* ed. Martin Price (Englewood Cliffs, N.J.: Prentice-Hall, 1967), p. 68.

[7]*"The Pickwick Papers," The Dickens Critics,* p. 109.

[8]"Dingley Dell and The Fleet."

[9]André Maurois, *Dickens* (New York: Ungar, 1967), p. 163.

[10]*Charles Dickens: The World of His Novels,* p. 27.

"AN ITEM OF MORTALITY" OLIVER TWIST

It is Christmas Day in the workhouse, and the cold, bare
walls are bright
With garlands of green and holly, and the place is a
pleasant sight;
For with clean-washed hands and faces in a long and
hungry line
The paupers sit at the table, for this is the hour they dine.

GEORGE R. SIMS

●

So now the whole thing has a happy end . . . In reality the end is usually bad. The reply to one kick in the pants is another kick in the pants. The queen's messenger doesn't come very often. . . . So don't pursue lawbreakers too eagerly; soon frost will come without any help, for it is cold—Remember the dark and the great cold in this valley that echoes with the sounds of misery.

BERTOLT BRECHT

●

Dickens wrote in 1865, almost three decades after *Oliver Twist*:

> But, that my view of the Poor Law may not be mistaken or misrepresented, I will state it. I believe there has been in England, since the days of the STUARTS, no law so often infamously administered, no law so often openly violated, no law habitually so ill-supervised. In the majority of the shameful cases of disease and death from destitution that shock the Public and disgrace the country, the illegality is quite equal to the inhumanity—and known languge could say no more of their lawlessness.[1]

By this time the horrors of the workhouse were so well established in the English scene that they were destined to become part of British social legend, a byword for total degradation. So, for the thirty-odd years of his productive career, Dickens was preoccupied with the use and abuse of the Poor Law. When he turned his full attention to the subject in his second novel, he did so with analytical intelligence and with an attempt to explore the relationships between the poorhouse and the laws pertaining to it, between the society that was willing to pass and support such laws and tolerate in its midst the consequent social horrors, and the existence in such a society of an elaborate underworld of thieves, rogues, murderers and fugitive children. In *Oliver Twist* Dickens combines a survey of the actual social scene with a metaphoric fiction designed to reveal the nature of such a society when exposed to a moral overview. "I had read of thieves by scores," says Dickens in his preface to *Oliver Twist,* ". . . but I had never met (except in Hogarth) with the miserable reality." (p. xv) It is after Hogarth that *Oliver Twist* is also called *The Parish Boy's Progress.* George Gissing, one of the earliest intelligent and serious Dickens critics, takes this influence into account:

> . . . the life of the English poor as seen by Dickens in his youth had undergone little outward change from that which was familiar to Hogarth, and it is *Oliver Twist* especially that reminds us of the other's stern moralities in black-and-white. Not improbably they influenced the young writer's treatment of the subject.[2]

He goes on, "half-a-dozen faces in *Oliver* have the very Hogarth stamp, the lines of bestial ugliness which disgust and repel."[3] Edgar Johnson tells us that at Gadshill there was a "staircase with its Hogarth prints."[4]

The mere recognition of one more eighteenth-century influence on Dickens would not in itself be especially significant, but a close look at the Hogarth illustrations themselves begins to throw a great deal of light, not only on *Oliver* but on the texture of all Dickens' work. For one thing, the illustrations of Cruikshank, and later of Browne, over which Dickens kept such rigorous control, and about which he became increasingly demanding and difficult to please,[5] reflect closely the qualities of the Hogarth engravings. Both present the spirit of satiric grotesquerie, the absurd juxtaposition of people and things, the comic savagery of social exposé. The gross kitchen-master, stunned by Oliver's famous request; the kittens playing before the fire with their mother, while Mr.

Bumble courts Mrs. Corney, the "mother" of the workhouse; the outrage and chaos of the scene wherein tiny Oliver "plucks up a spirit" and looms over the cowering Noah while the powerful Charlotte beats the child and screams for help: all of these are purely Hogarthian in spirit. But even more worthy of note is the very structure and intent of *Oliver Twist*. Dickens says in his preface that in spite of wide reading (and it must have been much wider than any critic has been able or willing to acknowledge) it was only in Hogarth that he found the "miserable reality" of the underworld (p. xv). Dickens had never *read* of this reality, and so he sets out to fill the literary gap and to present this reality in fiction as he had "met" it, that is, seen it, in Hogarth. The "reality" of which Dickens speaks was an underworld stripped of glamour. There was nothing before *Oliver,* indeed there is probably still nothing in English literature outside of Dickens' writing, that comes to grips so surely with the psychology and circumstances of the criminal, nothing else that presents the shabbiness, the fear, the terrifying *ennui,* with such power and clarity or with less pretense. "In every book I know, where such characters are treated of, allurements and fascinations are thrown around them." (p. xv) Nor has the material of popular entertainment altered this situation very much. The detective story, the Hollywood gangster, the vigilante, Batman's enemies and the prison escape and glamour of the human hunt reappear continually to suggest that the attraction of the criminal world is as strong as ever and the depiction of the criminal and his life as unrealistic as any escapist could wish. Dickens the moralist decided therefore to make a literary reversion to Hogarth—significantly retaining the terms for pictorial art in his statement of intention.

> It *appeared* to me that to draw a knot of such associates in crime as really did *exist;* to *paint* them in all their deformity, in all their wretchedness, in all the squalid misery of their lives; to *show* them as they really were, forever skulking uneasily through the dirtiest paths of life, with the great black ghastly gallows closing up their *prospect*, turn them where they might; it *appeared* to me that to do this, would be to attempt a something which was needed, and which would be a service to society. (p. xv, my italics)

The idea of a "Progress" is an ironic and satiric version of the picaresque novel, the most repeated form of eighteenth-century writing. In Hogarth the progress is towards disease, prison or death. Neither the Harlot nor the Rake is lucky or enlightened en route and they sink inexorably. Dickens has characteristically altered this movement into the form of the comic quest so that, true to his inveterate humanistic desire, he can take and offer the comfort and possibility of a wish-fulfillment ending. And yet this ending is deliberately ambivalent, coming as it does after some of the bitterest of social satire and some of the nearest brushes with disaster. We shall go into this later in more detail, but it is sufficient to say now that the shift from descent in the Hogarth hero to ascent in Oliver does not in any modal way alter the Hogarthian quality of the latter. Like the Rake or Harlot, Oliver is only his creator's pretext, a vehicle for social satire. The Progress technique provides the opportunity for a searching analysis of the society through which the hero passes, its values, its patterns of behaviour, its human consequences. Oliver is a touchstone of virtue whose passivity tests by its human presence the world it encounters.

It was no surprise to Dickens, and it should be no surprise to us, that the appearance of *Oliver* was greeted with various kinds of anger and dismay.[6] What Dickens actually did in *Oliver Twist* was to humanize the criminal. This was not readily forgiven, for to humanize the criminal is to show his relationship to the reader, who would prefer to regard him as another species. Dickens' intention was to break down the whole elaborate, abstract structure of moral and social cant which enables the remote, responsible, concerned and patronizing citizen to view the under-and-other-world from a distant pinnacle of respectability. Dickens violated the comfort of inverted-telescope morality, he destroyed the myth that the criminal is either gallant and amusing, and thus unreal and not a threat, or a monster, the "type" of evil, and thus, again, completely unrelated to "normal" people. Once make him merely pathetic, and the reader is threatened personally and socially. This was of course precisely Dickens' intention. If the criminal is simply human and humanly wrong, he must be related to the other figures of the society, to the underside of which he clings and off which he feeds. If the criminal is related to us, indeed is part of us, then we must examine ourselves to see how evil survives and flourishes. No sooner is Fagin or Sikes real than he begins to be felt and must be met, confronted, contended with, even, most difficult of all, understood. Illustrations of social blindness and comfortable self-delusion are contained within the novel itself. Nancy, for instance, represents a world of whose existence Rose was totally unaware. Not until she is aware of it can she be of proper use to Oliver, who is one of the links between Nancy's and Rose's worlds. Nancy and Rose both care for Oliver, but until they come together Oliver cannot be saved. Again, only Oliver sees Monks and Fagin in the country. For the others the menace exists by report only, just as Brownlow fails completely to comprehend the nature of the threat to Oliver. The boy cannot be saved until the evil around him ceases to be theoretical for his guardians. Thus it comes about that a great gulf develops between the reader's view of Fagin's world, a view permitted by Dickens, and the "respectable" characters' view of that world. Nor is this secret knowledge, shared by Oliver and the reader, ever attained by the others. The police, the crowd, the court, the mob, servants and hotel employees, all regard the thieves through a veil of convenient assumptions. The point is not so much that these particular assumptions are wrong, but that any assumptions prevent their possessor from ever looking at the individual. Not until Rose meets Nancy, face to face, and is forced to see, listen and understand, does she know that such a person not only exists, but is fully human, with her own story, hunger, pride, love and terror. Nancy in the hotel lobby is merely a shabby symbol of social evil and female degradation. Nancy in the room with Rose is flesh and blood. The same may be said of the Dodger's trial, Sikes' flight and Fagin's end. Even the retreat from the Maylies' house after the attempted burglary reveals a pathetically human terror and desperation which strips Toby Crackit of all pretense at glamour and shows how Sikes is forced to live. So it is seen that the criminal figures are just as human as the respectable citizens. Just as all parts of the plot, and all its characters collide finally in a kind of nuclear dispersion, so have they in reality been related parts of a nuclear cohesion all along. This human and social unity, the ironic pattern of which is in Hogarth, is, in Dickens' world, shown to be obscured only by the pretensions, assumptions, alienations, falsehoods and self-deceptions by which people isolate and blind themselves.

Where Hogarth is limited by his cynicism, Dickens, however angry, sad, satiric or frustrated he is, never becomes the cynic. His fiction puts its Hogarthian satire into perspective by adding to it a humanist vision of what society might be, if we could only see what it really is, not in an impossibly remote future, but in the here and now. Dickens makes this clear by an examination of the nature of love as the final refuge for the wandering Oliver, who en route encounters a whole range of characteristic social attitudes towards people. Love is merely a kind of perception. It is this double vision of a fallen world coincident with a world of grace, with Oliver passing between them, that gives the novel its mythological power and its overwhelming moral force. How the Parish Boy moves from being a statistical non-human neutrality, an "item of mortality," to an apprentice, a "pal," a foundling, a half-brother, a foster-child, a nephew, a brother, and finally a son, thus inheriting a world of love, is the subject of this chapter. The progress skirts the edge of a precipice, on the other side of which is disgrace and death, to which Oliver comes perilously close. Though Dickens' vision of human possibility grew and deepened in his later work, his technical mastery, his flawless structure and supremely wrought design are fully evident in *Oliver Twist.*

I

J. Hillis Miller has said that Oliver's search is for identity[7] and Steven Marcus has said that Oliver's search is for inheritance.[8] Perhaps they are saying the same thing, for there is no identity without inheritance. The family is society. The outcast of society is one who, for one reason or another, has no familial place. "Who is my mother?" is no step at all from "Who am I?" Oliver fights Noah Claypole, and will fight all the world if necessary, out of a desperate need to preserve all he has, an image of his mother, and thus a sense of origin and his very existence. But the jargon of "identity" and "inheritance" really does violence to what actually takes place in *Oliver Twist.* Oliver has, of course, no character. Dickens chooses in this case to avoid the whole vexed question of heredity and environment. Not that he is unaware of these problems. As a gesture to the one he offers the token comment, "But nature or inheritance had implanted a good sturdy spirit in

Oliver's breast." (p. 5) As an indication that he knows exactly what such an early treatment can produce in reality, Dickens tells us that "The simple fact was, that Oliver, instead of possessing too little feeling, possessed rather too much; and was in a fair way of being reduced, for life, to a state of brutal stupidity and sullenness by the ill-usage he had received." (p. 25) This is very close to what does happen to Smike in the next novel. But Dickens does not wish to pursue how Oliver might have attained his goodness in this "morality-play," so much as he is anxious to elaborate the consequences of Oliver's presence in the world. He is the child-touchstone and while he is really part of a satiric tradition, of which *Joseph Andrews* is another example, it is still necessary to point out why Dickens makes Oliver so passive a figure and so bland a personality. There are two principal reasons and they are central to Dickens' single design. In the morality-metaphor the passive goodness of Oliver is contrived to place all the emphasis in the novel on the reactions to him. As others respond to him so shall they be judged. No idea is more central to Dickens than that the world will be judged as it uses the children who inherit it. The passivity of Oliver leaves the responses of others to him unadulterated—there can be no confusion that he is somehow responsible for them, except by eliciting a response of any kind. He simply is. They must take him as they find him, and they find him as *they* are, not as he is. The second part of this design, not separate from it, is that the reader is almost totally prevented from involving himself emotionally with Oliver. Satire calls for a cerebral reader-response, not a visceral identification. This is its overriding characteristic. The neutrality of the reader's response to Oliver throws into relief the attitudes to those whom the hero encounters on his journey. Dickens gives enough hints to show that he could have indulged himself by painful and realistic portrayal of social horror. He prefers, and humour is part of this technique, to elicit a more detached moral understanding and judgement from his audience than such horror would produce. Oliver must remain therefore a signpost to society, a kind of geiger-counter to goodness. It is doubtful if Oliver can be said to go on a search at all. Oliver merely wanders, runs away, and things happen to him. The quest is Dickens'; Oliver is the compass, held, as it were, in his creator's hand.

If Oliver can be said to have any motivation it is mostly a negative one, the desire to avoid destruction. His goal is simply life itself, and in the terms of the novel this means quite literally the search for food and love, the two prerequisites to his survival. The single figure who embodies these provisions for the child is, of course, the mother, and we would expect the orphaned Oliver, in his desperate need to satisfy both kinds of hunger, to be intensely conscious of the absence of and need for a mother. The mother and the child form the primal image of the human community. The novel shows that the Progress is marked at every stage by a preoccupation with food and with some suggestion of parental relationships. Dickens shows as the novel proceeds, that society consists of two possible worlds, one sustained by love and the other surviving by indifference and exploitation. One world sees human beings as ends in themselves, the very measure of value, and the other does not *see* human beings, but only jostles against them like a crowd in a hurry, only uses creatures of incidental encounter as means to an abstract end, an end usually regarded as self-helpful, but in fact destructive of the self who uses it as it is of the means used. Simple though this fictional design is, it would be impossible to imagine it worked out with more care or detail. Every step, every contact, every degree of movement on the road to love contributes to the moral analysis and is an integrated function of the total structure.

The usual complaint about Dickens' sentiment is made about *Oliver Twist*. "The incursions of 'sentiment' (i.e. every reference to motherhood, the little scene between Oliver and Dick) are even more unsatisfactory."[9] But if sentiment in fiction is the attempt to elicit an automatic emotional response, Dickens is free of the crime here, for the systematic and continuous recall of motherhood is structurally functional and requires not our tears but our understanding that the mother concept is both embodiment and symbol of child-survival in a world so dehumanized that every child is the child that only a mother can love. Oliver soon learns that in his world the motherless child will probably not live alone; there is every chance he will die in company.

Oliver's birth is of no more significance in the workhouse world than the noting of a piece of merchandise during stocktaking in a commercial warehouse. Indeed, he is named Twist on precisely that kind of cataloguing principle, because he came after Swubble and before Unwin. The latter is yet only a name—who is Unwin, what is he, remains a mystery. Mr. Bumble, the "poet" who devises these names according to alphabetical necessity, thus disinherits and depersonalizes the children before they arrive—the local habitation and the name come first, the children after. All the foundlings are first conceived in the mind of the beadle and once so conceived so they will be born. Thus Oliver, the dehumanized, depersonalized "item of mortality," is born into a world of commercial principles, economic necessity, a commodity, a thing, and a surplus one at that. Oliver is made to undergo many years as an object, an exploitable "item." To become a human being he must encounter the Maylie world which takes its definition by contrast to the Bumble world. When Oliver is born he begins a struggle that presages his future. Balanced between life and death, alone by the birth-bed/death-bed, Oliver commences a career that inverts the norm. Most people in the comfortable middle-class world from which Dickens here departs are born, discover their mother and then seek independence. Oliver is born in isolation, must search for a mother and seek the family and dependence that others have been able to discard. Most fictional heroes before Oliver have grown up, married and become parents. Oliver must "grow down" and discover the childhood and love that he is denied.

The brilliance of this opening chapter lies in its symbolic or metaphoric synthesis of everything that will follow. The whole theme of the novel is contained here.[10] Oliver lies "rather unequally poised between this world and the next." (p. 1) This is one of three occasions in the novel where Oliver is poised in this way between life and death. There is also the illness at Brownlow's and the recovery from the gunshot wound at the Maylies'. Each of these is a progressive rebirth, a resurrection into a higher sphere of love. At each awakening he discovers the presence of some previously unknown ministering "mother." But while Oliver is subsequently fortunate with "mothers" the auguries for motherhood in the workhouse are gloomy indeed. The dying Agnes Flemming of the opening chapter, who has survived her journey on the "king's highway" only long enough to bear her child, receives "consolation" from the "old pauper woman . . . rendered misty" by beer. Her words of comfort are grimly ironic: "Think what it is to be a mother, there's a dear young lamb, do," (p. 2) is spoken by a mother whose children consist of eleven dead ones and two in the "workus." "Workus," for workhouse, augments the comic horror of the "young lamb" who has indeed been led, like a sacrifice, to the slaughter. Only later is this train of association confirmed by the discovery that her name is Agnes, which in fact means lamb. Oliver's mother dies in spite of the talk of "hope and comfort" offered her by way of life-encouragement. We are told that she and hope and comfort "had been strangers too long." Dickens here clearly suggests that life is dependent on some concept of a future (hope) and food and affection (comfort). The room of Oliver's birth now contains the baby, the corpse, the drunken woman and the surgeon. The absence of hope and comfort is strongly conveyed by the scene. The baby is (for us) nameless, the mother is nameless, there is no known father, and the surgeon pronounces death by saying "it's all over, Mrs. Thingummy." (p. 2) Suddenly the reader is struck with an overwhelming sense of isolation and anonymity. This is a world of total strangers thrown together by a necessity that is anything but an occasion of joy or celebration. Birth and death have come and gone and they leave not a ripple in this loveless setting. Dickens is relentless in depicting this atmosphere. The mother dead, the nurse picks up the baby, but *first* she picks up the cork to her precious green bottle. The surgeon put on his gloves "with great deliberation," suggesting that his concern with details of dress is in no way disturbed, and he predicts of the child, " 'It's very likely it *will* be troublesome. Give it a little gruel if it is.' " (p. 3) A "little" gruel is what will have to suffice Oliver for a long time. Troublesome he will be, whatever his nature, to a world that would prefer his non-existence. The rich irony of "a little gruel" is thus well established, for a "little," as we see later, has the advantage both of being less expensive than "more," and of eliminating the orphan's "troublesome" energy. The giving of a "little" will, moreover, satisfy the demands of "Christian" charity. "Give it a little gruel" but especially "if it is" troublesome, turns out to be the social panacea-punishment for the fact of the destitute in a Malthusian economy.

II

Oliver's first mother, after the death of the natural one, is Mrs. Mann, overseer of the baby-farm. To emphasize the irony of her name and rôle, Dickens has Mr. Bumble tell her,

> "You are a humane woman, Mrs. Mann." (Here she set down the glass.) "I shall take a early opportunity of mentioning it to the board, Mrs. Mann." (He drew it towards him.) "You feel as a mother, Mrs. Mann." (He stirred the gin-and-water.) (p. 7)

It is Bumble who is being "mothered" and bribed. Mrs. Mann is paid sevenpence-halfpenny "per small head per week." The animal husbandry image of "farm" and "head" is made quite explicit by the story of Mrs. Mann's similarity to the experimental philosopher who set out to prove that he could feed a horse on nothing at all. Like the horse, the child-livestock of the baby-farm usually frustrate the experiment by dying just at the point of the experiment's successful conclusion, whereupon each is "summoned into another world, and there gathered to the fathers it had never known in this." Dickens never permits the reader to forget this central theme of parentage and its meaning. Oliver miraculously survives the experience by virtue of "a good sturdy spirit that nature or inheritance had implanted" in his breast. At the age of nine he is removed back to his birthplace, the workhouse. He leaves the baby-farm with a piece of bread and butter, a gift designed to obscure nine years of hunger and which, like the embraces and tears of Mrs. Mann, and the rhetoric of Mr. Bumble, is part of a very elaborate system of falsehood. On arrival at the refuge of the poor, Oliver is taken before the "board," and once again the food imagery is subtly suggested both by the pun on the word and the fact that the board consists of eight or ten "fat gentlemen," sitting round a table. When told to bow to the board, Oliver bows to the table, for the abstract noun has no meaning for him. The board meets appropriately in a "whitewashed room." Oliver is then asked if he prays like a Christian for those "who feed him." This introduction of religious rhetoric and Dickens' comment on it must be understood if the subsequent events, especially the discovery of Fagin's world, are to be clearly seen.

> The gentleman who spoke last was unconsciously right. It would have been *very* like a Christian, and a marvellously good

> Christian, too, if Oliver had prayed for the people who fed and took care of *him*. (p. 10)

Dickens makes it clear that his idea of "Christian" is quite different from the board's. The latter think Oliver should be rhetorically religious. Dickens thinks it would perhaps take Christ himself to pray for them to be forgiven even if they know not what they do. "Like a Christian" in this context means the use of the ritual form and language only, so that in the novel "Christian" becomes synonymous with hypocrisy and falsehood. Later there are two compliments paid to Sikes' dog. Sikes himself is amazed at the dog's ferocity: " 'He's as willing as a Christian, strike me blind if he isn't!' said Sikes, regarding the animal with a kind of grim and ferocious approval." (p. 109) Charley Bates defines the dog as a Christian, a little later, when the Dodger has listed the animal's surly attributes in terms amounting to a description of Puritan gloom and religious bigotry.

> "He's an out-and-out Christian," said Charley.
>
> This was merely intended as a tribute to the animal's abilities, but it was an appropriate remark in another sense, if Master Bates had only known it; for there are a good many ladies and gentlemen, claiming to be out-and-out Christians, between whom, and Mr. Sikes' dog, there exist strong and singular points of resemblance. (p. 130)

These remarks emanate from the Fagin non-Christian camp, a fact that permits a certain clarity of view and which we shall examine at length further on.

It must be remembered at this point that the entire workhouse system represented the workings in a Christian society of the most reluctant form of social relief. Since the 1834 Poor Law was based on certain doubtful economic and psychological principles it had, strictly speaking, nothing to do with Christian charity, yet it doubtless acquired in its workings all the hypocritical rhetoric of philanthropy and generosity. In fact, the Poor Law was a token recognition of Christian principles, for it salved the social conscience that could not embrace an open policy of hostility and death to the poor. Dickens probably regarded this token as worse than nothing, on two counts, for it excused the individual from charitable concern and by its institutional veneer permitted the worst evils and inhumanity to flourish. Through the hypocritical machinery of a "benevolent" system, cruelty and neglect were given sanction and so absorbed into the establishment and made respectable. Under Dickens' urbanity and irony and the artistic restraint is a fury akin to Swift's in *A Modest Proposal*. Indeed, the board are like a group of men who have taken a kind of nineteenth-century "modest proposal" and seriously applied it.

> For the first six months after Oliver Twist was removed, the system was in full operation. It was rather expensive at first, in consequence of the increase in the undertaker's bill, and the necessity of taking in the clothes of all the paupers, which fluttered loosely on their wasted, shrunken forms, after a week or two's gruel. But the number of workhouse inmates got thin as well as the paupers; and the board were in ecstasies. (p. 11)

For us, this description is reminiscent of the concentration-camp image, where skeletal forms move in a silent nightmare to which the only response is bewilderment. Later, when Bumble meets Mrs. Mann again, he chats amiably about his paupers in economic terms that suggest again a dialogue appropriate to a "farm," where it does in fact take place.

> "They are both in a very low state, and we find it would come two pound cheaper to move 'em than to bury 'em—that is, if we can throw 'em upon another parish, which I think we shall be able to do, if they don't die upon the road to spite us. Ha! ha! ha!" (p. 120)

Dickens has been accused of vague philanthropy and naive radicalism,[11] but no other writer in English perceives so exactly the profundity of evil nurtured by the pretense of good in a heartless social system of charity.

As the surgeon predicted, Oliver persists in being troublesome by virtue of his survival, and is inevitably answered by the application of a little gruel. It is often forgotten that when Oliver reaches the crisis point in his "troublesome" career, when he asks for more, he does so on behalf of all orphans and because he is "desperate with hunger, and reckless with misery." The crisis is precipitated by the real threat of cannibalism among the boys, a possibility of which they are actually afraid. "To be or not to be" has somehow come to suggest the whole life-and-death question in a literary instant; Brecht's "eats first, morals after" deflates the balloon of philosophical cant with a knife-thrust of clarity; and Oliver's

"Please, sir, I want some more" contains all the poignant cries of all the hungry and unloved in the world. The child, David-like, addresses Goliath with the prescribed form, "Sir," challenges in his desperation all the inhuman repression and cruelty of the giant who towers unreachable above, Guardian of Gruel. It is the gesture of an infant Quixote. He asks not for better but simply for more—of everything. It goes without saying that no commentary can replace Dickens' words, a plea so small and so large at the same time. Nor can one ignore the rich humour which makes the scene tolerable, the presumption of the request and the exaggerated responses. Look at what happens when the request is made:

> "Please, sir, I want some more."
>
> The master was a fat, healthy man; but he turned very pale. He gazed in stupefied astonishment on the small rebel for some seconds, and then clung for support to the copper. The assistants were paralysed with wonder; the boys with fear.
>
> "What!" said the master at length, in a faint voice.
>
> "Please, sir," replied Oliver, "I want some more."
>
> The master aimed a blow at Oliver's head with the ladle; pinioned him in his arms; and shrieked aloud for the beadle. (p. 12)

To judge from the reaction of authority, Oliver might be a master revolutionary, but this is revealing as well as ridiculous. Oliver's request is nothing short of a challenge to the whole "parochial" system, and thus in turn to the whole social system and so to the entire economic values of society. The foundations quake. The seriousness of the matter calls for the judgement of the highest authority. Only the board can deal with a threat like this. It is interesting that Oliver's punishment is solitary confinement; his complaint may be catching. The isolation, cold and hunger which caused the crisis are now used openly to break his spirit, for the poor must be suppressed at all costs. If it were once revealed that the system of charity is in fact the cruel, destructive system that it is, the whole vast pretense would crumble, and economic laws and abstract theories held to be inviolable would count for nothing. It is easy to see how T. A. Jackson moves from this to a Marxian study of Dickens' radicalism.[12] But Dickens no more wished to introduce a new system than he wished to destroy the old one, for abstract system was itself anathema, and what Dickens goes on to show is that only the remedies of "humanity of heart," and thus the life and integrity of human beings as a supreme value, can alter the evils of exploitation and dehumanization. Isolated, beaten, and humiliated, Oliver is saved from suicide only by the exclusion of the means. But his temerity does produce a change, and in the world of the workhouse all change is for the better.

III

The board, in its wisdom, knows that anyone who asks for more must quickly be expelled from the parochial system and preferably from society altogether so that it may not be destroyed from within. Oliver is almost sold to Mr. Gamfield, the chimney-sweep. One of the most savagely ironic scenes in Dickens is that of the board solemnly bartering to save itself thirty shillings because Mr. Gamfield's is "a nasty business." If they are going to send Oliver to his death with Mr. Gamfield they are not so hard-hearted as to give away five pounds for the privilege. Three pounds, ten shillings seems quite enough.

> "The kind and blessed gentlemen which is so many parents to you, Oliver, when you have none of your own: are a going to 'prentice you: and to set you up in life, and make a man of you: although the expense to the parish is three pound ten!—three pound ten, Oliver!—seventy shillins—one hundred and forty sixpences!—and all for a naughty orphan which nobody can't love." (p. 18)

"Which nobody can't love" reminds one of the later "Nobody's fault" of *Little Dorrit* and shows how Dickens uses idiom and dialect for functional irony. But Gamfield is deprived even of his three pounds ten. When the magistrate is forced to pause and look for the inkstand he accidentally looks at Oliver. Dickens is at pains to point out that the magistrate's wandering gaze actually fastens on Oliver and he really sees him, that is, as a being with its own qualities, sees him with understanding or imagination, as he is: "and happening in the course of his search to look straight before him, his gaze encountered the pale and terrified face of Oliver Twist" (p. 20). Dickens suggests that even a "half-blind magistrate" could not mistake what he sees, yet no one else is moved at all and Bumble to this point in the novel has not seen Oliver or anything else. His predisposition to blindness costs him dear in his marriage. When the magistrate says "My Boy! . . . you look pale and alarmed," it sounds contextually unfamiliar because prior to this the adult world has been shown as blinded by its own desires and opinions. How Oliver has "looked" no one could have known, for no one has seen him, just as the magistrate almost didn't see him. Earlier Mrs. Mann has said, " 'I couldn't see 'em suffer before my very eyes, you know, sir,' " (p. 7) and not see them is what she and the others do.

The board, having failed to get rid of Oliver up England's chimneys, decides to follow the example of great families.

> The board, in imitation of so wise and salutary an example, took counsel together on the expediency of shipping off Oliver Twist, in some small trading vessel bound to a good unhealthy port. This suggested itself as the very best thing that could possibly be done with him: the probability being, that the skipper would flog him to death, in a playful mood, some day after dinner, or would knock his brains out with an iron bar; both pastimes being, as is pretty generally known, very favourite and common recreations among gentlemen of that class. The more the case presented itself to the board, in this point of view, the more manifold the advantages of the step appeared; so, they came to the conclusion that the only way of providing for Oliver effectually, was to send him to sea without delay. (p. 22)

At this point the undertaker steps in and takes Oliver and, this time, the whole five pounds is paid, presumably in view of the situation being so pleasant. It is worthy of note that prior to Oliver being deposited at the Sowerberrys' funeral parlour, he gives Mr. Bumble an uncomfortable moment and provides him the opportunity to become real. For the first time he, too, is forced to see Oliver, in response to the child's agonized cry of loneliness: "Mr. Bumble regarded Oliver's piteous and helpless look, with some astonishment, for a few seconds; . . ." (p. 26) The seconds pass unused, however; Mr. Bumble's emotion is explained away, presumably to himself, as "that troublesome cough" and he walks on "in silence." It is an appeal and an opening never to be offered to him again.

Oliver's move to the undertaker is accompanied by all the now-familiar characteristics of the novel's themes, the child as merchandise, the acquisition of non-parents and much reference to food. It is, however, a further step in the Parish Boy's Progress. When

Oliver is inspected at the undertaker's they complain of his smallness as though they are buying something, say a piece of meat, and are getting short measure. Mr. Bumble assures them that Oliver will grow and Mrs. Sowerberry predicts that her munificence will fatten him up. Oliver's diet does in fact improve, even though it consists of the dog's neglected scraps, and it is this meat that is later blamed for his vigorous rebellion, for having departed from "a little gruel," Oliver naturally grows more "troublesome." Mrs. Sowerberry, with her ironic over-provision of nourishment, and Mr. Sowerberry and his glimmer of kindness, are an improvement. Of the latter we are told that "To do him justice, he was, as far as his power went—it was not very extensive—kindly disposed towards the boy; . . ." (p. 47) Oliver leaves this setting, not because of the Sowerberrys, but because his sustaining mother-image is attacked.

At the funeral parlour, Oliver temporarily joins the living who feed off the dead, for undertaking is a profitable business.

> "I say you'll make your fortune, Mr. Sowerberry," repeated Mr. Bumble, tapping the undertaker on the shoulder, in a friendly manner, with his cane.
>
> "Think so?" said the undertaker in a tone which half admitted and half disputed the probability of the event. "The prices allowed by the board are very small, Mr. Bumble."
>
> "So are the coffins," replied the beadle: . . . (pp. 22-23)

The transition is thus made from the horrors of the inside of the workhouse to the horrors outside it and with extraordinary skill Dickens shows us how normal, respectable and economically satisfactory the whole system appears. Some are killed off in the name of charity and others grow fat in the name of parish service and those who survive the workhouse are made slaves to assist in burying the one group and fattening the other, and so a great many birds, as it were, are killed with one stony law. The ghoulish career in which Oliver is ironically a "mute" (a piece of expressionism which has all the earmarks of a modern absurdist play) comes to an end when Oliver is attacked, not physically as so often before, but verbally and in his weakest area. Once again the themes of food and love, the connection between survival and a mother-image are introduced and for the first time explicitly linked, ironically by Bumble who suggests that Oliver's defence of his mother's character is directly the result of his being fed on meat.

> "Meat ma'am, meat," replied Bumble, with stern emphasis. "You've over-fed him, ma'am. You've raised a artificial soul and spirit in him, ma'am, unbecoming a person of his condition: as the board, Mrs. Sowerberry, who are practical philosophers, will tell you. What have paupers to do with soul or spirit? It's quite enough that we let 'em have live bodies. If you had kept the boy on gruel, ma'am, this would never have happened." (p. 46)

Whatever the reason, Oliver's fight with Claypole is the only instance in the novel of his responding to any situation with total, insane outrage.

Dickens has already taken trouble to show the loneliness of Oliver.

> He was alone in a strange place; and we all know how chilled and desolate the best of us will sometimes feel in such a situation. The boy had no friends to care for, or to care for him. The regret of no recent separation was fresh in his mind; the absence of no loved and well-remembered face sank heavily into his heart. (p. 29)

The loneliness of Oliver will recur in later novels, in Pip and David, as though, from this very early case and up to the later work, Dickens is moved by the image of the lonely boy whose isolation is a haunting terror.[13] It becomes a central theme for Dickens, whose compassion for the child and whose indictment of the adult world grow from the most sensitive understanding in English literature of the child's mind. The attack on Oliver's most fragile psychic area, his only preserve of reassurance, is prefaced by a directive from the author, that its significance be not missed:

> And now, I come to a very important passage in Oliver's history; for I have to record an act, slight and unimportant perhaps in appearance, but which indirectly produced a material change in all his future prospects and proceedings. (p. 40)

It is interesting that one of the commonest forms of insult, and in turn of angry defense, is related to the character and reputation of the mother.[14] When Noah begins his taunts and introduces the subject of Oliver's mother, Oliver's colour rises and his breathing quickens, and "there was a curious working of the mouth and nostrils." It is, like many others of Dickens' descriptions, almost clinical. The foolhardy Noah mistakes these signs for the preliminaries to a fit of crying. In fact they are closer to the panic signs of hysteric reaction to a severe threat, in this case to the weak defenses of an insecure child. We discover now, what we did not know before. Oliver, on the basis of what he could glean of his mother in the workhouse, has constructed a conviction which sustains him in the midst of his desolation. We should remember that "He was alone . . ." (p. 29, quoted above.) Nor has this friendly ghost yet been replaced by Oliver's experience of real people who will later come to love him. Part of Oliver's progress will be this replacement. Little wonder that at this stage he should hold with desperation to the image he needs so badly, for this mother idea, ironically enough, is life itself to him, *his* "hope and comfort." The physical symptoms described above are very much akin to those of severe respiratory constriction, the kind that comes with suffocating fear. Without his mother, here under attack, he cannot breathe—she is the ground of his being, his identity and his motivation. When the victims of Oliver's mad attack cry "murder," they are in fact ironically closer to the truth than they know, even though their exaggerations appear laughable in view of Oliver's smallness, for Oliver is indeed in a murderous mood. This is the second time that a great comic power, threatening vastly greater forces, is attributed to Oliver.

> A minute ago, the boy had looked the quiet, mild, dejected creature that harsh treatment had made him. But his spirit was roused at last; the cruel insult to his dead mother had set his blood on fire. His breast heaved; his attitude was erect; his eye bright and vivid; his whole person changed, as he stood glaring over the cowardly tormentor who now lay crouching at his feet; and defied him with an energy he had never known before. (pp. 41-42)

Noah Claypole's threat to this area of Oliver's simple world-structure is the breaking point and drives the parish boy onward. Dickens feels no need to give further explanation of his departure. The situation at the undertaker's, physically more comfortable than anything preceding it, is now psychologically intolerable, for where almost any physical suffering can be borne, this cannot, and causes Oliver to run away.

Before he leaves he says goodbye to Dick, the only friend that he has, and receives from him, another orphan, who will not survive the baby-farm, the only blessing Oliver "had ever heard." But though Oliver has not heard another, the reader recalls the parting kiss of the dying mother. The link is thus made between the two dying goodbyes of Oliver's only well-wishers, one his kin by blood, the other by common suffering. This link with parental love and survival is kept explicitly before us on Oliver's journey, where the only instance of truly benevolent charity that Dickens records is the literally life-saving generosity of two more surrogate parents, a man and a woman.

> In fact, if it had not been for a good-hearted turnpike-man, and a benevolent old lady, Oliver's troubles would have been shortened by the very same process which had put an end to his mother's; in other words, he would most assuredly have fallen dead upon the king's highway. *But the turnpike-man gave him a meal of bread and cheese; and the old lady, who had a shipwrecked grandson wandering barefoot in some distant part of the earth, took pity upon the poor orphan, and gave him what little she could afford*—and more—with such kind and gentle words, and such tears of sympathy and compassion, that they sank deeper into Oliver's soul, than all the sufferings he had ever undergone. (p. 52, my italics)

Food and love sustain Oliver as he follows a journey much like his mother's before him, one on which she died. Oliver comes close to the same fate. One cannot help remembering Parson Adams, who, wandering like Oliver through England, makes the astonishing discovery "that it was possible in a country professing Christianity, for a wretch to starve in the midst of his fellow creatures who abounded."[15] A second observation from *Joseph Andrews* leads us directly to the world of Fagin, for Adams remarks that "he was glad to find some Christians left in the kingdom; for that he almost began to suspect that he was sojourning in a country inhabited only by Jews and Turks."[16] The next stage of the "progress" picks up the thread introduced by the workhouse and the Board as "Christian" and Dickens pursues a complex ironic design by turning his attention now to a world that is totally non-Christian.

When the Dodger picks up Oliver, the latter is in the gutter and likely to starve to death. From his point of view the Dodger's willingness to share his shilling, and his subsequent purchase of bread, ham and beer and the offer of shelter, is nothing less than magnanimity. Indeed, since the Dodger regards his life of crime as a jolly and rewarding life, any cynicism about his motives, even from the reader, seems entirely misplaced. Moreover, Oliver is about to be introduced to a brand new social situation. Prior to this his existence has been principally an irritation to everybody; at best he has been an exploitable "natural resource." Henceforth his existence will take on a special importance in that his survival comes to be central for others. Strangely enough, even Monks' hostility and the personal vendetta story lend to Oliver's existence for others a special significance and reality. He ceases to be anonymous. The negative dependency of the criminal world should not be cast aside by the reader as merely evil, but rather should be compared to the callous indifference of the workhouse.

If we look at the passage of Oliver's introduction to the Fagin gang and residence, suspending our subsequent knowledge and bearing in mind all that has gone before, we cannot help being relieved at Oliver's arrival.

> "We are very glad to see you, Oliver, very," said the Jew. "Dodger, take off the sausages; and draw a tub near the fire for Oliver. Ah, you're a-staring at the pocket-handkerchiefs! eh, my dear! There are a good many of 'em, ain't there? We've just looked 'em out, ready for the wash; that's all, Oliver; that's all. Ha! ha! ha!"
>
> The latter part of this speech, was hailed by a boisterous shout from all the hopeful pupils of the merry old gentleman. In the midst of which, they went to supper.
>
> Oliver ate his share, and the Jew then mixed him a glass of hot gin and water: telling him he must drink it off directly, because another gentleman wanted the tumbler. Oliver did as he was desired. Immediately afterwards he felt himself gently lifted on to one of the sacks; and then he sunk into a deep sleep. (p. 57)

Far from being sinister, the ending to this chapter is, ironically, full of comfort. The room is rich in handkerchiefs, and we are reminded that "pocket-handkerchiefs being decided articles of luxury, had been, for all future times and ages, removed from the noses of paupers by the express order of the board, in council assembled; . . ." (p. 14) Oliver partakes of gin and water and we remember that Mrs. Mann's gin and water was reserved for her own comfort and to soften Mr. Bumble. There is no reason to doubt the sincerity of the greeting "We are very glad to see you, Oliver." Once again the progress is marked by food, and now, for the first time in the novel, Oliver "ate his share" of the sausages and hot gin and water. He is "gently" put to bed, and not alone, and he no doubt goes to sleep more comfortably than he ever did before. Fagin combines the rôles of mother and father. The Fagin den is a parody of domestic bless, as was the "workus," which was much less congenial. It is not insignificant that the following morning Oliver is in a prewaking dream-state when his mind has "some glimmering conception of its mighty powers." Half-asleep and half-awake, Oliver combines the present and the past in a single vision that signalizes a kind of detachment or self-realization, marking a new stage of his progress. Indeed, it is made quite clear on his first morning that nothing in his treatment has led Oliver to doubt the kindness of his new master.

> Oliver thought the old gentleman must be a decided miser to live in such a dirty place, with so many watches; but, *thinking that perhaps his fondness for the Dodger and the other boys,* cost him a good deal of money, he only cast a deferential look at the Jew, and asked if he might get up. (p. 60, my italics)

If I am right in suggesting that Dickens intends Fagin's world, in spite of its moral dangers, to be an improvement over the workhouse, then clearly Dickens is intending an elaborate and ironic comparison and contrast. William F. Axton makes the point that the parochial workhouse and the Fagin underworld are smitten with the same disease.

> Behind experimental philosophy there lies the theatrical figure of Monks, black cloak, slouch hat, glittering eye, manic guilt, and all, who embodies in himself the motives underlying the moral position occupied by the Workhouse Board—i.e., respectable society—and the criminal underworld: that is to say, consuming self-interest.[17]

But the differences between these two worlds are more interesting than their similarities. One of these primary distinctions is the attitude toward survival. Dickens explicitly shows that the death of the poor is essentially what is aimed at in a workhouse world. So hard are the conditions in order to discourage the applicants, and so parsimonious the administration in order to maintain the beauty of its bookkeeping, that the number of dead seems to be a kind of testimonial to the efficiency of the system. In the underworld, on the contrary, survival is of paramount importance. To avoid the rope and the jail becomes the prime objective and the code of honour works well for a long time. But the overriding difference between the underworld and the workhouse world is that one is outside and one is inside authorized society. The master of the ladle, symbol of rule and authority itself, turns pale when Oliver asks for more, and the child is imprisoned. Fagin, master of the underworld is, like Oliver, an outcast, whose entire creed is to ask for more and to take more and in this he and his subjects are one. Their "consuming self-interest" gives them at least an initial parity. The community of fear and greed is, frighteningly enough, more unified than the jungle of the predatory "respectable" world. The fact that the underworld is outside the pale produces another important distinction between it and the world of Bumble. The one is real, the other false. It is for this reason that the two worlds are given two different religious authorities, Christian and Jewish. The Jew, both historically and in the novel, was excluded from the respectably established world, first by his religion and sometimes as a consequence of the first exclusion, by his activities. Fagin thus becomes a kind of Satanic master,[18] excluded from the society of Christian "heaven," ruling a group of fallen angels as it were, the children who might have been innocently happy, had they not had to be rescued by evil from the starvation-gutters of goodness. Fagin is father-figure and devil combined. Ernest Jones speaks of the Devil as friendly father in the following way:

> It is important to note that the Devil's power especially related to *secret* and *magical* affairs. He was the master of all forbidden arts, the so-called "black arts." This was why he was the chief resort of magicians and other people who wanted either knowledge they were forbidden to have, or power to perform deeds beyond ordinary human capacity.
>
> These powers would be put at the service of human beings in despair, usually on certain conditions, such as that they would henceforth belong to the Devil and do his bidding: just like the parents who do something for a child on condition that he is "good," i.e. do what they want. In many legends he appears as a friendly helper of mankind who protects those in distress—*particularly widows and orphans!*—and aids them over their

> difficulties; Conway and Wunsche narrate a large number of such stories. We here see the Devil playing the part of the friendly father, and the correspondence between the two conceptions is at times extraordinarily close in detail. (my italics)[19]

The parallels to Oliver's situation are not only obvious but uncanny. For the outcast it is satisfying to find an omnipotent father figure who specializes in outcasts. To sell oneself to the Devil is to be well looked after and to demonstrate one's hatred of society at one and the same time. However, the Devil as benevolent father will never cease to be Devil for the person who has not fully yielded to his power and protection. There is no more freedom in one dependency than in another. Thus Fagin is not the father for Oliver. The Devil/Jew figure of medieval myth can also be viewed as the bad and punishing father, just as Fagin is feared by the boys who lose Oliver and feared by all those to whose secrets he is privy.[20]

From Dickens' "Christian" point of view, however, Fagin and his world are freed from one great danger, the danger of hypocrisy. All possibility of social pretension, position and respectability is denied Fagin and he has no means of entering that "over-world" where Bumble is destined to become master. The one is a world of darkness, of hidden workings in secret rooms and passages. The other is a daylight world basking in its social rôle and thoroughly enjoying its pretensions. On two occasions figures from Fagin's world significantly parody the respectable society. Fagin, like Mr. Peachum of Gay's *Beggars' Opera,* keeps a whole set of costumes and disguises on hand. On one occasion Nancy dresses up in costume and pretends to look concernedly for her poor "brother" Oliver at the jail, thoroughly convincing everyone that she is indeed respectable. In fact she finds it very easy. Later, when she goes on a truly Christian errand to visit Rose Maylie, but dressed as herself, she is treated with the utmost contempt and humiliation by the hotel servants. On the second occasion Toby Crackit has been trying in vain to set up the "crib at Chertsey" as an "inside job:"

> "But do you mean to say, my dear," remonstrated the Jew, "that the women can't be got over?"
>
> "Not a bit of it," replied Sikes.

> "Not by flash Toby Crackit?" said the Jew incredulously. "Think what women are, Bill."
>
> "No; not even by flash Toby Crackit," replied Sikes. "He says he's worn sham whiskers, and a canary waistcoat, the whole blessed time he's been loitering down there, and it's all of no use."
>
> "He should have tried mustachios and a pair of military trousers, my dear," said the Jew.
>
> "So he did," rejoined Sikes, "and they warn't of no more use than the other plant." (p. 138)

The fact that Fagin is astounded at this failure only shows how commonly these disguises worked and how unusual the Maylie household is.

If Fagin is the Jew-Devil-Father figure of ancient Christian mythology, Bumble is the Christian-Father-Saint of modern Christian industrialism. Bumble has power over *his* fallen angels, though he provides nothing in return. This is the principal distinction between them. The world of Bumble is respectable. While its evil is no less, its dependence on the poor and its exploitation of them just as great, it is an infinitely more dangerous world. There is no danger in nineteenth-century England that Fagin will attain public office, but Bumble becomes master of the workhouse, the bureaucratic symbol of government, and one of a long Dickensian line of Doodles and Coodles, Barnacles and Podsnaps. The world of Bumble is all appearance. Mr. Bumble of the cocked hat is, for instance, entirely and solely his dress:

> Oliver was completely enshrouded by the skirts of Mr. Bumble's coat as they blew open, and disclosed to great advantage his flapped waistcoat and drab plush knee-breeches. (p. 26)

The costumes worn by the gang when pretending to be other than themselves are worn by the Bumbles of the world all the time.

While Fagin may deceive others he does not deceive himself. He fully understands and explains the avowed philosophy of Number One and its social implications. He knows he is confined to the dark. He knows he looks awful, or rather there is no evidence that he is ever conscious of his appearance. His workers begin to play rôles only when they enter the respectable world of London's daylight streets and when they assume one of the many disguises in Fagin's wardrobe. Even Oliver's innocent face is seen as a powerful weapon to exploit a world totally taken in by appearances. Bumble on the other hand has a wildly inflated idea of his own ability. He lives by playing rôles.

> "Do you think this respectful or proper conduct, Mrs. Mann," inquired Mr. Bumble, grasping his cane, "to keep the parish officers a waiting at your garden-gate, when they come here upon porochial business connected with the porochial orphans? Are you aweer, Mrs. Mann, that you are, as I may say, a porochial delegate, and a stipendiary?" . . .
>
> Mr. Bumble had a great idea of his oratorical powers and his importance. He had displayed the one, and vindicated the other. He relaxed. (p. 6)

His courtship observes all the exaggerated gentility of the drawing room, wildly funny yet somehow painfully sick in a context where outside the door is a world of starving half-naked wretches.

> "The day afore yesterday, a man—you have been a married woman, ma'am, and I may mention it to you—a man, with hardly a rag upon his back (here Mrs. Corney looked at the floor), . . ." (p. 167)

When it comes to love and seeing people, Mr. Bumble measures Mrs. Corney's worth in domestic commodities, a parody of fortune-hunting: " 'Coals, candles, and house-rent free,' said Mr. Bumble. 'Oh, Mrs. Corney, what a Angel you are!' " (p. 199) Contrast all this with Fagin's end, the simple address and answer, "Fagin!" "That's me."

Mr. Bumble, however, has no identity. When he becomes master of the workhouse, he is discovered to have laid aside his manhood with his dress:

> The laced coat, and the cocked-hat; where were they? He still wore knee-breeches, and dark cotton stockings on his nether limbs; but they were not *the* breeches. The coat was wide-skirted; and in that respect like *the* coat, but, oh, how different! The mighty cocked-hat was replaced by a modest round one. Mr. Bumble was no longer a beadle. (p. 267)

To make the point quite explicitly universal Dickens adds, "Strip the bishop of his apron, or the beadle of his hat and lace; what are they? Men. Mere men. Dignity, and even holiness too, sometimes, are more questions of coat and waistcoat than some people imagine." (p. 267) In the unreal parochial world the real suffering of the outcast can be totally obscured. The poorhouse under its

Christian master not only leads to the non-Christian world of Fagin, by Oliver's exemplary route, but it perpetrates and preserves a system of monstrous evil precisely because of its "Christian" forms and has this vast disguise. Fagin's world is under. Bumble's is on top. Fagin's world is inviolable, and the gothic imagery of dirt and darkness and secrecy emphasizes this. It runs from the light. It becomes clear then that Fagin is used for satiric counterpoint as a non-Christian (the Jew being the only reasonable choice for this purpose in nineteenth-century England) and not because Dickens was really interested in Jews at all. His principal interest is in exposing a world of pretended values, a world built on the cross made where national economic policy intersects with national religion, at which juncture both conspire to produce a vast national hypocrisy which claims to satisfy with one stroke of politic genius the twin ends of economic necessity and religious obligation.

The Fagin stage of Oliver's career is no less a part of Dickens' systematic progress-design than what follows. That the thieves should accidentally produce the encounter with Brownlow is part of this brilliant design. The beggars of Gay's opera would never have been seen or heard had they been incarcerated in a poorhouse system. Only the thieves will wake Brownlow from his brown study at the bookstall, by forcing themselves on his notice. The poor do not exist in a system of organized charity. They are effectively eliminated in such a system. They exist only when they ask for more.

IV

Brownlow has been seen by critics as undifferentiatedly benevolent and really indistinguishable from the Maylies, just as Fagin has been undifferentiated from the workhouse.[21] Brownlow, however, is not Oliver's final refuge because in his own way, better though he is, he uses Oliver and is unwilling or unable to fully accept with total trust and love what he sees. With characteristic subtlety Dickens plants the tiniest seeds of doubt in the reader's mind. This is how Brownlow starts the hue and cry:

> Seeing the boy scudding away at such a rapid pace, he very naturally concluded him to be the depredator; and, shouting "Stop thief!" with all his might, made off after him, book in hand. (p. 66)

The phrase "very naturally" might go unnoticed were it not that a little further on Dickens repeats the word nature in an explanatory way. "Although Oliver had been brought up by philosophers, he was not theoretically acquainted with the beautiful axiom that self-preservation is the first law of nature." (p. 66) In other words, the survival of the fittest requires the proper respect for jungle law. Brownlow, acting "very naturally," shouting "with all his might," feels greatly wronged. It is on second glance surprising that his response should be so vengeful and automatic over a handkerchief. It becomes less surprising as we see later how disillusioned and cynical he has become with age. Brownlow shouts out "stop thief" with great alacrity, thereby accusing the wrong person. He himself runs off with an unpaid-for book in his hand, suggesting the ease with which one might in a vindictive and ungenerous world be charged with theft, as Mr. Fang, the magistrate, is quick to point out to him. Mr. Brownlow is helpless and silent at the trial, apparently paralyzed with indignation at his own mistreatment, while Oliver is sentenced to three months hard labour; the boy is not even conscious at the time. This is the first of three trials in the novel, and in each case we may apply my earlier remarks about the respectable world of daylight and its relation to the underworld. In each trial, Oliver's, the Dodger's and Fagin's, the proceedings are summary, the consequences brutal and the bystanders totally unmoved by compassion. Indeed, in all cases the results are foregone conclusions, the accused already condemned by being outcast. No spectator sees the remotest connection between himself and the victim of the process of law. This is a Christian world but one that is characterized in every area by its jungle view of man. Oliver is condemned by the workhouse board member in the white waistcoat as inevitably doomed to be hanged. In the court the prediction is again repeated: " 'Must go before the magistrate now, sir,' replied the man. 'His worship will be disengaged in half a minute. Now, young gallows!' " (p. 69) The Dodger is caught and tried for putting back a handkerchief and sentenced on circumstantial evidence. Having been condemned by description he quite rightly washes his hands of the whole business and will not lend dignity to the court by his cooperation, for he sees how hopeless it all is.

"I never see such an out-and-out young wagabond, your

> worship," observed the officer with a grin. "Do you mean to say anything, you young shaver?"
>
> "No," replied the Dodger, "not here, for this ain't the shop for justice; . . ." (p. 335)

Fagin cannot believe that a world as corrupt as the one he has lived in can really sort out whom to hang and whom not to: "What right have they to butcher me?" Christ or Devil would alike win no sympathy from this crowd with its lunches and knitting, for "they might as well have been of stone." This is like pagan Rome, only now the Christians are in the grandstand seats and what they want is blood.

> But in no one face—not even among the women, of whom there were many there—could he read the faintest sympathy with himself, or any feeling but one of all-absorbing interest that he should be condemned. (p. 404)

To return to Brownlow, he is first a false accuser, second a helpless bystander and then suspicious about the name Tom White, thrust upon Oliver in court, and is convinced only by Oliver's look of innocence. Nevertheless, the move to Brownlow's house is in fact a major progress and as such it is marked principally by Mrs. Bedwin rather than by Brownlow. Oliver awakes from his second life-and-death-bed struggle to find a new mother. She is described as a "motherly old lady." Now, however, for the first time, the natural mother of the imagination whose "face has always looked sweet and happy" when Oliver dreamed of her is brought together with a real and present, loving woman.

> "Save us!" said the old lady, with tears in her eyes, "What a grateful little dear it is. Pretty creetur! What would his mother feel if she had sat by him as I have, and could see him now!"
>
> "Perhaps she does see me," whispered Oliver, folding his hands together; "perhaps she has sat by me. I almost feel as if she had." (p. 77)

It is at this point, moreover, that the presence of the mysterious picture reinforces the theme. Oliver is closer to home than he knows. The theme of sustenance, of love and security as symbolized by and embodied in a loving mother, is once again accompanied by an elaboration of some food emblem. Mrs. Bedwin takes a great deal of trouble with a broth for Oliver and in case the reader is not aware of the distance Oliver has come from gruel to broth, Dickens makes it explicit:

> And with this, the old lady applied herself to warming up, in a little saucepan, a basin full of broth: strong enough, Oliver thought, to furnish an ample dinner, when reduced to the regulation strength, for three hundred and fifty paupers, at the lowest computation. (p. 79)

And two pages later:

> "He has just had a basin of beautiful strong broth, sir," replied Mrs. Bedwin: drawing herself up slightly, and laying a strong emphasis on the last word: to intimate that between slops, and broth well compounded, there existed no affinity or connexion whatsoever. (p. 81)

Mr. Brownlow is not so totally accepting in his confrontation of Oliver as Mrs. Bedwin, and it will improve our understanding of the novel to discover why.

> ". . . you need not be afraid of my deserting you, unless you give me cause."
>
> "I never, never will, sir," interposed Oliver.
>
> "I hope not," rejoined the old gentleman. "I do not think you ever will. I have been deceived, before, in the objects whom I have endeavoured to benefit; but I feel strongly disposed to trust you, nevertheless; *and I am more interested in your behalf than I can well account for, even to myself.* The persons on whom I have bestowed my dearest love, lie deep in their graves; but, although the happiness and delight of my life lie buried there too, I have not made a coffin of my heart, and sealed it up, for ever, on my best affections. Deep affliction has but strengthened and refined them." (p. 96, my italics)

The words I have italicized suggest that Mr. Brownlow is surprised at his own interest in Oliver. He obviously has enough self-awareness to know that it is not normal or characteristic of him to care for passing waifs and strays. In the light of these lines his following protestations are of interest. Mr. Brownlow speaks a large part of this to himself.

> As the old gentleman said this in a low voice: more to himself than to his companion: and as he remained silent for a short time afterwards: Oliver sat quite still. (p. 96)

It is rather as though his protestations about trust and affections are efforts to convince himself. He admits that Oliver could be a deceiving "object" like the others. The conflict in Brownlow is augmented and clarified by the introduction of Grimwig, who appears to be a kind of under or repressed side to Mr. Brownlow's ego. Grimwig is in fact an early instance of Dickens' expressionistic technique. Though Mr. Grimwig is "a worthy creature at bottom" he seems to express verbally every doubt that Brownlow has tried to push aside, with the result that they squabble persistently like two halves of the same creature. It is interesting that Grimwig is described as a parrot:

> He had a manner of screwing his head on one side when he spoke; and of looking out of the corners of his eyes at the same time: which irresistibly reminded the beholder of a parrot. (p. 97)

and later as a ventriloquist:

> "A bad one! I'll eat my head if he is not a bad one," growled Mr. Grimwig, speaking by some ventriloquial power, without moving a muscle of his face. (p. 311)

Mr. Grimwig is a cynic who has no use for boys, among other things. His cynicism is designed to protect him against being disappointed and hurt, for if nothing is good at the start, one cannot be surprised when it turns out bad. It is for this reason that Dickens provides him with the curious oath-threat, "I'll eat my head," as though to say that he will in fact sacrifice his head to his heart if his cynicism is proved wrong. "This was the handsome offer with which Mr. Grimwig backed and confirmed nearly every assertion he made." (p. 97) This must therefore be taken as a wish as well as a dread, but it is a hope veiled by his mistrust of human nature. Mr. Grimwig will destroy his false outlook when the world proves him wrong. After Oliver's return late in the novel Mr. Grimwig kisses Rose, assumes a paternalism quite alien to him earlier and refrains thereafter from his threat to eat his head, his heart in fact having taken over, which the three turns of the chair and the kiss symbolize. Thereafter he is "all smiles and kindness, and not offering to eat his head—no, not once; . . ." (p. 394) Mr. Brownlow sends Oliver out on his disastrous errand to prove to himself that he is right and Grimwig, his negative alter ego, is wrong.

> The old gentleman was just going to say that Oliver should not go out on any account; when a most malicious cough from

> Mr. Grimwig determined him that he should; and that, by his prompt discharge of the commission, he should prove to him the injustice of his suspicions: on this head at least: at once. (p. 101)

Once again Oliver momentarily becomes the pawn in someone else's game. It is Mrs. Bedwin, who does not require proofs and reason and whose desire to keep him in her sight grows out of love, who is proved right. But it is necessary that Oliver leave Browlow's, for that kind but hurt old man is not yet a fit guardian. Oliver must proceed on his social progress to find a home where he can exist entirely in his own right, for no other reason than that he is Oliver, a child who takes up space in this world and thus earns a place by virtue of his independent human dignity.

Before meeting the Maylies, Oliver makes a further "social" progress in the acquisition of an "older sister" and ally in Nancy. In his "quest" for a family Oliver acquires the pretended sister that Dickens significantly provides for him. She saves him from a savage beating and promises him allegiance and he in his turn elicits from her the latent goodness that has become obscured by her brutal life and associates. Oliver's next acquisition is a real aunt and a real guardian, the two Maylie women. Just as Oliver narrowly and almost accidentally escaped disaster at his meeting with Brownlow, so his short life is almost ended at the time of his encounter with the Maylies. But Dickens quite deliberately represents his meeting with Rose so as to contrast it with the Brownlow meeting.

> With a footstep as soft and gentle as the voice, the speaker tripped away. She soon returned, with the direction that the wounded person was to be carried, carefully, up stairs to Mr. Giles's room; and that Brittles was to saddle the pony and betake himself instantly to Chertsey: from which place he was to despatch, with all speed, a constable and doctor.
>
> "But won't you take one look at him, first, miss?" asked Mr. Giles, with as much pride as if Oliver were some bird of rare plumage, that he had skilfully brought down. "Not one little peep, miss?"
>
> "Not now, for the world," replied the young lady. "Poor fellow! Oh! treat him kindly, Giles, for my sake!"
>
> The old servant looked up at the speaker, as she turned away, with a glance as proud and admiring as if she had been his own child. Then, bending over Oliver, he helped to carry

him up stairs, with the care and solicitude of a woman. (p. 211)

The refusal to look at Oliver, having the pretext of Rose's feminine frailty, her abhorrence of blood, in fact has the effect of depriving her of any motivation at all. Her directions come from her natural compassion, uninfluenced by family likenesses or the innocence of Oliver's appearance. Mr. Brownlow only mistakenly thought he was robbed by Oliver. The Maylies know that he "broke" into the house, as do we. Rose's simple and complete response of "good nature" is the first instance of its kind in the novel and it is here, rightly, that Oliver must stay, and from here in fact he never again departs in the novel, for the Maylies are already fit to receive the outcast. As though to make quite clear the contrast in his receivers, Dickens permits Oliver no chance to corroborate his story and the Maylies every chance to doubt him. Brownlow is quite certain he has been duped and trusts neither Oliver nor his own best instincts. The Maylies, however, have not a second's doubt as to Oliver's veracity, or if they do, their own generosity is not a whit affected by it. Oliver fails to produce Barney and fails again to produce Brownlow but "The circumstance occasioned no alternation, however, in the behaviour of his benefactors." (p. 237) Later when Oliver sees Monks and Fagin and no one else sees any sign of them, it never occurs to anyone to doubt for a second the boy's sincerity.[22]

Mr. Brownlow's final conversion is achieved when he and Rose are brought together and is beautifully clarified by the conversion of Grimwig and the conduct of Mrs. Bedwin. Brownlow wants a sign: " 'if you have it in your power to produce any evidence which will alter the unfavourable opinion I was once induced to entertain of that poor child, in Heaven's name put me in possession of it.' " (p. 311) He is deceived by appearances because he has lost his faith in human beings and has failed to realize that his soured vision will distort all he sees. It is interesting that while Brownlow remains suspicious of Oliver and is quite ready to believe Bumble's story of Oliver's character, never for a moment entertaining a doubt as to Bumble's honesty or judgement, Mrs. Bedwin categorically refuses to believe in Oliver's badness.

"Mrs. Bedwin," said Mr. Brownlow, when the housekeeper appeared; "that boy, Oliver, is an impostor."

> "It can't be, sir. It cannot be," said the old lady, energetically.
> "I tell you he is," retorted the old gentleman. "What do you mean by can't be? We have just heard a full account of him from his birth; and he has been a thorough-paced little villain, all his life."
> "I never will believe it, sir," replied the old lady, firmly. "Never!" (p. 125)

Her response seems, from the evidence, just as valid as the other. Brownlow's soured vision is further illustrated by his reception of Rose on their first meeting. Having failed to show her the normal courtesies, he explains, " 'I beg your pardon, young lady—I imagined it was some importunate person who—I beg you will excuse me. Be seated, pray.' " (p. 310) Rose does not know the rule that Brownlow has made regarding the mention of Oliver's name, and when she introduces this subject it produces the most disturbing effect. Mr. Brownlow, however, exercises his reason, he asks for evidence. Mr. Grimwig, as cynical as ever, verbalizes Brownlow's doubt and suspicion: " 'A bad one! I'll eat my head if he is not a bad one,' growled Mr. Grimwig, . . ." (p. 311) Brownlow and Grimwig then engage in a dialogue that symbolizes an inner conflict and is full of ironies:

> "Do not heed my friend, Miss Maylie," said Mr. Brownlow; "he does not mean what he says."
> "Yes, he does," growled Mr. Grimwig.
> "No, he does not," said Mr. Brownlow, obviously rising in wrath as he spoke.
> "He'll eat his head, if he doesn't," growled Mr. Grimwig.
> "He would deserve to have it knocked off, if he does," said Mr. Brownlow.
> "And he'd uncommonly like to see any man offer to do it," responded Mr. Grimwig, knocking his stick upon the floor. (p. 311)

Mr. Grimwig would not only not object to anyone's knocking off his head—he would metaphorically *like* to see someone do it and make him a whole man. Rose in fact does it with her information, which is why he kisses her. To make the application of the Brownlow-Grimwig morality play quite clear, Dickens shows the contrast with Mrs. Bedwin's reception of Oliver. " 'God be good to me!' cried the old lady, embracing him; 'it is my innocent boy!' " (p. 313) To prevent the reader from suspecting that Mrs. Bedwin has received any knowledge of Oliver prior to her entry, Dickens uses her poor eyesight, which prevents her even seeing that Oliver is present; it is a device similar to Rose's dislike of the sight of blood. When she does speak there is a marvellous assurance in her faith and in the way she waves aside the passage of time, as though Oliver's absence has been a matter of hours only, the prank of a mischievous child.

> "He would come back—I knew he would," said the old lady, holding him in her arms. "How well he looks, and how like a gentleman's son he is dressed again! Where have you been, this long, long while?" (p. 313)

Oliver later will finally become a son, not through birth but through the love of others: "he [Brownlow] gratified the only remaining wish of Oliver's warm and earnest heart, and thus linked together a little society, . . ." (p. 412)

Oliver's progress is now complete except for the need to return to the scene of his birth. The world of *Oliver Twist,* of poor, rich, good and evil, has come full circle, for these are not separate worlds, but states of mind that exist side by side, open to change by a shift of angle or vision, and all these worlds have been connected intricately all through the novel. The links of Nancy and Monks and Bumble and Brownlow are used to show that none of them is exclusive of the others—family being no guarantee of goodness and love, and a gang of thieves no certain excluder of virtue. Love, totally unmotivated by any purpose whatsoever and arising only in response to the beauty of humanity of the object, the instinctive compassion of good-nature, only this is necessary to transform the poorhouse world into the garden of grace with which the novel ends. But Dickens is under no illusion that his ending is anything more than a fairy-tale conclusion. Dick is dead and Oliver might easily have been Dick. There is a latent dark ending to this novel no less present for not being stated. Just as Brecht made explicit the darkness of Gay's opera, so Dickens never forgets the Hogarthian origins of his novel while imposing his happy ending. Oliver's statement to Rose is redolent of late Shakespearian plays, the first few words suggesting a whole world of secret suffering, traditionally more appropriate to an old Lear than a young child.

"It will make you cry, I know, to hear what he can tell; but

> never mind, never mind, it will be all over, and you will smile again—I know that too—to think how changed he is; you did the same with me. He said 'God bless you' to me when I ran away," cried the boy with a burst of affectionate emotion; "and I will say 'God bless *you*' now, and show him how I love him for it!" (p. 393)

To hear what Dick could tell would be indeed a heartrending experience. But Dick is dead.

> "Oliver, my child," said Mrs. Maylie, "where have you been, and why do you look so sad? There are tears stealing down your face at this moment. What is the matter?"
>
> It is a world of disappointment; often to the hopes we most cherish, and hopes that do our nature the greatest honour.
>
> Poor Dick was dead! (p. 403)

It is no wonder that Oliver and his aunt should pass "whole hours together in picturing the friends whom they had so sadly lost; . . ." (p. 415) for their past suffering is more real than anyone else knows and is made more poignant by their present consolations. The reader should remember that only he has been privy to the early life of Oliver. He and the child thus share a special kind of secret, a perspective of worlds within worlds that amounts to a moral vision denied to the others in the novel who represent stages of humanity in Oliver's tour of society, a journey that takes him to the underworld. On each occasion he survives through the love of those with whose help he re-enters life, when on the brink of death. This novel, as Dickens clearly states, is a moral metaphor celebrating "strong affection and humanity of heart." (p. 415)

What are we to make of Oliver's final visit to Fagin? Oliver is the only person in the entire novel who shows any compassion for Fagin. Following the total alienation revealed in the court and the crowd, Oliver calls for God's forgiveness for Fagin. How can he do this? I suppose we are meant to understand this as an instance of Oliver's goodness, but we cannot help remembering also that Oliver is the only surviving member of the gang who can visit Fagin, and he is the only member of the happy society of the novel's ending who has seen and shared what Fagin saw and was. The scene they play out together is in a way a totally private one. Only Oliver, now that Dick is dead, is fully a party to the suffering and savagery that is Fagin's world. Nancy, Sikes, the Dodger are all gone. Oliver, in his new good fortune, cannot forget the underworld he knew; only *he* knows now the distance between it and what he now enjoys. He cannot forget that Fagin was right when he "laid great stress on the fact of his having taken Oliver in, and cherished him when, without his timely aid, he might have perished with hunger." (p. 127) Oliver knows that but for luck and the kindness of a few he too might have been languishing in a prison cell and facing transportation or death, like the man before him. It is another instance of the mirror image that is seen earlier when Nancy and Rose face each other, two young girls, worlds apart, yet fundamentally the same, separated by the one being loved and the other being brutalized; the one was lucky enough to meet Mrs. Maylie, the other met Fagin and Sikes. It is a picture of two worlds bridged by Oliver who has known both:

> "Thank Heaven upon your knees, dear lady," cried the girl, "that you had friends to care for and keep you in your childhood, and that you were never in the midst of cold and hunger, and riot and drunkenness, and—and—something worse than all —as I have been from my cradle. I may use the word, for the alley and the gutter were mine,. as they will be my death-bed." (p. 302)

Noah and Charlotte, seen on their way to London, are introduced to reinforce certain patterns that are inevitable parts of these novels. They represent precisely the parallel case to Nancy and Sikes.

> "Where do you mean to stop for the night, Noah?" she asked, after they had walked a few hundred yards.
>
> "How should I know?" replied Noah, whose temper had been considerably impaired by walking.
>
> "Near, I hope," said Charlotte.
>
> "No, not near," replied Mr. Claypole. "There! Not near; so don't think it."
>
> "Why not?"
>
> "When I tell yer that I don't mean to do a thing, that's enough, without any why or because either," replied Mr. Claypole with dignity. (p. 318)

If this novel is about love and its absence, and the search for it in family and in marriage, and its redeeming powers, then the pairs of "lovers," Nancy and Sikes and Noah and Charlotte, are parodies of lovers and find their contrast in Rose and Harry. Rose hesitates to marry her lover because, out of her regard for him, she is afraid of carrying the stigma of her illegitimacy into his life, and perhaps even more she knows that it could damage their relationship if it becomes a source of resentment to her husband. As if to make this question of marriage and its powers for good and evil quite clear we are given the story of Monks' parents.

> "I know that of the wretched marriage, into which family pride, and the most sordid and narrowest of all ambition, forced your unhappy father when a mere boy, you were the sole and most unnatural issue. . . ."
>
> "But I also know," pursued the old gentleman, "the misery, the slow torture, the protracted anguish of that ill-assorted union. I know how listlessly and wearily each of that wretched pair dragged on their heavy chain through a world that was poisoned to them both. I know how cold formalities were succeeded by open taunts; how indifference gave place to dislike, dislike to hate, and hate to loathing, . . ." (p. 374)

Monks' loathing for Oliver is seen to be no mystery but the natural outcome of a learned hate, the resentment born of deprivation of love. Monks cannot love, but it is interesting that his fits at the sight of Oliver bear all the marks of hysterical convulsions resulting from inhibition; he cannot bring himself to an act of personal violence on Oliver, a sign perhaps that self-hate is at work, a loathing for the loveless self.[23]

Love then can transform the world of *Oliver Twist* and link "together a little society." But the death of Dick and Agnes and Fagin is never far away, for the absence of love can as surely poison and turn a "little society" into a jungle as its presence transforms the very same ground into a garden.

All Dickens' subsequent novels deal with heart and humanity and affection as well. It is perhaps enough for the writer to show how things are, though it proves to be not enough for Dickens, who like his characters, seems in his whole canon to be reaching for the garden of peace of his endings. Evil must first be analyzed and examined in every phase and mode, in all its manifestations. Thereafter the means to eschew evil, to attain the vision of human beauty and dignity as well as the means to acquire the "humanity of heart" will increasingly occupy the novels. The exploration of the human confusion and the means for its resolution are the themes of Dickens' work. In *Oliver Twist* Dickens is content to set out the terms and materials of his whole subject and plunge us, as he plunged his contemporaries, into the nineteenth century, where, without a theological framework he must convey images of redemption. He does this by humanizing the suffering of evil, the learning of hate, the blindness of indifference, and the transforming powers of love. The gratitude of which Dickens speaks "to that Being whose code is Mercy" is a gratitude for life. Having been born we are on our own, we and those who receive us, according to their kind.

[1]"A Postscript in lieu of a Preface," *Our Mutual Friend,* New Oxford Illustrated Dickens, 1952, p. 822.

[2]*Critical Studies of the Works of Charles Dickens* (New York: Haskell House, 1965), p. 55.

[3]Gissing, p. 55.

[4]*Charles Dickens: His Tragedy and Triumph,* 2 vols. (Boston: Little, Brown, 1952). Since completing this manuscript I have read F. R. Leavis' assertion of the inescapable influence of Hogarth on Dickens, though Leavis gives no details (*Dickens the Novelist,* p. 26).

[5]See various complaints by Browne about Dickens' exacting demands and his insistence on the drawings conforming to the projections of his own imagination, as recorded in *Life and Labours of Hâblot Knight Browne* by David Croal Thompson (London: Chapman & Hall, 1884).

[6]See George H. Ford, *Dickens and His Readers* (New York: Norton, 1965), for a survey of critical reaction.

[7]*Charles Dickens: The World of His Novels.*

[8]*Dickens: From PICKWICK to DOMBEY.*

[9]Arnold Kettle, "Dickens: Oliver Twist," reprinted in *The Dickens Critics,* ed. by George H. Ford and Lauriat Lane Jr. (Ithaca, N.Y.: Cornell Univ. Press, 1961), pp. 257-8. The "more" here refers to Kettle's preceding comments on Fagin. The critic objects to Dickens' "attempts" at irony and cites as his example the description of Fagin as a "kind old gentleman." He misses completely the depth of irony in "kind" and takes no account of the old devil-worship tradition in which the "old gentleman" description figures, nor does Kettle seem aware of the richness of parody in Dickens' language as it is applied to the English class scene. See below for my discussion of Fagin.

[10]It is worth noting that Dickens frequently makes his opening chapters symbolic miniatures for everything that follows. The most famous example is in *Bleak House,* but I suspect the same is true of *Little Dorrit, Our Mutual Friend, Great Expectations, Hard Times, A Tale of Two Cities,* perhaps, indeed, all the novels.

[11]This is true even of his apologists. I am thinking of several remarks by André Maurois in his *Dickens* (New York: Ungar, 1967).

[12]Thomas A. Jackson, *Charles Dickens: Progress of a Radical* (London: Lawrence & Wishart, 1937).

[13]One of the most extraordinary features of Dickens criticism is the persistence of the use of the ubiquitous and now boring story of Dickens' childhood and blacking-warehouse experience to explain his portraits of lonely little boys. This piece of biography-sleuthing takes no account, as an explanation, of what Dickens does with his children in the novels. The sense of alienation in the child is universal, not peculiar to Dickens, and he shows how fundamental love is to the overcoming of or compensating for the human sense of isolation discovered in the process of growing up. Dickens tries to make it clear enough—"we all know how chilled and desolate the best of us will sometimes feel"—that what interests him is the dependency of the child and what this reveals of adult values. Forget, censor, or hate what one was as a child and one will be forever insensitive to children. When Dickens looked back on his childhood he saw another creature, remote, strange and different, yet perfectly understood, as Pip and David looked back. It is not self-pity. It is compassion for everybody.

[14]The term "bastard" has traditionally been one of great opprobrium, especially among schoolboys. Insults about mothers are among the most offensive in most languages, it seems. Arabic, I understand, is particularly rich in family insults. I imagine the same is true for oriental idiom, though I only surmise.

[15]Henry Fielding, *Joseph Andrews,* Riverside ed. (Boston: Houghton Mifflin, 1961), p. 143.

[16]*Joseph Andrews,* p. 151.

[17]William F. Axton, *Circle of Fire* (Lexington: Univ. of Kentucky Press, 1966), p. 97.

[18]The best collection of evidence for Fagin as devil is provided by Lauriat Lane, Jr. in "The Devil in *Oliver Twist,*" *The Dickensian* 52 (June 1956): 132-6.

[19]*On the Nightmare* (London: Hogarth, 1931), pp. 167-8.

[20]Ernest Jones' study is given further historical substantiation by another very important work, Norman Cohn's *Pursuit of the Millenium* (New York: Harper, 1961). Both these books, in different ways, concern themselves with the rôle of psychology in social history. By their enquiry into the social repercussions of fear, superstition, and the psychic aberration at the roots of fanaticism they provide us with a useful link between anthropology and literature. This kind of consideration seems to me central for a full understanding of Dickens. Mr. Cohn's comment on the Jew-image of Christian history is strikingly apposite to a consideration of Fagin:

> But the Jew and the Cleric could also themselves very easily be seen as father-figures. This is obvious enough in the case of the cleric, who after all is actually called "Father" by the laity. If it is less obvious in the case of the Jew it is nevertheless a fact, for even today the Jew—the man who clings to the *Old Testament* and rejects the *New,* the member of the people into which Christ was born—is imagined by many Christians as typically an "old Jew," a decrepit figure in old, wornout clothes. If one examines the picture of Jews torturing and castrating a helpless and innocent boy (Plate 4), one appreciates with just how much fear and hate the phantastic figure of the bad father could be regarded. (p. 72)

If one turns to the illustration in the Cohn text cited in the above quotation, "Plate 4," one sees an almost shockingly brutal picture to which the author puts the following comment: "A medieval version of the ritual murder of a Christian boy by Jews. A striking example of the projection on to the Jews of the phantastic image of the torturing and castrating father." (p. 72) The illustration from *Oliver Twist,* "Oliver introduced to the Respectable Old Gentleman," shows a whole group of Christian boys with a Jew-figure portrayed in the precise terms of medieval conceptions as described by Mr. Cohn. Fagin even has the Devil's toasting fork, evoking all the associations of torture and power. The trident is the fishing-power symbol to give inverse equation to Christ's kindly net.

[21]Lane ("The Devil in *Oliver Twist,*" p. 135) provides in a passing comment the only clear statement I know suggesting that Brownlow is clearly the moral inferior of the Maylies. He calls this the "difference between partial and total redemption."

[22]It is interesting that in order for Oliver to encounter the attention of the respectable world the thieves have to violate the isolation of that world. In the Chertsey "rape" scene (interestingly the house is called a "crib"), the house has to be torn open and Oliver forcibly pushed through the window, and placed in the "crib." It is then that Oliver undergoes a new kind of "baptism by fire" and thus arrives at the last stage but one of his progress. The last stage will occur when Oliver acquires a father and is adopted by Mr. Brownlow, who must first be converted.

[23]This kind of case is explored much more fully in Estella of *Great Expectations.*

"TRIUMPHS OF AERIAL ARCHITECTURE" NICHOLAS NICKLEBY

Is this a holy thing to see
In a rich and fruitful land,
Babes reduced to misery,
Fed with cold and usurous hand?

And their sun does never shine,
And their fields are bleak and bare,
And their ways are filled with thorns:
It is eternal winter there.

WILLIAM BLAKE

•

The awareness of human separation, without reunion by love—is the source of shame. It is at the same time the source of guilt and anxiety.

The deepest need of man, then, is the need to overcome his separateness, to leave the prison of his aloneness. The absolute failure to achieve this aim means insanity. . . .

ERICH FROMM

•

The weather was intensely and bitterly cold; a great deal of snow fell from time to time; and the wind was intolerably keen.

NICHOLAS NICKLEBY

•

The early work, less obviously but no less forcefully than the later, for example, *Little Dorrit,* depends for its meaning and force on the author's awareness of human isolation, his awareness of the absence of a genuine community, and his presentation of this vision of separateness in various images of imprisonment. If critics have noticed little else about *Nicholas Nickleby* they have seen that isolation, or fragmentation, is one of its central themes. One says it displays an "atomistic world,"[1] another a "kaleidoscopic world,"[2] and a third speaks of "illusion, isolation and solipsism."[3] *Oliver Twist* presents us with a passive hero whose treatment exposes the characteristics and possibilities of a society. *Nicholas Nickleby,* dealing with precisely the same society, shifts its point of view to an active hero who must discover ways to integrate himself into society. While Oliver wanders, waiting to encounter a community that will accept him, Nicholas charges ahead encountering and discarding various communities until he meets the Cheerybles, who, like the Maylies before them, take in the helpless hero, whereupon he discovers that he too must help forge the community of his choosing. Both novels end in familial images. Both novels indicate that what is required is the structuring of new societies out of new impulses. To build a new society may require the growth of sufficient maturity to enable the old one to be rejected.

The central metaphor of *Nicholas Nickleby* is acting and the model by which Dickens explains the truth of human relationships is marriage or sexual pairing. This remains the most critically neglected of Dickens' novels, probably because the images do not produce a sufficiently integrating cohesion in spite of what seems to me the clarity of the author's intention. The structural problems of *Nicholas* seem to have discouraged critical answers to the question of how the Squeers' school, the acting episodes, the uncle and nephew plot and the pervasive marriage theme are all related. It is instructive to compare this situation to the large body of excellent criticism addressed to a highly unified and integrated novel like *Great Expectations.* Yet answers to the above questions can be seen. The key, I think, lies in the discovery, as revealed in this novel, that acting is not confined to the stage and that through the playing of rôles, people are able to perpetrate the most inhumane acts. Yet this idea is explored through apparently disparate plot lines. The Yorkshire school is begun and dropped. The Crummles are introduced and dropped. Nicholas' adventures (and Kate's) seem to proceed without precise integration with the other elements in the novel. What has the school to do with Crummles? What connection is there between Madeline Bray and Madame Mantalini? Philip Collins suggests that "Simply, Dickens wanted to write about

Yorkshire schools and theatrical companies and the rest. Nicholas has virtually no character upon which these experiences might impinge."[4] There is some truth in this, yet Oliver has no more "character" than Nicholas, while *Oliver Twist* is a much more successful novel. The difference, I think, is that the central themes of the later novel do not accord happily with the plot structure and are not sufficiently explicit or elaborated to hold the plot together. Oliver fits nicely into his picaresque journeying. Nicholas is, I believe, a comic version of *Hamlet*, and here the plot of *Hamlet* suffers from too much stretching. It is moreover true that Dickens wanted to write of the schools and that this section is the most forceful and vivid in the novel. But does this necessarily mean that there is no relationship between Yorkshire and all the rest? It is incumbent on us to see if we can perceive and explain how all the elements fit together. Not that when we have done so we necessarily have made a wholly successful novel out of one that may be loosely constructed, obscure or weakly peopled. We shall, however, have raised some interesting possibilities about the novel's meaning, about the distance between Dickens' intention and realization and about the relationship between *Nicholas* and the rest of Dickens' work. Nicholas may not be the character to fulfill the task Dickens had in mind for him, but his rôle is more complicated than has been generally thought. He is an inverted Oliver, the passive made active. Dickens fully intended Nicholas to be more complex and varied than most readers find him:

> If Nicholas be not always found to be blameless or agreeable, he is not always intended to appear so. He is a young man of an impetuous temper and of little or no experience; and I saw no reason why such a hero should be lifted out of nature. (p. xix)

To summarize the critical problem then, we must see if we can account for the juxtaposition of the pseudo-picaresque hero and structure with the Yorkshire schools, the company of actors, the villainy of Ralph, the surfeit of marriages and the story of Smike. I have said that *Nicholas* is a version of *Hamlet*. True, it is a version inimitably Dickensian, with happy ending and poetic justice complete, but the elements of Shakespeare's plot seem nevertheless inescapable. I know of no external evidence for this, for though Dickens' letters show him to be intimately familiar with the play there is no clue of a specific connection between these two works. All we have as the faintest clue is the novel's original dedication to Macready. Nevertheless I find it fruitful to read the novel bearing Shakespeare's play in mind. Uncle Ralph, like Claudius, seems to have acquired an economic "kingdom" by whatever means are at his disposal. His brother, neglected and forgotten, dies of a broken heart or world-weariness and Ralph finds himself with a sister-in-law whom he does not, indeed, marry, but whom he agrees to take into his "protection" on the condition that her son, his nephew, is sent away. During his sojourn "abroad," that is, in Yorkshire, the nephew discovers his uncle's design, later joins with a company of actors, and takes part in a Shakespearian play within the novel, *Romeo and Juliet*. There is a fight over a sister, Kate, as the result of Nicholas' accidentally overhearing another man speak of her, just as Hamlet overhears Laertes. This man is Sir Mulberry Hawk, like Laertes a rake and gallant, similarly a conspirator with the hero's uncle, and, where Laertes is a fencing-master, Hawk is a former pugilist of some distinction. Both men are associated with France (the seat of high-living) into which place Hawk finally retreats. While certain relationships are altered, the similarity of event is clear. Two scenes confirm this suspicion. In the scene of confrontation between Claudius and Hamlet there are three principal subjects of discussion: one is the past career of Hamlet and the necessity of ceasing his education; the second is the reaction to the death of old Hamlet, and third is the requirement that henceforth Hamlet should do what Claudius tells him to do. Turning to the novel we find that " 'Nicholas has not long completed such education as his poor father could give him, . . .' " (p. 25) This is no satisfaction to his uncle, who regards him as worthless and useless and who hates him on the irrational grounds of simple contrast: "The old man's eye was keen with the twinklings of avarice and cunning; the young man's bright with the light of intelligence and spirit." (p. 24) Nicholas, like Hamlet, must now, because of his father's death, give up all thoughts of continuing his education. This seems to be, in both cases, the result of the uncles' desire to have a more repressive control over the youthful nephews. As to the discussion of the father's death, readers will remember the elaborate dialogue in *Hamlet* on the subject of death as "common."

For what we know must be, and is as common
As any the most vulgar thing to sense,
Why should we in our peevish opposition
Take it to heart?
(*Hamlet,* I, ii, 98-101)

In the novel we find Ralph saying:

"You must bear up against sorrow, ma'am; *I* always do."
"Mine was no common loss! . . ."
"It was no *un*common loss, ma'am. . . . Husbands die every day, ma'am, and wives too." (p. 23)

Ralph, like Claudius, seems to suggest that in his case "discretion fought with nature" and discretion won. Indeed, his whole career has been such a fight and one that "nature" has lost more and more easily.

One other scene must be mentioned. Later in the novel Mrs. Nickleby is courted by the madman next door. When Nicholas discovers this and discusses it with her we witness a scene remarkably close to that between Hamlet and Gertrude. Nicholas tells his mother that she should "vindicate" herself, "especially one of your age and condition, in circumstances like these, which are unworthy of a serious thought." (p. 484) Hamlet rebukes his mother:

You cannot call it love; for at your age
The heydey in the blood is tame, it's humble.
(*Hamlet,* III, iv, 68-9)

Again compare Nicholas' " 'I would not shame you by seeming to take them to heart or treat them earnestly for an instant,' " (p. 484) with Hamlet's " 'O Shame! where is thy blush?' " (III, iv, 82) and " '. . . sure that sense / Is apoplex'd.' " (III, iv, 72-73) As to the suitor himself, he is an "absurd old idiot" while Claudius is " 'A slave that is not twentieth part the tithe / Of your precedent lord.' " (III, iv, 97-8) Mrs. Nickleby asks " 'What am I to do?' " (Gertrude: "What shall I do?") and Nicholas answers, " 'Do what your good sense and feeling, and respect for my father's memory, would prompt,' " and do not tell Kate, he says, " 'for Heaven's sake.' " (p. 484) Hamlet tells *his* mother,

Confess yourself to heaven,
Repent what's past; avoid what is to come;
(III, iv, 149-50)

Both scenes take place at night and end with "So saying, Nicholas kissed his mother, and bad her good night" and Hamlet's " 'Good night, Mother.' " This brief account will by no means be as convincing as a reading of Chapter XXXVII itself. The sense of *déjà vu* is strong indeed.

Aside from this being interesting as a literary curiosity, there is much greater significance in a comparison of the two works. Beyond the superficial similarity of framework, both seek to explore the problem of how corruption in society may be exorcised and cleansed and what sort of individual and what kind of qualities are necessary for this moral purge. Stripped to its two most obvious levels, both integrally related, *Hamlet* is a story of bitter struggle between a nephew and an uncle. At the same time it is a struggle for the future of the State, the act of cleansing away evil, restoring rightful and good rule and exposing the lies on which the state is currently built. The intense and immediate opposite of the older man is the younger, and the desire to keep him under control is not merely instinctive but political. The youth is both an inheritor (neither uncle has a legitimate heir) and a force for change. Ralph's rôle is economic and his link with Squeers' school direct. Claudius wishes to retain power and his queen. By the use of the hold they have over political tributaries (Squeers and England), both rulers intend to prevent their nephews from disturbing their tyranny. The nephews are placed in rebellious positions naturally. They must oppose where they are harassed and must protect their own interests and seek their own growth and ambition. To effect this end the hero must cleanse himself, gain perspective, discover the truth, achieve self-awareness and self-control and finally act dispassionately so as to avoid tainted motivation. He must act, that is, in the rôle of divine agent. Stripped of its supernatural elements, then, one might say that *Hamlet* puts the proposition relentlessly, without compromise and in all its apocalyptically remote difficulty, that a wholesome state is ruled and inhabited by good people, the task of each generation being to free itself of lies and deceit and the iron grip of the past. To do this requires in the individual a degree of perception, perspective and total awareness that is universally rare.[5] I have tried to suggest that in *Oliver Twist* Dickens began to explore the beginnings of this vision by creating metaphors around the interdependence of society and the individual's perception. *Nicholas Nickleby* continues this idea. Where *Oliver Twist* finds its prototype of society in the family and in attitudes towards children, *Nicholas Nickleby* explores its moral vision of society through the theme of sex and marriage, through the relationship of adults. The Yorkshire schools might, from one perspective, be seen to exist in the service of certain kinds of sexual relations. Claudius and Gertrude could have been, had they occurred in the nineteenth century, ideal patrons of such schools. Hamlet, if younger, might easily have found himself a kind of royal Smike.

No other Dickens novel seems to present such a proliferation of married couples.[6] At least, while other novels do have famous pairs (the Gargerys, the Dombeys, the Merdles, the Lammles) they seem memorable as separate figures or as unique couples. In *Nicholas Nickleby* the impressive array of pairs seems to illustrate some theme about marriage itself. Moreover, since marriage precedes children, and the Yorkshire schools are a repository for unwanted children, what more natural than for Dickens to seek to explore a dozen examples of this most interesting institution. It is through Squeers' continuous re-entry and the permanent presence of Smike, that the schools are kept in our awareness from beginning to end. Dickens was not interested merely in exposing the horrors of the schools themselves. As scholars have pointed out, these had been well known for many years.[7] He was driven to explore beyond the fact to the cause, to the purposes they served and to the customers who sustained them. The Yorkshire schools were in fact an important feature of England's social life, like brothels in a puritan culture. They were a symptom of a moral horror, a monstrous attitude, more even than they were horrible in themselves.

What sort of places were these Yorkshire schools, and why do they represent for Dickens in his novel something profoundly rotten in the heart of England? Philip Collins tells us,

> That the schools were Spartan at best, and often harsh and cruel, and that many of them advertised 'No vacations' and were therefore much used as a depository for orphans, bastards and other unwanted children . . . .[8]

Their teachers were

> Traders in the avarice, indifference, or imbecility of parents, and the helplessness of children; ignorant, sordid, brutal men, to whom few considerate persons would have entrusted the board and lodging of a horse or a dog; they formed the worthy corner-stone of a structure, which, for absurdity and a magnificent high-minded *laissez-aller* neglect, has rarely been exceeded in the world. (p. xv)

Out of sight, out of mind, the schools were a way of making non-love blind. Their customers are men like Snawley whose motive is avarice and Ralph Nickleby whose motives are shame, greed and guilt. The children are given into the care of Squeers, himself significantly one-eyed, a sadist in power, one more keeper of a Dickensian concentration camp.

> "Half-past three," muttered Mr. Squeers, turning from the window, and looking sulkily at the coffee-room clock. "There will be nobody here to-day."
>
> Much vexed by this reflection, Mr. Squeers looked at the little boy to see whether he was doing anything he could beat him for. As he happened not to be doing anything at all, he merely boxed his ears, and told him not to do it again. (p. 31)

Dickens knows that such a man can only pursue his tendencies by an elaborate form of self-deceit and by an insane greed.

> . . . Squeers covered his rascality, even at home, with a spice of his habitual deceit; as if he really had a notion of some day or other being able to take himself in, and persuade his own mind that he was a very good fellow. (p. 87)

Power, too, is an inevitable part of the desire of such a man.

> "Now I'll tell you what, Mrs. Squeers. In this matter of having a teacher, I'll take my own way, if you please. A slave-driver in the West Indies is allowed a man under him, to see that his blacks don't run away, or get up a rebellion; and I'll have a man under me to do the same with *our* blacks, . . ." (p. 99)

And the boys must be regarded as not human at all, as of less value than domestic animals:

> "How is my Squeery?" said this lady in a playful manner, and a very hoarse voice.
>
> "Quite well, my love," replied Squeers. "How's the cows?"
>
> "All right, every one of 'em," answered the lady.
>
> "And the pigs?" said Squeers.
>
> "As well as they were when you went away."

> "Come; that's a blessing," said Squeers, pulling off his greatcoat. "The boys are all as they were, I suppose?"
>
> "Oh, yes, they're well enough," replied Mrs. Squeers, snappishly. "That young Pitcher's had a fever." (p. 78)

What Nicholas sees on his arrival is an image of every reject that a loveless society can gather together for the purposes of their slow elimination.

> Pale and haggard faces, lank and bony figures, children with the countenances of old men, deformities with irons upon their limbs, boys of stunted growth, and others whose long meagre legs would hardly bear their stooping bodies, all crowded on the view together; there were the bleared eye, the hare-lip, the crooked foot, and every ugliness or distortion that told of unnatural aversion conceived by parents for their offspring, or of young lives which, from the earliest dawn of infancy, had been one horrible endurance of cruelty and neglect. . . . With every kindly sympathy and affection blasted in its birth, with every young and healthy feeling flogged and starved down, with every revengeful passion that can fester in swollen hearts eating its evil way to their core in silence, what an incipient Hell was breeding here! (p. 88)

These are not the orphans of *Oliver Twist*. They are more positively rejected, the outcasts of a society whose values have become totally dehumanized. Dickens well knew that he was creating Squeers as a type:

> . . . Mr. Squeers is the representative of a class, and not of an individual. Where imposture, ignorance, and brutal cupidity, are the stock in trade of a small body of men, and one is described by these characteristics, all his fellows will recognise something belonging to themselves, and each will have a misgiving that the portrait is his own. (p. xviii)

The system of Dotheboys Hall can actually be made to fall like a house of cards at a touch, in this case the touch of love. This in fact happens by virtue of the mixture of compassion and gratitude that grows up between Nicholas and Smike, for Squeers and his institution are doomed once somebody cares and opens the cage. Inexorably the novel moves towards the moment when all the birds fly in a kind of frenzied dispersion, as though the whole had been held together only by illusion. But Nicholas has much to learn before he rounds off the novel by his return visit to Yorkshire as liberator. Like Hamlet, Nicholas must undergo a period of maturation and suffering before he can act as a reforming agent. Both heroes suffer a domestic exile, pushed aside from the centre of power and unable to realize their heroic destinies until they are able to see clearly what rôle is proper and natural for them. Both must first play other parts on and off the stage: both Shakespeare and Dickens explore the entire question of rôle-playing in their respective works. Gilbert Murray's comments on Stoicism seem especially relevant here.

> Life becomes, as the Stoics more than once tell us, like a play which is acted or a game which is played with counters. Viewed from outside, the counters are valueless; but to those engaged in the game their importance is paramount. What really and ultimately matters is that the game shall be played. God, the eternal dramatist, has cast you for some part in His drama and hands you the rôle. What interests Him is the one thing which He cannot determine—the action of your free and conscious will.[9]

Nicholas' first trip is as a subscriber to the system and he lends his own illusions to those others carefully constructed to sustain the Schools: "Parental Care" (payment of fees), "boarded, clothed, booked" (kept in prison in rags), "instructed in all languages living and dead" (the language of brutality, the rod and abuse), "no extras, no vacation" (not allowed to escape), "diet unparalleled" (not fit for human consumption). Nicholas goes to Yorkshire repressing all wise judgment and misgiving about the job itself and about the care that his uncle will lavish on his sister and mother. Newman Noggs, the Horatio of this tale, knows the truth. Kate has the courage to raise doubts: " 'But the salary is so small, and it is such a long way off, uncle!' faltered Kate." (p. 26) Only Nicholas feeds himself on "a thousand visionary ideas." As soon becomes clear, Nicholas deludes himself thoroughly not only by reason of his ignorance and his castles in the air, but also by virtue of a pride that aspires to real power and riches quickly. He gives Newman Noggs a "fervent and glowing description of all the honours and advantages to be derived from his appointment at that seat of learning, Dotheboys Hall." (p. 41) When he arrives there, Nicholas quickly undergoes the process of disillusionment, but he runs the risk of becoming inured to the scenes around him.

He engages in a social exchange, a parody of drawing-room courtship that seems wildly grotesque in the setting. He succeeds in making enemies of Miss Squeers and John Browdie:

> This state of things had been brought about by divers means and workings. Miss Squeers had brought it about, by aspiring to the high state and condition of being matrimonially engaged, without good grounds for so doing; Miss Price had brought it about by indulging in three motives of action: first, a desire to punish her friend for laying claim to a rivalship in dignity, having no good title: secondly, the gratification of her own vanity, in receiving the compliments of a smart young man: and thirdly, a wish to convince the corn-factor of the great danger he ran in deferring the celebration of their expected nuptials; while Nicholas had brought it about, by half an hour's gaiety and thoughtlessness, and a very sincere desire to avoid the imputation of inclining at all to Miss Squeers. (pp. 111-12)

It is worth noting that Dickens accounts for this paradigm of social confusion by citing silliness, pretense, deceit and pride in all cases. Only Browdie is excluded from blame and it will be important to notice that the "honest Yorkshireman" is always himself, open, candid, and entirely unmotivated by anything except his own good nature. This quality of candour will continue to be of central moral significance in Dickens' work. Nicholas pays for his error of pretension and realizes quickly that his games have no place in this world of horror:

> "I was glad," he murmured, "to grasp at any relief from the sight of this dreadful place, or the presence of its vile master. I have set these people by the ears, and made two new enemies, where, Heaven knows, I needed none. Well, it is a just punishment for having forgotten, even for an hour, what is around me now!" (p. 113)

It is a dramatic recognition of false and real worlds juxtaposed. But Nicholas still has much to learn. He shows an unrealistic and inappropriate pride, a concern for his own dignity and image on other occasions. When asked to join Crummles for supper he says: " 'It is more than probable, I think, that the gentleman may not relish my company; and although I am the dusty figure you see, I am too proud to thrust myself into his,' " (p. 277) and after joining the company of actors Nicholas objects to canvassing for the performance: " 'I am very sorry to throw a damp upon the prospects of anybody, and more especially a lady,' replied Nicholas;

'but really I must decidedly object to making one of the canvassing party,' " (p. 306) though he is not led by this attitude to hardness of heart or stubbornness and he reveals a growing self-awareness. " 'It is not in my nature,' said Nicholas, moved by these appeals, 'to resist any entreaty, unless it is to do something positively wrong; and, beyond a feeling of pride, I know nothing which should prevent my doing this.' " (pp. 306-7) After beating Squeers, Nicholas leaves for London with Smike, but not before he has been able to apologize to Browdie and seal his friendship with him. Smike and Nicholas are cousins. The former is so brutalized, so ignorant and so neglected that he resembles a clear case of retardation. He reminds us of what Oliver might have become. His relationship to Nicholas is a revelation of contrast between the same materials treated differently, the one accepted, loved and educated, the other rejected and treated as we have seen. Love comes to Smike too late and his love of Kate remains undeclared and unfulfilled. Nicholas and his family reclaim Smike sufficiently so that he sees what might have been.

To return to Nicholas and his adventures is to bring us to Ralph, the ruler of the "kingdom" to which the hero returns, like Hamlet coming back from his abortive trip to England. He returns to confront his uncle, who is not only the wicked uncle of the fairy-tale but a much more carefully drawn figure, symbolic paradigm of self-alienation and avarice. The power and riches of Ralph are compensations to him for the absence of love and kinship and fellow-feeling. Indeed the novel persistently raises the question of outlook, of values, of joy and gloom as postures towards the world. Dickens suggests that one's response to the world is really a matter of decision; for that reason he places together, early on, the two stories of the "Five Sisters of York" and "The Baron of Grogzwig."

> "If our affections be tried, our affections are our consolation and comfort; . . ." (p. 65)

> "And my advice to all men is, that if ever they become hipped and melancholy from similar causes (as very many men do), they look at both sides of the question, applying a magnifying glass to the best one; and if they still feel tempted to retire without leave, that they smoke a large pipe and drink a full bottle first, and profit by the laudable example of the Baron of Grogzwig." (pp. 74-75)

But Dickens goes much deeper than this by suggesting that in order to laugh like the Baron one must enjoy life itself (the pipe, the bottle and people) and in order to do that one must really be at peace with oneself. The man who does not like himself cannot like anyone else. To put it another way, a man who has thoroughly deceived himself about his own nature and consequently about his values must then undertake a view of life in conformity with his earlier deceptions, to sustain his false creation. The cynical, hard-bitten, avaricious con-man must insist that everyone else is similarly inclined and thus justify himself. This way of regarding the world is perhaps more widespread than any other and Dickens illustrates his profound understanding of this throughout the novel. The relationship between the central acting metaphor, the role of deceit and the world view of Ralph and Arthur Gride may not be obvious, but it is clear enough on reflection. Nicholas' family, we are told, were "wholly unacquainted with what is called the world—a conventional phrase which, being interpreted, often signifieth all the rascals in it." (p. 28) In this sense they never become acquainted with "the world," for they never sour or despair. Their capacity to love sustains and protects them and keeps their vision clear. Ralph Nickleby, on the other hand, has decided that the supreme value is money. Now this would be, as satire, the supreme cliché were it not for Dickens' awareness and revelation that the great danger of passionate money-getting is that it requires the disregard of one's own nature and that of others, a distortion of view productive of personal and social disaster.

> On the death of his father, Ralph Nickleby, who had been some time before placed in a mercantile house in London, applied himself passionately to his old pursuit of money-getting, in which he speedily became so buried and absorbed, that he quite forgot his brother for many years; and if, at times, a recollection of his old play-fellow broke upon him through the haze in which he lived—for gold conjures up a mist about a man, more destructive of all his old senses and lulling to his feelings than the fumes of charcoal—it brought along with it a companion thought, that if they were intimate he would want to borrow money of him. So, Mr. Ralph Nickleby shrugged his shoulders, and said things were better as they were. (p. 4)

The fact that Ralph "said" things were better as they were does not mean that he believed it. But the haze inevitably gets thicker.

The early lies produce new rationalizations to protect the old and the real man gets buried deeper and deeper in the fog of self-denial. It is no accident that all this is explained in the first chapter called "Introduces all the Rest," for once again Dickens clearly sets up the terms for the entire novel at the start. All that happens thereafter will illustrate the consequences of and the answers to these distorted values. As I have said above, the world will conform like a mirror to the mind which looks at it and those who dislike themselves and have opted for deceit and money-getting will find themselves surrounded by greed and hate.

> The only scriptural admonition that Ralph Nickleby heeded, in the letter, was "know thyself." He knew himself well, and choosing to imagine that all mankind were cast in the same mould, hated them; for, though no man hates himself, the coldest among us having too much self-love for that, yet most men unconsciously judge the world from themselves, and it will be very generally found that those who sneer habitually at human nature, and affect to despise it, are among its worst and least pleasant samples. (pp. 567-68)

I am interested in the phrase "in the letter," a reservation made wisely by the author who is aware that the spirit of self-knowledge is a thing quite different and one which he will explore with increasing perception in later novels.

Ralph, however, is human after all. Somewhere in Ralph there are remnants of feeling, compassion and regret which persistently struggle for realization against the overwhelming odds of habitual suppression and self-deceit. The best image of this is given as the description of the scene that faces the usurer from his office window:

> Some London houses have a melancholy little plot of ground behind them, usually fenced in by four high whitewashed walls, and frowned upon by stacks of chimneys: in which there withers on, from year to year, a crippled tree, that makes a show of putting forth a few leaves late in autumn when other trees shed theirs, and, drooping in the effort, lingers on, all crackled and smoke-dried, till the following season, when it repeats the same process, and perhaps if the weather be particularly genial, even tempts some rheumatic sparrow to chirrup in its branches. People sometimes call these dark yards "gardens;" it is not supposed that they were ever planted, but rather that they are

> pieces of unreclaimed land, with the withered vegetation of the original brick-field. . . .
>
> It was into a place of this kind that Mr. Ralph Nickleby gazed, as he sat with his hands in his pockets looking out of a window. (p. 8)

It is an allegorical passage. Ralph is after all "the crippled tree" imprisoned by "four high walls." The tree just grew but the walls were made around the "unreclaimed land." His world of commerce and deceit is "unreclaimed land" and his rationalizations are the "four high walls" to keep people out and himself isolated. The leaves and the sparrow are the remnants of human love and feeling that keep Ralph human and alive. Ralph suffers some pangs of conscience about Kate and his use of her as a pawn in his economic game of chess with Sir Mulberry Hawk. Dickens shows us Ralph debating with himself in a passage reminiscent of Claudius' attempt at prayer which ends, "Words without thoughts never to heaven go."

> To say that Ralph loved or cared for—in the most ordinary acceptation of those terms—any one of God's creatures, would be the wildest fiction. Still, there had somehow stolen upon him from time to time a thought of his niece which was tinged with compassion and pity; breaking through the dull cloud of dislike or indifference which darkened men and women in his eyes, there was, in her case, the faintest gleam of light—a most feeble and sickly ray at the best of times—but there it was, and it showed the poor girl in a better and purer aspect than any in which he had looked on human nature yet.
>
> "I wish," thought Ralph, "I had never done this. . . ." (p. 341)

But Dickens presents an exemplary instance of the rationalization that makes Ralph's "reasoning" come out on the side of expedience, leaving him "free" of the most obvious guilt.

> He sat down, and told the chances, for and against, on his fingers.
>
> "If I had not put them in the right track to-day," thought Ralph, "this foolish woman would have done so. Well. If her daughter is as true to herself as she should be from what I have seen, what harm ensues? A little teazing, a little humbling, a few tears. Yes," said Ralph, aloud, as he locked his iron safe. "She must take her chance. She must take her chance." (p. 341)

Ralph would not be an interesting case did he not suffer some torment from hate, envy, bitterness and contempt as the price for his self-denial. Even Gride with his lust, which adds spice to his greed, is more alive than Ralph. Gride sees himself as satisfying both avarice and lust at once by the possession of the beautiful Madeline. Ralph is so isolated that even the inducement of vast riches cannot make the most pleasant of companions a possible temptation to him. His encounter with the Mantalinis on one occasion reveals the depths of his bitterness:

> "Oh! Nothing, ma'am, nothing," replied Ralph. "I know his amiable nature, and yours,—mere little remarks that give a zest to your daily intercourse—lovers' quarrels that add sweetness to those domestic joys which promise to last so long—that's all; that's all."
>
> If an iron door could be supposed to quarrel with its hinges, and to make a firm resolution to open with slow obstinacy, and grind them to powder in the process, it would emit a pleasanter sound in so doing than did these words in the rough and bitter voice in which they were uttered by Ralph. Even Mr. Mantalini felt their influence, and turning affrighted round, exclaimed: "What a demd horrid croaking!" (p. 126)

It should be remembered, however, that once upon a time Ralph did marry for money, but so sealed were his affections, so impossible was communication that he lived mostly alone and remained totally unmoved by the existence of his child. This child is Smike, the senior pupil of the Squeers school, a kind of symbolic founding member. Ralph then becomes in the novel the prototype of loveless parenthood, more deeply involved with the Squeers establishment than even he knows. He is the novel's centre of anti-social destructiveness, the king of a metaphoric state in which love is everywhere distorted into sexual arrangements for greed, lust, appearance or convenience. If, in *Hamlet*, something is rotten in Denmark, in *Nicholas* there is some spiritual sickness in England, where Ralph is the figure of manipulating and loveless power, a kind of sterile Fisher-King watching over the wasteland of the benighted garden behind his house.

If greed, money-lust and hunger for power are forms of self-deceit contributing to a social system of lies and inhumanity, then the novel may be said to present such deceit in an elaborate variety of forms. From the silliness of the Lillyvicks to the absurd pretensions of the Wititterlys we have examples of marriage based on every kind of unreality. Mr. Mantalini deceives Mrs. Mantalini in order to spend her money and she deceives herself in order to be able to believe Mr. Mantalini. The Kenwigses play at middle-class pretensions, Gride lusts for Madeline Bray, but more for her riches than her person, and the whole world of suitors and courtship and bribery is superbly parodied by the mad neighbour who courts Mrs. Nickleby, for Dickens leaves no one out of the marriage-aspiring vision of how the world is generated and organized.

> "I have estates, ma'am," said the old gentleman, flourishing his right hand negligently, as if he made very light of such matters, and speaking very fast; "jewels, lighthouses, fish-ponds, a whalery of my own in the North Sea, and several oyster-beds of great profit in the Pacific Ocean." (p. 536)

All of this is sustained and borne out in the novel by the image of acting, a metaphor that conveys precisely the folly of a world bent on deluding itself into a comfortable fantasy that produces the suffering of which the schools are the chosen example. Nicholas joins the acting company of Crummles. Hamlet, like Nicholas, plays many parts in a drama that is in a sense about drama. We might regard *Hamlet* as presenting the view that all life-situations are plays within the play. Hamlet and Nicholas must find a way to play a determinant rôle in the drama in which they involuntarily find themselves. Both play stage-parts in the process as though this gives some perspective as they work their way towards a natural life-rôle. Perhaps in *Hamlet*, more than anywhere else in Shakespeare, people are shown as playing rôles and giving performances. From the opening "staging" of a court celebration, the appearance of the ghost and the various parts played by Polonius and Osric, through to the "staged" duel at the end, *Hamlet* presents versions of the drama of which the "Mousetrap" is only the most obvious. Similarly the presence of the Crummles' acting company serves a highlighting purpose in *Nicholas*. It exposes and explains the pervasive metaphor of the novel, by throwing into relief the pretensions that are taken for reality by the "amateur performers" who people the society, the audience as it were. This is perhaps most perfectly illustrated in the visit of the actors to the Curdles, who proceed to give a fine performance as "critics" without any awareness that *they* are acting. It is further borne out by the

Wititterlys and the performance in the boxes at the play to which Kate and her mother are taken. The second function of the Crummles episode is to form a bridge for Nicholas to cross. We have seen how Nicholas has twice deluded himself that his family is best served by his absence and that he can make his fortune away from home. He has never truly confronted his circumstances. Somehow, like Hamlet, his perception of reality is improved by involvement with the drama. He now returns to London not to act a part, written by someone else, but for action as himself in a part of his own making, attacking Sir Mulberry Hawk, confounding his uncle and looking squarely at the world in which he is placed.

> But now, when he thought how regularly things went on, from day to day, in the same unvarying round; how youth and beauty died, and ugly griping age lived tottering on; how crafty avarice grew rich, and manly honest hearts were poor and sad; how few they were who tenanted the stately houses, and how many those who lay in noisesome pens, or rose each day and laid them down each night, and lived and died, father and son, mother and child, race upon race, generation upon generation, without a home to shelter them or the energies of one single man directed to their aid; how, in seeking, not a luxurious and splendid life, but the bare means of a most wretched and inadequate subsistence, there were women and children in that one town, divided into classes, numbered and estimated as regularly as the noble families and folks of great degree, and reared from infancy to drive most criminal and dreadful trades; how ignorance was punished and never taught; how jail-doors gaped and gallows loomed, for thousands urged towards them by circumstances darkly curtaining their very cradles' heads, and but for which they might have earned their honest bread and lived in peace; how many died in soul, and had no chance of life; how many who could scarcely go astray, be they vicious as they would, turned haughtily from the crushed and stricken wretch who could scarce do otherwise, and who would have been a greater wonder had he or she done well, than even they had they done ill; how much injustice, misery, and wrong there was, and yet how the world rolled on, from year to year, alike careless and indifferent, and no man seeking to remedy or redress it; when he thought of all this, and selected from the mass the one slight case on which his thoughts were bent, he felt, indeed, that there was little ground for hope, . . . (p. 693)

The parallels to various observations in *Hamlet* are widespread.

How the actors produce the effect of throwing a critical and revealing light on others in the novel is worthy of examination. Steven Marcus has drawn attention to this phenomenon:

> The Crummles possess both the openness and warmth of Miss LaCreevy and the vitality of the *croupier*. They are the professional actors in a novel which has as one of its primary themes the cultivation of self through imitation; and they represent vis-à-vis the Kenwigses and Mantalinis what the Cheerybles are intended to represent vis-à-vis Ralph and Mrs. Nickleby. Crummles stands for them all when, having first met Nicholas but five minutes before, he lays "open his affairs without the smallest reserve" (ch. 22). Since impersonation is the essence of their lives, they have nothing to conceal, and they are ingenuous about their jealousies and snobberies, which has the interesting result of neutralizing them.[10]

To understand this it may be helpful to remember how thoroughly Dickens was skilled in and involved in the art of acting. He clearly had a great respect for the professional actor. The actor could do with the presentation of character what Dickens the writer did in creating his thoroughly convincing fictional characters. How could Dickens imagine his great variety of characters while maintaining his overall control and vision, never losing sight of his objective? How can the actor play rôle after rôle with total conviction? Presumably by the possession of a highly integrated, realized self. The rôles can be assumed without the actor becoming the person he plays. He knows he plays a rôle. His real self is untouched and protected by the knowledge that a rôle is a rôle. It is no accident that this century saw an explicit relationship develop between psychoanalysis and the art of acting. The self must develop sufficient freedom from rôle-playing to be free to play rôles by conscious choice and control. In *Nicholas Nickleby* we are shown the absence of such control of awareness in the "amateur" performers, the audience, the unwitting participants in the social drama. These people become the rôles they play, they are the distorted grotesques of Dickens' fiction. The grotesque appears to be an effect achieved by concentrating one's perception on the folly and pretension of unwitting rôle-playing. The distortion is then in the character, not in the perception. One might illustrate this by trying to imagine a distorting mirror throwing back a just satiric portrait of some aspect of oneself rather than a false image.[11]

"What a bad mirror," it [the world] exclaims; "it must be con-

> cave or convex; for surely I never looked like that. Mere caricature, farce, and horse play. Dickens exaggerates; *I* never was so sentimental as that; *I* never saw anything so dreadful; *I* don't believe there were ever any people like Quilp, or Squeers, or Serjeant Buzfuz." But the polite world is lying; there *are* such people; we are such people ourselves in our true moments, in our veritable impulses.[12]

The aim, it seems, is to be rôle-free and to be able to act, like the Cheerybles, out of the continuous total responsiveness of undisguised good-nature. This is not to say that the benevolent brothers do not act. They do indeed play games and act parts continuously. They are not however imprisoned in any one of these parts, nor do they take themselves or their games with absolute seriousness. This quality of the playful has considerable moral significance for Dickens.

Dickens will not let us forget the degree to which the playing of rôles off the stage interferes with real relationships, with love, with sincerity and with the remedies that are necessary to cure social evils. Crummles is capable of ceasing his performances:

> When he [Nicholas] had said good-bye all round and came to Mr. Crummles, he could not but mark the difference between their present separation and their parting at Portsmouth. Not a jot of his theatrical manner remained; he put out his hand with an air which, if he could have summoned it at will, would have made him the best actor of his day in homely parts, and when Nicholas shook it with the warmth he honestly felt, appeared thoroughly melted. (pp. 635-36)

This kind of comment is so conscious and so much part of the creative theme that we must not underestimate its significance to the whole. Unlike Crummles there are others incapable of distinguishing the performance from the reality. Ralph can no longer tell the difference between desperate hunger and deceiving beggary: " 'Don't make fine play-acting speeches about bread, but earn it.' " (p. 573) Newman Noggs, the most sincere of souls, who keeps his own secret council, expresses his hatred of Ralph in his own silent way outside the office door, but this would be seen by Ralph as a bizarre piece of acting, though in fact Noggs is desperately earnest, and frustrated, Ralph being closed away, shielded by a door.

> As the usurer turned for consolation to his books and papers, a performance was going on outside his office-door, which would

> have occasioned him no small surprise, if he could by any means have become acquainted with it.
>
> Newman Noggs was the sole actor. (p. 373)

Newman Noggs is Horatio to Nicholas' Hamlet. He is the only man Nicholas can trust, the man at court, remaining there while Nicholas travels. It is Newman who counsels his friend to patience when things seem at their worst; it is he who says, "the greater necessity for coolness, for reason, for consideration, for thought." Like Horatio, Newman is

> As one, in suff'ring all, that suffers nothing;
> A man that Fortune's buffets and rewards
> Hast ta'en with equal thanks;
> (*Hamlet,* III, ii, 71-73)

Newman is always himself and his tears at Nicholas' good fortune are the Dickensian hallmark of the genuine. The realm of performance on the other hand goes from ladies fainting to enemies embracing:

> These facts were no sooner thoroughly ascertained than the lady gave several indications of fainting, but being forewarned that if she did, she must be carried on some gentleman's shoulders to the nearest public-house, she prudently thought better of it, and walked back with the rest. (p. 54)

Hawk meets someone who is "the person of all others whom Sir Mulberry most hated and dreaded to meet. They shook hands with excessive cordiality." (p. 657) And Dickens shows us how these tricks are perpetrated. "Morleena fell, all stiff and rigid, into the baby's chair, as she had seen her mother fall when she fainted away." (p. 465) Morleena has an expert teacher: "Mrs. Kenwigs meanwhile clasping them alternately to her bosom, with attitudes expressive of distraction, which Miss Petowker herself might have copied." (p. 167) All this is playful enough but it is integrally related in the novel to more vicious deceit with more disastrous consequences. Walter Bray is Dickens' principal vehicle for presenting this aspect of his subject. Comic and tragic deception are only different sides of the same coin:

> When men are about to commit, or to sanction the commission of some injustice, it is not uncommon for them to express pity for the object either of that or some parallel pro-

> ceeding, and to feel themselves, at the time, quite virtuous and moral, and immensely superior to those who express no pity at all. This is a kind of upholding of faith above works, and is very comfortable. (p. 713)

Ralph naturally recognizes Bray's self-deception clearly, a deception enabling him to use and abuse his daughter cruelly.

> "He is trying to deceive himself, even before our eyes, already. He is making believe that he thinks of her good, and not his own. He is acting a virtuous part, and is so considerate and affectionate, sir, that his daughter scarcely knew him." (p. 624)

In the case of such play-acting the performer is never far from the recognition of the truth, a fact which only makes more horrible his desperate rationalizations.

> There was a gleam of conscience in the shame and terror of this hasty action, which, in one short moment, tore the thin covering of sophistry from the cruel design, and laid it bare in all its meanness and heartless deformity. The father fell into his chair pale and trembling; Arthur Gride plucked and fumbled at his hat, and durst not raise his eyes from the floor; even Ralph crouched for the moment like a beaten hound, cowed by the presence of one young innocent girl! (p. 622)

Nicholas, himself, though having a quite different motive, and out of a very different nature, is not free from self-deception:

> . . . persuading himself that he was a most conscientious and glorious martyr, nobly resolved to do what, if he had examined his own heart a little more carefully, he would have found he could not resist. Such is the sleight of hand by which we juggle with ourselves, and change our very weaknesses into most magnanimous virtues! (p. 603)

This last quotation reveals how profoundly Dickens understands the ranges and significance of rationalization, an understanding of note when one sees how vigorously he explores this subject in later novels.

But just as there is deceit and lust and greed, so there is honesty and love and generosity. The novel is plentifully supplied with examples of constancy and open-heartedness. The Browdies for example, along with the Crummles and subsequently Frank and Kate and Nicholas and Madeline, are open, generous-hearted and loving people. Indeed, Nicholas' first friend in the novel is John

Browdie, whose affection and admiration he wins by his declaration that he has beaten the schoolmaster, for he proves by having done so that his sense of justice is stronger than his "interest." The Cheeryble brothers are of course the most celebrated (and critically denigrated) exponents of love and philanthropy in the novel and they seem in many respects remarkably like Browdie. What they have in common is a totally undisguised nature. This quality of openness is catching, so that the Cheerybles reach people as surely as Ralph shuts people out.

> There was something so earnest and guileless in the way in which all this was said, and such a complete disregard of all conventional restraints and coldnesses, that Nicholas could not resist it. Among men who have any sound and sterling qualities, there is nothing so contagious as pure openness of heart. Nicholas took the infection instantly, . . . (p. 451)

Having decided on presenting such "selves," Dickens must present them as unchanging and unchangeable. Whether we are convinced or not by the goodness of "good" characters we are meant to recognize them as whole people, acting out of their basic good nature, content with themselves, accepting the existential conditions of life and undistorted by any false aims or values. They cannot be threatened for they have no defenses and no disguises and need none.

> "The time was, sir, when my dear brother Ned and I were two poor simple-hearted boys, wandering, almost barefoot, to seek our fortunes; are we changed in anything but years and worldly circumstances since that time? No, God forbid!" (p. 812)

Charles' cry "God forbid!" suggests the importance here being attached to the ability to remain oneself through all vicissitudes. Again we are reminded of Hamlet's description of Horatio's character, freedom from the tyranny of "passion," a quality to which Hamlet aspires and which he demonstrates on his return from England. Hamlet at Ophelia's grave is able to rebuke Laertes for a display of passion that mirrors his own former self. *Nicholas Nickleby* likewise seems to celebrate this Stoic necessity for equilibrium. Those characters are also the open-hearted, earnest, and genuine whose security gives them freedom to be themselves. Such are the Cheerybles. Browdie is, too, the same man first and last. Crummles, we are told, not only "laid open his affairs without the smallest reserve," (p. 280) but is able to perceive Nicholas' distress and speak to him of it with no trace of self-consciousness: " 'Why, so I saw,' observed Mr. Crummles. 'You're uneasy in your mind. What's the matter?' " (p. 282) Miss LaCreevy must be included in this group for she wins her battle between middle-class pretensions and her own natural kindness of disposition when she is "plainly wavering between her good-nature and her interest." (p. 22) Kate, too, is whole, but so used to a world of lies and social pretension and tension that she can hardly adjust to the liberating atmosphere of naturalness when she meets it through Frank and his uncle:

> . . . the usual stiffness and formality of a first meeting showed no signs of appearing, and Kate really more than once detected herself in the very act of wondering when it was going to begin. (p. 565)

Kate, like all thoroughly sincere and guileless people, trusts her own instincts and is sensitive to honesty or guile in others. Her cry of protest at the accusation brought against Nicholas sounds very much like Mrs. Bedwin's in *Oliver Twist*. " 'I never will believe it,' said Kate, indignantly: 'never. It is some base conspiracy, which carries its own falsehood with it.' " (p. 249) There is indeed about the Cheerybles, Frank, Crummles, Kate, and Browdie a kind of tranquillity.

There is no doubt that "tranquil" characters are less interesting than disturbed ones. A novel about an asylum is more fascinating, I assume, than one about a Buddhist monastery. Nevertheless, the function and meaning of such characters should be clear. The Maylies indicate Dickens' early interest in the image, the impact of such characters, what their presence "feels like." He quickly begins to explore the distinctions between the characteristics of grotesque neuroticism and those of the ordered, tranquil and creative personality. Ralph is not monstrous, dangerous and evil simply because he loves money above all else. He is so because he is incapable of loving anything else, anything that can love back, because he is isolated, full of hate, mistrust and anger, and as his suicide finally suggests, because he is miserable and totally at odds with life. The Yorkshire schools exist because society is not simply cruel but made up of those who are soul-sick. Sadism, lust, fear and loneliness take the thousand social forms of a "respectable" society and habitually wear the disguises of marriage, business and education. Dickens will never be satisfied merely to present the appearances of goodness and evil. In this sense *Nicholas Nickleby* is an ambitious novel, more ambitious, if less neat and well-structured, than the simple allegory of *Oliver Twist*. I make no attempt to catalogue its weaknesses, its failure to endow Nicholas with a character complex enough to sustain the rôle designed for him. Other critics have frequently pointed out the faults of this early work. Rather I am interested in suggesting the strands of thought, the moral framework on which the confusing tapestry of *Nicholas Nickleby* is wrought. The vision to which Dickens is working can be seen to take form here, its salient features begin to be discerned. The Yorkshire Schools, *Hamlet* and the single individual seeking harmony in and with the State, Ralph—the business jungle and the Muffin Company, Mr. Gregsbury and politics, Squeers and education and Nicholas seeking to find himself and a world with which to harmonize: all these things *are* related, however disparate they may appear at first. The new society of friends and lovers, Kate and Frank, Matilda and John, Tim and LaCreevy, Nicholas and Madeline point to a new world, like the lovers who find their true partners to create a new order at the end of *A Midsummer Night's Dream*. It is not as simple-minded as it might appear.

Nor is there anything arbitrary about the novel's ending. If there is a structural weakness it is that suspense ends with the early introduction of the Cheerybles. Thereafter we witness a long dénouement. There are no real surprises. Everything follows from the conditions that were set up in the first half of the novel. Ralph commits suicide, thus logically fulfilling a process of self-destruction that was clearly suggested even when his fortunes were in the ascendant. He dies in the room of Smike's earliest recollection of isolated imprisonment, thus making a connection between self-destruction and the treatment of Smike, both characters suffering and dying because of the father's failure to love. Nicholas returns to Yorkshire to announce his marriage to his friends and the announcement produces almost directly the break-up of the school, suggesting again the connection between the school and the indifference and sadism which sustain it and the destruction of the school and the love and marriage which accompany it. The themes are thus consistently borne out to the end, but once again Dickens is not satisfied to produce a purely fairy-tale ending. He is anxious to indicate in producing the idyll of the end, that this is a deliberate choice imposed on the novel, and he shows that he has not forgotten the tragic consequences of what has gone before:

> There were a few timid young children, who, miserable as they had been, and many as were the tears they had shed in the wretched school, still knew no other home, and had formed for it a sort of attachment which made them weep when the bolder spirits fled, and cling to it as a refuge. Of these, some were found crying under hedges and in such places, frightened by the solitude. (p. 827)

The last image moreover is that of Smike's grave to remind us clearly that the happy children who sometimes mourn for their lost cousins are blessed by a love between their parents that is discovered only with great difficulty and that without it they might all be Smikes appointed prematurely to their own inevitable graves. So once again Dickens ends a novel as though to say that some live happily ever after and more have been beaten and starved to death and he has shown us how both fates may be determined by the minds of men.

Nicholas engages in an argument with a "literary gentleman" on the subject of dramatic material, and speaking of Shakespeare's genius and the eternal pleasure of his metaphors when placed against the trivia of contemporary concerns, the hero says,

> ". . . for, whereas he brought within the magic circle of his genius, traditions peculiarly adapted for his purpose, and turned familiar things into constellations which should enlighten the world for ages, you drag within the magic circle of your dullness, subjects not at all adapted to the purposes of the stage, and debase as he exalted." (p. 633)

Dickens is revealing not only his dependence on Shakespeare and their common literary tradition, but more specifically, in writing a comic nineteenth-century *Hamlet*, he is using "familiar things," like the Yorkshire schools, and in so doing showing once again that Hamlet's dilemma is the universal struggle of the individual mind with corrupt social forces and ultimately with itself.

[1]Bernard Bergonzi, *"Nicholas Nickleby,"* in *Dickens and the Twentieth Century*, ed. John Gross and Gabriel Pearson (London: Routledge & K. Paul, 1962), p. 66.

[2]Miller, *Charles Dickens: The World of His Novels,* p. 93.

[3]Marcus, *From PICKWICK to DOMBEY,* p. 108.

[4]*Dickens and Education* (London: Macmillan, 1963), p. 2.

[5]See my article, "Hamlet's Sea-Change," in *English* 15 (Summer 1964): 53-5.

[6]The following list may not be complete: Kate participates in three pairings (Hawk, Verisopht and Frank), Nicholas in two (Fanny and Madeline); the Kenwigses, the Lillyvicks, the Browdies, the Squeers, the Mantalinis, the Crummles, the Wititterlys, Miss LaCreevy and Tim Linkinwater; Gride pursues Madeline; Ralph was once married; the Cheerybles were disappointed early; Smike secretly adores Kate; the Snawleys.

[7]Especially Philip Collins, *Dickens and Education,* and John Manning, *Dickens on Education* (Toronto: Univ. of Toronto Press, 1959).

[8]*Dickens and Education,* p. 100.

[9]Gilbert Murray, *Stoic, Christian and Humanist* (London: C. A. Watts, 1940), pp. 108-9.

[10]*From PICKWICK to DOMBEY*, p. 116.

[11]In practice, however, most of us perceive images of ourselves projected by a flattering fantasy:

> . . . Miss Squeers, looking in her own little glass, . . . saw—not herself, but the reflection of some pleasant image in her own brain. (p. 135)

[12]George Santayana, "Dickens," in *The Dickens Critics,* p. 144.

"FOR LOVE OR MONEY"
THE OLD CURIOSITY SHOP

The Giants who formed this world into its sensual existence and now seem to live in it in chains, are in truth the causes of its life and the sources of all activity; but the chains are the cunning of weak and tame minds which have power to resist energy.

WILLIAM BLAKE

•

"What becomes of the old giants?" said Short, turning to him again after a little reflection.

"They're usually kept in caravans to wait upon the dwarfs," said Mr. Vuffin.

THE OLD CURIOSITY SHOP

•

We have seen how Dickens in his early work explores modes of evil and presents images of goodness. We have also seen how he begins his exploration of the relationship between the individual and his perception of the world (psychology) and the state of society (morality). What makes Dickens a radical then is his awareness that nothing short of a profound alteration in individual perception will change the social state of affairs. This Dickensian view produces the emphasis on children, on education and on interpersonal relationships. *The Old Curiosity Shop* extends the analysis, placing a new degree of importance on personal relations and the destructive power of rationalization. The failure to perceive immediate, present human reality stems from guilt, fear and illusion, and the destruction of others may be and frequently is pursued under the name and guise of love.

Nicholas Nickleby chooses a metaphor of acting and the stage to expose states of destructive rôle-playing in all human affairs. *The Old Curiosity Shop* carries the metaphor one stage further. People can kill their Selves by the assumption of rôles which become fixed, and the process has many degrees to it, signified by the move from actors to puppets. We move from the stage to the country fair, from the Crummles to Codlin and Short and from *Romeo and Juliet* to Punch and Judy. We are witnessing in these two novels a process of *reductio ad absurdum*. Nell's world is much more weird and grotesque and considerably more surreal than Nicholas's. She moves in a society where the child leads and cares for the man, where the giants wait on the dwarfs, where puppets and wax works have replaced people. It is a topsy-turvy world where "all the ladies and all the gentlemen were looking intensely nowhere, and staring with extraordinary earnestness at nothing." (p. 214) As Mrs. Jarley puts it, " 'I won't go so far as to say, that, as it is, I've seen wax-work quite like life, but I've certainly seen some life that was exactly like wax-work.' " (p. 203) It is a world where human beings are not seen as ends-in-themselves or not seen at all. It is exactly the same world that by extension can produce in this century gas ovens for the elimination of whole races of people in one decade, and quiet discussions about megadeaths in the next. It is a world gone truly mad. In this novel Dickens adds one more dimension to his search for the sources of moral aberration, throwing new light on the ways in which people destroy themselves and each other and disguise this process to themselves.

That Dickens knew he was writing about an absurd world peopled by dead figures, dominated by the past and blind to the present, is perfectly clear.

> I will merely observe, therefore, that, in writing the book I had it always in my fancy to surround the lonely figure of the child with grotesque and wild, but not impossible, companions, and to gather about her innocent face and pure intentions, associates as strange and uncongenial as the grim objects that are about her bed when her history is first foreshadowed. (p. xii)

And when old Master Humphrey finds Nell's home this is what he sees:

> There were suits of mail standing *like ghosts* in armour, here and there; *fantastic carvings* brought from *monkish cloisters;* rusty weapons of various kinds; *distorted figures* in china, and wood, and iron, and ivory; tapestry, and strange furniture *that might have been designed in dreams.* (pp. 4-5, my italics)

This novel conducts the experiment of placing a human embodiment of innocence in the midst of a fallen world and watching its systematic destruction. The innocence cannot survive but it is also incorruptible. The juxtaposition produces a moral commentary on the nature of that corruption which cannot recognize and value the innocence it destroys. For the moralist the innocence and the corruption are both part of the human character and their separation into emblematic figures like Nell and Quilp necessarily produces allegory, allegory being to the novelist what dissection is to the biologist. Both put parts of the whole under a microscope, so to speak. It is the purity, the wholeness of Quilp's evil that gives it the unadulterated energy which proves compelling and even attractive to the reader. Likewise it is the unabused goodness of Nell that has often offended the critics. But if this allegory produces this artificial separation of human qualities, we must bear in mind the moral question lying behind the exercise, namely, how can goodness and evil be integrated so that the former dominates and determines the world? Those who respond sympathetically to Nell do so because of their perception of her innocence, a response which evidences their own goodness. It is the sign of "kindred." Those who in looking at Nell, cannot see the suffering and mortality that is common to their humanity see Nell as an exploitable "alien." I have carefully documented a similar reading of *Oliver Twist*, but here a psychological dimension is added to show how even those who believe themselves motivated by love, may destroy the "object" of their love when they are thwarted by delusions that block a liberated perception.

I have suggested that the acting metaphor of *Nicholas Nickleby* becomes the puppet metaphor of *The Old Curiosity Shop*. We shall see also that while *Hamlet* is helpful in finding our way through *Nicholas Nickleby* and in giving clues to Nicholas' character, so *Lear* is helpful in apprehending *The Old Curiosity Shop*. But before we turn to this let us ask how far we can pursue the puppet theme, how deeply has Dickens applied it? Punch and Judy came to their peak of popularity in the eighteenth century rather than the nineteenth; but by that time the story and character of Punch had become part of English life and their show was still a commonplace at country fairs. No one in Dickens' audience was unaware of a whole set of detailed associations when they read of the work of

Codlin and Short. They knew that Punch was a master of evil, a classic impudent sadist who beat his wife, a grotesque rascal who defied everyone, believed no one, took his principal pleasures in other people's discomfort and even sometimes cheated the very gallows, which was not his only resemblance to the devil himself. Who is Quilp? Quilp is Punch.[1] If a close look at the original illustrations is not sufficient to convince the reader of this, let him consider the stick with which Quilp is wont to beat others, his tormenting of his wife, the lolling, puppet-like tongue, the draping of himself over window-sills and furniture, his sitting on the backs of chairs, his fun with dogs (Toby) and his lascivious descriptions of Nell: " 'Such a fresh, blooming, modest little bud, neighbour,' said Quilp, nursing his short leg, and making his eyes twinkle very much; 'such a chubby, rosy, cosy, little Nell!' " (p. 73) Compare this with actual Punch dialogue as recorded between 1828 and 1939. "What a pretty creature!" "Ain't she a beauty?" "Oh, what beautiful lips!" "Oh! You little beauty! Oh! You little bit of jam!" "Oh! you little darling!"[2] Punch spoke in a shrieking high voice as Quilp does often, "Mr. Quilp finished in a shrill squeak, . . ." (p. 356) There is a Punch in *The Old Curiosity Shop* and there is Quilp. Their relationship is a moral theme in the novel. Quilp has great power in his world, not just over Trent but presumably over many others whose stories are untold. Quilp gathers to himself and expresses all those sadistic libidinous qualities latent or repressed in the world around him. This use of expressionism, the bodying forth of latent and often ferocious impulses, is a marked characteristic of this novel. Like Punch, Quilp functions satirically as parody and deflator of the naïve, hypocritical world inhabited by and embodied in the Brasses and in Mrs. Jiniwin, his mother-in-law. The audience identification with Punch and with Quilp can be explained by the relief experienced in witnessing those aspects of man which society or self-interest requires to be kept hidden, and as I have said above, in the purity of their presentation. There is a good deal of Quilp in the wildness of Dennis and Hugh later in *Barnaby Rudge* and perhaps even in the entire mob itself in that novel when license replaces order.

What we see in Punch and Quilp is both pleasing and frightening, for however attractive the image of total rebellion and unfettered subterranean energy may be, we know that we might in such a world be victim as well as tyrant. Passion, without compassion, renders us mechanical. Destruction becomes inevitable and almost routine. A whole world of Quilps probably leads to the chateau of Sade's *120 Days of Sodom*, which begins with sexual perversion and ends with the literal decimation and murder of almost all the inhabitants. All sadistic lust requires the depersonalization of the sex-object. Mrs. Quilp and Nell have this bond. Quilp proposes to make Nell his wife, presumably after murdering the present Mrs. Quilp. Quilp (and Punch) are amusing up to a point where Dickens knows he must stop; push him beyond that point and one would find oneself at the centre of a monstrous nightmare rather than at the fringe of a bizarre dream. One would be in a world where the power of the sadistic, the uncompassionate, the dead of heart, controlled events, and a fantasy world where men and women of wax, had attained power through the indifference of those who only pretend that they care for the well-being and dignity of others. I am aware that this suggestion brings Dickens' novel close to the world of much science fiction. I believe they are indeed similar, science fiction being the modern gothic novel. I am sure one could trace a clear line from *The Old Curiosity Shop* to *The Midwich Cuckoos* or *The Chrysalids* of John Wyndham. In contemporary terms we would say, as modern satire frequently does, that machines or robots run the world or one day will, if we persist in our current values and illusions. What this means is that the day may come (is already here?) when the distinction between men and robots is no longer clear. Dickens chooses puppets and figures of wax for a similar warning.[3]

King Lear finds himself in just such a world, where all the normal, dependable human sympathies have suddenly been eroded and replaced by unfeeling and brutal responses from totally unyielding and sadistic manipulators. Perhaps it is for this reason that critics have often recognized echoes of *Lear* in this novel. George Ford has written:

> The death scene which Dickens most admired in all literature was that of King Lear, as acted by Macready. In *The Old Curiosity Shop,* a reader senses again and again that the author was making a bid to write another Lear—which incidentally may account for some of the intensity of Macready's own emotions in reading the novel.[4]

In the novel, Sampson Brass describes Mr. Garland, rather than old Mr. Trent, as King Lear:

> "He quite realizes my idea of King Lear, as he appeared when in possession of his kingdom, Mr. Richard—the same good humour, the same white hair and partial baldness, the same liability to be imposed upon. Ah! A sweet subject for contemplation, sir, very sweet!" (pp. 423-24)

The reader knows, however, that this ironic and sneering description is more appropriate to Trent. Only the false Brass would suggest that Mr. Garland is imposed upon by Kit. The echoes from *Lear* are sometimes quite precise: " 'Her voice was ever soft/Gentle and low' " from *Lear* becomes " 'There was ever something mild and quiet about her, I remember, from the first; . . .' " (p. 537). These lines are spoken by old Lear and old Trent respectively. The words spoken by Kent about Lear's death, " 'He hates him/ That would upon the rack of this tough world/Stretch him out longer, . . .' " become a comment on Nell's death: " 'if one deliberate wish expressed in solemn terms above this bed could call her back to life, which of us would utter it!' " (p. 539) There are other less obvious echoes of *Lear,* but this latter quotation leads us to what I believe is the most central consideration in *The Old Curiosity Shop. Lear* is a play about a king who was old before he was wise. It is certainly not Cordelia's play. Lear, wilful, weak, deluded, mistaking appearances for reality, projecting his own version of the world onto others, brings his family and the state to ruin. In his wanderings he learns some truths: that life conforms to no abstract plan, that love trusts implicitly and absolutely and requires no pre-ordained ritual, that the truth of the heart is more profound than the phantasms of reason. Cordelia, best-loved daughter, is brought to an untimely death in the service of her father. Lear is the principal sufferer in the play. Nell is the principal sufferer in the novel, and this has led the critics almost uniformly to underestimate the Grandfather's rôle in the novel. For what Dickens has done is to elevate the Nell-Cordelia rôle while retaining all the evil of Lear's early delusion, so disguised by pathos as to require the most careful reading to perceive it. It is as though we have a play in which Cordelia, called upon to express her love as she is in *Lear,* does so and thus permits the parent-figure to sustain the delusion that all he does is beneficent and born of love. When the subject is blind to the reality and individuality of others the love-object disappears and is replaced by a fantasy figure of his own making. The old man uses the words of the child (and the devotion) as a basis for self-indulgence. Nell's innocent acquiescence sustains the old man's fantasies, his complete lack of self-knowledge. Cordelia exposes her whole situation by refusing to participate in the charade, by remaining true to herself and by holding to the truth that nothing that she says will affect the actual love-relationship, will not create it if it does not exist or be necessary if it does. Ironically, it is true that "Nothing can come of nothing" and that something is self-sufficient. Cordelia can say quietly and with a clear conscience, " 'So young, my lord, and true,' " thus producing a "dragon and his wrath" for Lear is thrown back upon a self, hedged round with monumental defenses. He would destroy those who would expose what lies behind because what lies behind is isolated insecurity. The sicknesses of the individual and of the state are one. Nell, however, is given a different rôle; she is required to reveal by her suffering the destructive effects of self-delusion in one who uses her without seeing her. Having abdicated from reality, the old man becomes a child in his dependency, in his helplessness, while the child is turned into an old woman, having omitted childhood altogether, and longing for death from world-weariness. Nell loves life, but worn out by premature responsibilities and anxieties and physical hardship, she has not the energy to engage in it. *King Lear* is tragic by virtue of Lear's sickness producing Lear's suffering. *The Old Curiosity Shop* is pathetic by virtue of Trent's sickness producing Nell's suffering. His own late discovery of what he has done is too late to be significant in the novel's structure. In fact, the grandfather's response to Nell's death is reinforced pathos by virtue of the continuing illusion about Nell. When alive she was unregarded, when dead she is the only present reality. It is a horrible irony. For Nell, as for Cordelia, her value is discovered too late.

The novel begins with Master Humphrey and his encounter with Nell, and this is a very precise design by Dickens. They meet by accident so that Nell's dependence and Humphrey's good nature are in no way prejudiced by any knowledge of each other. Humphrey thus becomes our touchstone figure and there is no reason thereafter to doubt the accuracy of his initial perceptions, no matter what we learn of Trent or how involved we become. We are asked to hold on to the "objective" account rendered by an early identification with Humphrey who begins the story in the first person and then disappears. He exposes at the start his and Dickens' response to the Child, the only proper response and the only one that makes any sense in parent, teacher or any loving adult.

> I love these little people; and it is not a slight thing when they, who are so fresh from God, love us. As I had felt pleased, at first, by her confidence, I determined to deserve it, and to do credit to the nature which had prompted her to repose it in me. (p. 4)

The respect and love of children must be earned by those who value them highly and are fully conscious of their beauty and dependence in the here and now. Nell first appears as a lost child. She has been sent out on a night errand. Consider what this means in terms of London in the 1830's. While Nell is a child and is lost like a child, she acts with the accustomed responsibility of a mature adult:

> She put her hand in mine, as confidingly as if she had known me from her cradle, and we trudged away together: the little creature accommodating her pace to mine, and rather seeming to lead and take care of me than I to be protecting her. (p. 3)

On arrival at Nell's home we are taken fully into the world of "curiosities" and the very existence of this world springs entirely from the mind of Old Trent.

> The haggard aspect of the little old man was wonderfully suited to the place; he might have groped among old churches, and tombs, and deserted houses, and gathered all the spoils with his own hands. There was nothing in the whole collection but was in keeping with himself; nothing that looked older or more worn than he. (p. 5)

This is a world of the past, a world of death and decay, a world of fantasy.

> We are so much in the habit of allowing impressions to be made upon us by external objects, which should be produced by reflection alone, but which, without such visible aids, often escape us, that I am not sure I should have been so thoroughly possessed by this one subject, but for the heaps of fantastic things I had seen huddled together in the curiosity-dealer's

> warehouse. These, crowding on my mind, in connection with the child, and gathering round her, as it were, brought her condition palpably before me. I had her image, without any effort of imagination, surrounded and beset by everything that was foreign to its nature, and farthest removed from the sympathies of her sex and age. (p. 13)

The old man may be "wonderfully suited to the place" but what has a child to do with such a world? She, like the rubbish collected by the old man (a foretaste of Krook in *Bleak House*) has become reified. There is plenty of evidence that the grandfather lives entirely in a world where the real Nell never enters and where his principal feelings are for and about himself: " 'Ah! it's a weary life for an old man—a weary, weary, life—but there is a great end to gain, and that I keep before me.' " (p. 10) Nell is the means to gain the end rather than the end itself—she has been abstracted out of his existence. There are two occasions on Humphrey's brief visit when Trent actually drifts off into a private schizophrenic-like world.

> "I am very happy as I am, grandfather," said the child.
>
> "Tush, tush!" returned the old man, "thou dost not know—how should'st thou!" Then he muttered again between his teeth, "The time must come, I am very sure it must. It will be all the better for coming late;" and then he sighed and fell into his former musing state, and still holding the child between his knees appeared to be insensible to everything around him. (p. 9)

And again, "The old man had again relapsed into his former abstraction and took no notice of what passed; . . ." (p. 8) On being confronted by the charge that he might take more care of Nell the old man replies by an evasion—that he loves Nell very much, though his actual words convey a significant irony as to the strangeness of his love: " 'More care!' said the old man in a shrill voice, 'more care of Nelly! why who ever loved a child as I love Nell?' " (p. 5) Who indeed? A similar irony is evident when he confronts Nell on her return: " 'Why bless thee, child,' said the old man, patting her on the head, 'how couldst thou miss thy way? What if I had lost thee, Nell!' " (p. 5) His reason for concern is naturally great and related to himself since she is his *raison d'être*, the means by which he sustains his fantasy about a future. " 'She is not my child, sir,' returned the old man. 'Her mother was, and she was poor. I save nothing—not a penny—though I live as you see, but' —he laid his hand upon my arm and leant forward to whisper— 'she shall be rich one of these days, and a fine lady.' " (p. 6) One day, Nell, her childhood lost and never realized, worn out by care and work and responsibility, will be a "fine lady." Nor in fact is the suggestion about poverty, as excuse for a withdrawal from the present, permitted by Dickens to be more than a rationalization. Humphrey, observing Nell acting like a housewife and mother, says that it grieves him to see children, "scarcely more than infants," initiated into the hard ways of life:

> "It checks their confidence and simplicity—two of the best qualities that Heaven gives them—and demands that they share our sorrows before they are capable of entering into our enjoyments." (p. 6)

Old Trent has squandered some substantial resources on his illusion, depriving Nell of ordinary comforts while seeking to make her "rich." Later in the novel Quilp calls Nell his "duck of diamonds," a phrase explicable only by reference to a passage in proof omitted before publication in which, when Humphrey meets the lost Nell, she has been on an errand bearing diamonds to Quilp as collateral for the loans which Trent needs for his gambling. From Quilp's point of view Nell is like the golden goose, except that she lays diamonds. Even with the passage omitted it is clear that Quilp is much too shrewd to lend money without some pretty impressive security. He must be convinced that Trent is not poor. Later, when Trent reveals to Quilp what he has done with the money Quilp is amazed at his own blindness: " 'That I should have been blinded,' said Quilp, looking contemptuously at him, 'by a mere shallow gambler!' " (p. 74) There is no surprise for us, however, in his being fooled, for Quilp is so totally scheming and avaricious that he is incapable of imagining a different sort of madness by which one might impoverish oneself in pursuit of a private illusion. He cannot conceive of a scheme as wild as Trent's. That the gambling compulsion is madness is made perfectly clear: " 'When did you first begin this mad career?' " Quilp asks, naturally failing to recognize his own sadistic possessiveness as madness in its own right. What is not clear is whether the obsession with some illusory future "Nell" actually precedes and causes the gambling or whether the compulsion to play comes first and then Nell is found to rationalize it. Whatever the answer, Nell is the supreme loser. We are not to take seriously the old man's denial of pleasure in his gambling.

> "Then I began. I found no pleasure in it, I expected none. What has it ever brought me but anxious days and sleepless nights; but loss of health and peace of mind, and gain of feebleness and sorrow!" (p. 74)

Quilp asks if gambling has always been Trent's El Dorado. " 'Yes,' cried the old man, turning upon him with gleaming eyes, 'it was. It is. It will be, till I die,' " (p. 74) thus giving the lie to his denial of being possessed by the mad lust to play, the gambler's disease. Many or most compulsives will deny that they experience any pleasure, indeed the sense of being driven is presumably part of the suffering. Yet the very sense of compulsion, the "it was. It is. It will be, till I die," is a device for the evasion of the present, of making choices, and of seeing and participating in present reality. It is not my fault, says the gambler, the thief, the murderer, I was driven to it, it was Fortune, it was bad luck, it was my son-in-law.

Nell knows nothing of these activities. She suffers in a private world, hidden from the grandfather by his blindness and his own preoccupations.

> And so he went on, content to read the book of her heart from the page first presented to him, little dreaming of the story that lay hidden in its other leaves, and murmuring within himself that at least the child was happy. (pp. 68-69)

As the money supply dwindles, and as the luck never changes, she sees in him the "dawning of despondent madness." She has been shut out from his heart all along and now she has no clue as to why he is declining.

> "If you are poor, let us be poor together; but let me be with you, do let me be with you; do not let me see such change and not know why, or I shall break my heart and die. Dear grandfather, let us leave this sad place to-morrow, and beg our way from door to door." (p. 71)

They are poor now but they were not poor before. Either the old man can confess the wasted years, admit his folly and indifference and share his lot with Nell or he can withdraw further into dependence and privacy and nurse his sense of self-pity. It is not really a choice and there is no reason to expect that he will ever confront Nell as she is, for to do so would require self-confrontation, a prospect too painful to be endured. As though to corroborate Humphrey's earlier fears, Dickens shows us what it is really like to be Nell, what goes on behind the smiles and efficiency in the secret thoughts of her nightmare existence:

> If he were to die—if sudden illness had happened to him, and he were never to come home again, alive—if, one night, he should come home, and kiss and bless her as usual, and after she had gone to bed and had fallen asleep and was perhaps dreaming pleasantly, and smiling in her sleep, he should kill himself and his blood come creeping, creeping, on the ground to her own bedroom door! These thoughts were too terrible to dwell upon. . . . (pp. 69-70)

I would suggest that part, however small, of this terror is the element of wish-fulfillment in such a thought, a wish that reflects perhaps the author's barely disguised anger and dislike for her grandfather. Certainly in her circumstances such a terrifying thought could hardly be more natural. I think it of central importance to us to hold onto one of Humphrey's inner monologues:

> His affection for the child might not be inconsistent with villany of the worst kind; even that very affection was, in itself, an extraordinary contradiction, or how could he leave her thus? Disposed as I was to think badly of him, I never doubted that his love for her was real. I could not admit the thought, remembering what had passed between us, and the tone of voice in which he had called her by her name. (p. 12)

What passes for love may produce the strangest consequences. We mean well but can we trust our actions? A clear perception, the capacity to see the beauty and fragility of what is before us, is our only guarantee of our proper evaluation of it. The instant we abstract we kill. This is what *The Old Curiosity Shop* reveals to us and this is why we are told that Nell "seemed to exist in a kind of allegory." (p. 13) Surely nothing could be clearer than Dickens' noted intention that he is about to present an allegory, the terms of which are all set up before Humphrey takes his leave. It is the story of beauty and the beast, but here beauty dies because the beast cannot be converted as long as it refuses to live and join the human race. The parent who claims that everything he does is for his child may well be speaking of some other child than the one who stands before him, some brain-child, made to measure and perfectly behaved and much less troublesome than the real live separate human being who demands by its actual presence the response of another human heart.

It is a long time before any glimmering of Nell's real state penetrates the old man's darkness. When they leave London, all pretense of his being responsible for her disappears for them both.

> The old man looked, irresolutely and helplessly, first at her, then to the right and left, then at her again, and shook his head. It was plain that she was thenceforth his guide and leader. The child felt it, but had no doubts or misgiving, and putting her hand in his, led him gently away. (p. 96)

If we have understood the early part of the novel the grandfather's dependency is no surprise. Not only does he not see her needs and her suffering but he does not see and trust her love for him: " 'Don't leave me, Nell; say that thou'lt not leave me. I loved thee all the while, indeed I did. If I lose thee too, my dear, I must die!' " (p. 117) He sees enough, perhaps, to be aware of her grounds for deserting him and this increases his terror, for her removal not only would leave him physically helpless (perhaps it would not) but would force him to an awareness of what he has done and how he has driven her away. This is in fact what happens at her death. It is because of the doubts about his past conduct that he feels compelled to assure her (and himself?) that he has loved her all along. He strikes this selfish and guilty note on two further occasions, each tinged with recrimination and self-pity.

> "Nothing to fear!" returned the old man. "Nothing to fear if they took me from thee! Nothing to fear if they parted us! Nobody is true to me. No, not one. Not even Nell!" (p. 180)

Mrs. Jarley is amazed at this relationship.

> "Do you want a good situation for your grand-daughter, master? If you do, I can put her in the way of getting one. What do you say?"
>
> "I can't leave her," answered the old man. "We can't separate. What would become of me without her?"
>
> "I should have thought you were old enough to take care of yourself, if you ever will be," retorted Mrs. Jarley sharply. (p. 205)

But he never will be, and because he is not he cannot take care of Nell.

It is not long after they leave London that Nell and her ward meet the puppet men and the link is formed between the old man and the world of puppets and later waxworks, a link with moral implications inherent in its symbolism. A puppet is dead, animated only from outside. The absence of feeling, the inability to perceive the other, the incapacity to relate is an aspect of the world in which Nell finds herself. The sadism of the Punch-Quilp figure is recalled at the meeting with Codlin and Short. The old man is fascinated, which not only reaffirms for us his child-like state but also reveals to us that he responds more to their antics than he does to Nell. He seems suddenly to be animated in a way not seen before and to be in consequence even more oblivious to Nell's needs.

> Among the laughter none was more loud and frequent than the old man's. Nell's was unheard, for she, poor child, with her head drooping on his shoulder, had fallen asleep, and slept too soundly to be roused by any of his efforts to awaken her to a participation in his glee. (p. 126)

The puppets are after all no threat to him. He joins them in a stereotypic world where all manipulation is by outside forces and one is thus freed from all responsibility, a world where no demands are made on one's personality or on one's humanity. It is a world where the giants wait on the dwarfs.

> The supper was very good, but she was too tired to eat, and yet would not leave the old man until she had kissed him in his bed. He, happily insensible to every care and anxiety, sat listening with a vacant smile and admiring face to all that his new friends said; and it was not until they retired yawning to their room, that he followed the child up stairs. (p. 126)

Codlin and Short are in keeping with this state of affairs for when they encounter Nell they instantly regard her as a possible means to their own benefit. Nell and the old man are made virtually captive and it is only later that Codlin and Short, through their greed, are in turn used by another to get word of Nell.

Not only is Nell used by her grandfather and by Codlin and Short, but she is also used by the boatmen who insist that she sing to them as they pursue their drunken way:

> In this way, with little cessation, and singing the same songs again and again, the tired and exhausted child kept them in good humour all that night; and many a cottager, who was aroused from his soundest sleep by the discordant chorus as it floated away upon the wind, hid his head beneath the bedclothes and trembled at the sounds. (p. 324)

Nell is literally worn out like a much-employed utensil. Only those who are themselves neglected can see themselves in Nell and thus see her at all, as she sees the abused and exploited child at the boarding school.

> . . . and although some ladies smiled gently as they shook their heads, and others cried to the gentlemen beside them "See, what a pretty face!" they let the pretty face pass on, and never thought that it looked tired or hungry.
>
> There was but one lady who seemed to understand the child, and she was one who sat alone in a handsome carriage, while two young men in dashing clothes, who had just dismounted from it, talked and laughed loudly at a little distance, appearing to forget her, quite. (pp. 150-51)

Quilp regards Nell as a lust-object and young Trent and Swiveller also fall into the category of those who regard her as a means to some material end of their own.

Dickens will not let us forget this link between the grandfather and the absence of human perception that murders by its blindness. Old Trent is akin, not only to the puppets he so much admires, and to Quilp, who is merely the exposed unrationalized expression of the destructive forces of less obvious "lovers;" he is also like the waxwork images that Mrs. Jarley exhibits. The children ". . . were fully impressed with the belief that her grandfather was a cunning device in wax." (p. 211) When does the old man come alive? When he revives his passion for gambling.

> "Do you hear what he says?" whispered the old man. "Do you hear that, Nell?"
>
> The child saw with astonishment and alarm that his whole appearance had undergone a complete change. His face was flushed and eager, his eyes were strained, his teeth set, his breath came short and thick, and the hand he laid upon her arm trembled so violently that she shook beneath its grasp. (p. 221)

The old man hears Nell's voice and does not hear what she says:

> "Aye, aye, I'll listen," returned the old man, *still without looking at her*; "a pretty voice. It has always a sweet sound to

> me. It always had when it was her mother's, poor child." (p. 232, my italics)

The mother, Trent's daughter, and the child have become an unwholesome conglomerate in the man's mind. Dickens, as though not satisfied with all the hints as to the nature and significance of the grandfather's state of mind, finally has him steal from Nell. The passage describing the old man's nocturnal visit to Nell's darkened room is one of Dickens' great scenes of Gothic horror but it is also rich in irony. Nell finds that the thing she fears most, the unrealized source of her nightmares, the greatest threat to their peace and quiet, the marauder in her room, is her grandfather after all, driven to steal money from the very person he claims to wish money for. Man does *not* destroy the thing he loves. *He destroys the thing he does not see and he chooses not to see those things that challenge most his hidden self.* Only after it is too late and after they have been driven into physical hardship does the old man, like Lear in the storm, begin to question himself.

> "Ah! poor, houseless, wandering, motherless child!" cried the old man, clasping his hands and *gazing as if for the first time* upon her anxious face, her travel-stained dress, and bruised and swollen feet; "has all my agony of care brought her to this at last? Was I a happy man once, and have I lost happiness and all I had, for this?" (pp. 327-28, my italics)

The temptation to escape blame is still strong, however, and Dickens will not permit any sudden conversion. When they meet the man from the foundry he cross-examines the old man who continues to see himself as anything but a helpless victim.

> "How came you to think of resting there?" he said. "Or how," he added, looking more attentively at the child, "do you come to want a place of rest at this time of night?"
>
> "Our misfortunes," the grandfather answered, "are the cause."
>
> "Do you know," said the man, looking still more earnestly at Nell, "how wet she is, and that the damp streets are not a place for her?"
>
> "I know it well, God help me," he replied. "What can I do?" (pp. 328-29)

A little later, however, a fuller acceptance of his earlier blindness dawns on him:

> "She is quite exhausted," said the schoolmaster, glancing

> upward into his face. "You have taxed her powers too far, friend."
>
> "She is perishing of want," rejoined the old man. "I never thought how weak and ill she was, till now." (p. 340)

Finally, Dickens gives the game away. Death itself and the dawning likelihood of Nell's death produce in the old man the existential awareness that it is almost too late and if amends are to be made they must be made now. Here is the passage which explains all that has been presented indirectly by Dickens before.

> From that time, there sprung up in the old man's mind, a solicitude about the child which never slept or left him. There are chords in the human heart—strange, varying strings—which are only struck by accident; which will remain mute and senseless to appeals the most passionate and earnest, and respond at last to the slightest casual touch. In the most insensible or childish minds, there is some train of reflection which art can seldom lead, or skill assist, but which will reveal itself, as great truths have done, by chance, and when the discoverer has the plainest end in view. From that time, the old man never, for a moment, forgot the weakness and devotion of the child; from the time of that slight incident, he who had seen her toiling by his side through so much difficulty and suffering, and had scarcely thought of her otherwise than as the partner of miseries which he felt severely in his own person, and deplored for his own sake at least as much as hers, awoke to a sense of what he owed her, and what those miseries had made her. Never, no, never once, in one unguarded moment from that time to the end, did any care for himself, any thought of his own comfort, any selfish consideration or regard distract his thoughts from the gentle object of his love. (p. 409)

This then is the story of Nell and her grandfather, the puppet-man who finally comes alive in the allegory and who after, in effect, killing his grandchild can say of the dead girl, " 'I would not vex my darling, for the wide world's riches.' " (p. 535)

In the novel Nell is undoubtedly strongly connected with a death-wish. Her death is prepared for at length and very gently, but the preparation also has the effect of convincing the reader of the appropriateness of her premature demise. Her preoccupation with graves, mourners and the old suggests the heavy weariness which life has been for her. Death is even horribly prefigured by Nell's employment as a guide to waxen corpse-like images. Not only does she fear death—she descries it. If life depends on a life-wish, life-impulse or life-motive then such a response must come from somewhere, must be sustained by love, nurtured by laughter and nourished by the ability to imagine a future. Kit, whom Humphrey calls Nell's "good angel," is early removed from her life by the same blindness in the old man that abuses the girl. It is the old man who first suggests Kit's name to Quilp when looking for a scapegoat and then receives the same name back from Quilp with a kind of grim satisfaction. Kit, like Kent, is banished. Kit, however, represents life and love and joy. It is he who makes Nell laugh—I cannot recall her laughing again after they are separated. It is Kit who watches the house and invisibly guards her at night. It is honest Kit who brings hope and joy and laughter into his own home. It is Kit who is privileged to utter the marvellous speech for Dickens against all the posing hypocritical solemnity of Little Bethel and all it symbolizes in England.

> "I know who has been putting that in your head," rejoined her son disconsolately; "that's Little Bethel again. Now I say, mother, pray don't take to going there regularly, for if I was to see your good-humoured face that has always made home cheerful, turned into a grievous one, and the baby trained to look grievous too, and to call itself a young sinner (bless its heart) and a child of the devil (which is calling its dead father names); if I was to see this, and see little Jacob looking grievous likewise, I should so take it to heart that I'm sure I should go and list for a soldier, and run my head on purpose against the first cannon-ball I saw coming my way."
>
> "Oh, Kit, don't talk like that."
>
> "I would, indeed, mother, and unless you want to make me feel very wretched and uncomfortable, you'll keep that bow on your bonnet, which you'd more than half a mind to pull off last week. Can you suppose there's any harm in looking as cheerful and being as cheerful as our poor circumstances will permit? Do I see anything in the way I'm made, which calls upon me to be a snivelling, solemn, whispering chap, sneaking about as if I couldn't help it, and expressing myself in a most unpleasant snuffle? on the contrairy, don't I see every reason why I shouldn't? Just hear this! Ha ha ha! An't that as nat'ral as walking, and as good for the health? Ha ha ha! An't that as nat'ral as a sheep's bleating, or a pig's grunting, or a horse's neighing, or a bird's singing? Ha ha ha! Isn't it, mother?" (p. 167)

So much for kill-joy religion. Kit and laughter and Astleys and oysters all go together while Nell moves inexorably towards death. Once Kit is removed from Nell's world she is abandoned to a suffering and hardship reminiscent of *Oliver Twist* and particularly of little Dick in that novel. Dick and Oliver both manifest strong death-wishes and the whole aura of the poorhouse is one of waiting for death. The death of little Dick and little Nell (and to some extent, later, of little Paul) is a logical extension of their reification.

Kit's career is part of the counterpoint Dickens uses to explore the themes of life and death in two antithetical stories. Kit and his close, loving family acquire friends and extend their love in a kind of upward spiral. Kit fights against Little Bethel, which is a death-force in opposition to him in his struggle for his mother's good nature. Kit defeats Quilp with the aid of love that exists between people hardly known to him at all. As death and hate spread and destroy, so life and love spread and grow. Christopher Nubbles' Christian name suggests virtues that he demonstrates in his life, a name suggestive of the love which Dickens saw as the essence of the Christ—love—life—resurrection story, a theme explicitly expanded later in Sidney Carton's much repeated "I am the resurrection and the life." Kit's story is set against that of Nell, the pun on knell, the story of sacrifice and crucifixion, the other, death-side of the Christ story in which the universal Mass, the Human Being incarnate is murdered by custom, ritual, logic, rationalization and blindness. Kit and Nell, representing antithetical careers and fates, live in different worlds by virtue of the perceptions of those who inhabit those worlds. The Garlands, like the Cheerybles before them and the Maylies even earlier, not only inhabit but produce a world of life and love. The machinations of the Brasses are no more able to destroy this world than the schoolmaster is able to prevent Nell's death.

In the network of relationships and effects, Kit is saved from injustice and destruction by the results of love in a relationship with which he has nothing to do. This brings us to Swiveller, who is perhaps the most interesting character in the novel and certainly the one who points to things to come in Dickens' work. Up to this point the fiction has presented characters who by and large are good or evil. Now, however, we see an instance of Dickens' interest in the question of moral conversion. The two divergent paths of life and death, of creativity and destruction, of indifference/

selfhood versus compassion/love come to a focus in the individual, Swiveller, and Dickens here for the first time begins to indicate his concern to move from the morality-play structure of emblematic stories and figures to an analysis of conflict and resolution in a single personality. Swiveller, like Trent, is characterized at the start by carelessness rather than malice. His comic irresponsibility is the light-hearted equivalent of the old grandfather's failure to take account of Nell's (or anyone's) individual humanity and present reality. The girl becomes a pawn in a scheme of which Swiveller is part.

> In this hatching of their scheme, neither Trent nor Quilp had had one thought about the happiness or misery of poor innocent Nell. It would have been strange if the careless profligate, who was the butt of both, had been harassed by any such consideration; for his high opinion of his own merits and deserts rendered the project rather a laudable one than otherwise; and if he had been visited by so unwonted a guest as reflection, he would—being a brute only in the gratification of his appetites—have soothed his conscience with the plea that he did not mean to beat or kill his wife, and would therefore, after all said and done, be a very tolerable, average husband. (p. 179)

Swiveller can conceive of Nell, or at least speak of her, as a creature whose entire life is devoted to his well-being, and comic though it is, it is a suggestive element in the pattern of purposes that Nell fantastically plays in the minds of other people.

> "It's a gratifying circumstance which you'll be glad to hear, that a young and lovely girl is growing into a woman expressly on my account, and is now saving up for me." (p. 67)

The statement amounts to a comic version of Trent's similar view of the girl he "saves." Swiveller, when he complains of fortune and its treatment of him, leads Dickens to an observation that could equally well apply to Old Trent, in its substance if not in its tone:

> As he was entirely alone, it may be presumed that, in these remarks, Mr. Swiveller addressed himself to his fate or destiny, whom, as we learn by the precedents, it is the custom of heroes to taunt in a very bitter and ironical manner when they find themselves in situations of an unpleasant nature. (p. 254)

We thus have an image of a young man who is dangerously careless, indifferent, self-indulgent, self-deluded and rôle-playing, the prototype of the London Pip or the Eugene Wrayburn of later novels. Swiveller, as his name suggests, is capable however of making a switch, and he does this, appropriately enough, by letting his good nature have its way when he actually confronts the extraordinary figure of Sally Brass' imprisoned kitchenmaid. The Marchioness is Sally's illegitimate daughter (Sally confesses this in a proof passage omitted before publication) and is used to being beaten by her mother, in whom she elicits a vicious mixture of guilt, fear and frustrated desire. Swiveller witnesses such a beating and by befriending the starving nameless creature actually creates a human being. He names her, he teaches her and he makes her aware that she is real. Naturally she will worship her creator and in saving his life by her nursing care and fidelity she in turn re-creates him, for that part of him that found her now is reaffirmed and given ascendancy by reciprocal gratitude. Swiveller is able to be generous to the scullery maid because he can feel so superior to her that she threatens him not at all. Subsequently, the extent and intensity of her devotion quite shakes him. He has created, not a monster, but a ministering angel. Quilp is the monster and he feeds off the self-tormenting like the old man, but Nell the unseen is the true victim.

Swiveller's conversion during illness is the first of many such conversions in Dickens' work. But Swiveller is a relatively simple character compared with the psyches in conflict who embody the life-death struggle in subsequent novels. Nevertheless, we are already a long way from *Oliver Twist,* where, on the whole, good was good and bad was bad. In *The Old Curiosity Shop* destructive powers are shown to appear often in the name of love. But a world where people do not see, hear, touch and meet each other, a world of secret places where people are not open to each other, is seen as a world of puppets, of wax figures, of graveyards and corpses.

> Thus, it will always happen that these men of the world, who go through it in armour, defend themselves from quite as much good as evil; . . . (p. 500)

Death is not in the future. The world may be peopled with the dead who create the doll-like illusion that they move and talk and feel. But life is also here and now for it is the creative imagination capable of seeing the beauty beneath the grime and ugliness, the human being in the beaten effigy. What is a mere symbolic hate-object, a caged puppet to Sally Brass, becomes a human being to Dick Swiveller. There is even afterlife here and now in the testimony of the living to the good that went before.

> "There is nothing," cried her friend, "no, nothing innocent or good, that dies, and is forgotten. Let us hold to that faith, or none." (p. 406)

Those who live in an abstract future destroy the present; God resides in the human breast; the poor but loving man lives, like Kit, in a world of immense value and meaning to him.

> His household gods are of flesh and blood, with no alloy of silver, gold, or precious stone; he has no property but in the affections of his own heart; and when they endear bare floors and walls, despite of rags and toil and scanty fare, that man has his love of home from God, and his rude hut becomes a solemn place. (pp. 281-82)

Kit marries Barbara and Dickens is fully aware that so prosaic a conclusion to his tale of suffering requires some explanation. The marriage, the home, the love of children, far from being clichés of happiness are indeed rarities in their fullest realization and precisely antidotal to the horrors of living isolation and death into which so many fall.

> And it is pleasant to write down that they reared a family; because any propagation of goodness and benevolence is no small addition to the aristocracy of nature, and no small subject of rejoicing for mankind at large. (p. 550)

This might be a fitting description of Dickens' subject from first to last. The continuing quest of Dickens' artistry, however, is how to translate this conviction into process. From modes of good and evil to modes of meaning to modes of being—this is the progress of a moralist.

[1]I am grateful to Prof. Maurice Elliott of York University for a substantial amount of corroborating evidence. He has pointed out to me the coincident origins of *The Old Curiosity Shop* and the magazine *Punch* (see Marion H. Spielmann, *The History of PUNCH* (London: Cassell, 1895)) and that Cruikshank was commissioned to do 24 etchings for a book, *Punch and*

Judy, in 1828 for S. Prowett. Among many items, Prof. Elliott has particularly mentioned to me references in *Tom Jones* Bk. 12, chap. 5; Dion Clayton Calthrop, *Punch and Judy. A Corner in the History of Entertainment. With an Essay on the Pleasant Art of Keeping People Amused* (London: Dulan, 1926); Maurice Baring, *Punch, Judy and Other Essays* (New York: Books for Libraries Press, 1968); Martin C. Battestin, "Fielding and 'Master Punch' in Panton Street," *Philological Quarterly* 45(1966):191-208

[2]George Speaight, *The History of the English Puppet Theatre* (London: Harrap, 1955), p. 190.

[3]William Faulkner's Popeye (*Sanctuary*) for instance, or perhaps Flem Snopes (*The Hamlet*) are twentieth-century equivalents of Quilp but frighteningly and appropriately much more mechanical; the ferocious wit and energy has significantly disappeared.

[4]*Dickens and His Readers,* p. 69.

"THE LONG ROSARY OF REGRETS" BARNABY RUDGE

They cannot *both* be unreal and non-existent, real and exist, unreal and exist, or real and not exist. *They* exist to be destroyed and are destroyed to be reinvented.

We need not worry that the kill ratio between Them and Us will get too high. There are always more where *they* came from. From *inside Us*.

RONALD D. LAING

•

"We hear the world wonder, every day, at monsters of ingratitude. Did it ever occur to you that it often looks for monsters of affection, as though they were things of course?"

BARNABY RUDGE

•

Barnaby Rudge carries us into an examination of how the fate of a nation may depend on choices that man makes in his life or death responses to others. Reconciliation is life; alienation is death. Both have their origins in the mind of man.

Dickens was nothing if not thoroughgoing in his search for the modes of evil, in his anatomy of society. *Barnaby Rudge* is an ambitious novel. It is historical because it is intended to be political. Dickens is attempting by analysis of historical event to understand the nature of political structure. Perspective is possible only through historic distance. Now he seeks to show how the structure of society is related to individual character and to present the symbolic rôle of inter-personal relations in the quality of human affairs. A glance at some of the scholarly history of the Gordon Riots[1] quickly shows how accurate Dickens was in his uses of history, even down to the borrowing of dialogue from the trials of the rioters. A sentence in a letter to Forster reveals Dickens' familiarity with the original sources for his background work on *Barnaby Rudge*. In defense of his sympathetic portrait of Gordon, Dickens says,

> *He never got anything by his madness, and never sought it. The wildest and most raging attacks of the time, allow him these merits*: and not to let him have 'em in their full extent, remembering in what a (politically) wicked time he lived, would lie upon my conscience heavily.[2] (my italics)

The novel is more than an oblique commentary on current unrest, though it is clearly this as well.[3] Beyond the immediate causes, beyond high prices and unemployment and wide class disparity, there must be reasons for social indifference, for prejudice and the toleration of poverty and violence and there must be some explanation of those who use and benefit from social disorder. The explanation for this concern for accuracy, is Dickens' anxiety to find out the real causes of real events and the proper solutions for actual human problems. That this theme is of central concern to Dickens is illustrated by the fact that he began it very early (*Oliver Twist*) and returned to it very late (*A Tale of Two Cities*). A number of critics have pointed out the contemporary relevance of *Barnaby Rudge* to the 1840's (House, Tillotson and Marcus, among others). Dickens saw that intolerable social conditions produce ample fuel for riot, destruction and social chaos. He deplored such conditions on these as well as on humanitarian grounds. More than this he believes that social evil is first caused and then exploited by those who see no common human bond between themselves and others or those who are blind to the present or to the nature of men in general. His novel is, then, a presentation of the causes of the conditions that make riot possible as well as of the riots themselves. If the novel may be said to be built on one central idea it is that " 'All good ends can be worked out by good means. Those that cannot, are bad; and may be counted so at once, and left alone.' " (p. 607) It should be remembered, in attempting to understand the full impact of *Barnaby Rudge*, that its subject was riot rather than revolution and that the above aphorism spoken by Haredale applies as much to government, social repression, and the law as it does to the rioters. Dickens identifies in the novel, and invites the reader to identify, only with Gabriel Varden, the locksmith, whose name and whose habitat, "The Golden Key," are symbolic of the central rôle he occupies. It is possible for him to have made the lock of Newgate, in spite of the horrors associated therewith, because his guardianship of social order is the act of a man of good nature, of tolerance, of good humour, of love. He is no Puritan but then neither is he a church-man of any kind. He is Dickens' man of large heart, his religion is humanism. Dickens knows that the lock and key are primary symbols of a fallen world. But he also knows that if all men were Gabriel Vardens the lock and key would disappear. The paradox of the good locksmith is itself the key to an understanding of the novel.

Dickens had already shown his fascination with murder, guilt and the agonies of the fugitive with the Sikes story in *Oliver Twist*. He would do so again with Jonas in *Martin Chuzzlewit*, his next novel. Now he makes the theme of murder and guilt seminal to his novel and adds elements to it that he used again and again. This is perhaps the earliest full-blown detective fiction in English. There has been a murder, two in fact, and the novel begins with the telling of the event that has now become a folk tale of Chigwell. In other words the murder is now part of the culture of this society and the novel begins as though the entire fictional metaphor stems from this event. Unknown to the tellers, Rudge, the murderer, is one of the listeners. The killing involved confused identity, and the use of a stream where the body was deposited. It was identified by clothes, watch and ring. Almost all of these elements are repeated later in *Our Mutual Friend* (three times in different ways) and in *Edwin Drood,* where only the watch is found after a disappearance and supposed death by drowning. One of the murdered men in *Barnaby Rudge* was Reuben Haredale, whose brother survives to mourn him and seek revenge for about twenty-seven years. Haredale is a Catholic. The murderer, Rudge, has been fugitive all that time. The story of Cain and Abel is the story of the first crime against humanity after the fall. The murder of a brother is the primary and supreme act of man against man and began the course of events that led to the flood: "The earth also was corrupt before God, and the earth was filled with violence."[4] Rudge, the murderer, is marked by a deep scar on his face, as Cain was marked. If we remember Haredale's remark, and it is he whose brother was murdered, " 'The men who learn endurance, are they who call the whole world brother,' " (p. 605) and if we add to this the division in England between Catholic and Protestant, we begin to see the theme of the novel taking shape. The murder is the symbolic centre of a story about human strife. The Bible is, after all, archetypal history and there is no shortage of Biblical names to substantiate such a reading of this historical novel.

Barnaby is the simple-minded offspring of Rudge, and we must explain why Dickens chose him as the central title-figure. Barnaby plays the rôle that children play elsewhere in Dickens' fiction. He is the innocent, the touchstone and the moral mirror. Somehow neutralized by his monstrous father and his angelic mother, he comes to reflect the world around him. The struggle for him is between the forces of destruction represented by his father and the rioters and those represented by his mother and Gabriel, who is victorious in the end and bears him off bodily from the gallows itself in an image of resurrection. As though to reinforce this mirror or clay quality of the impressionable and parodying Barnaby, Dickens attaches to him the pet raven Grip. Like Barnaby, Grip repeats with enthusiasm, but without comprehension, what he learns by rote. Grip cries "I'm a devil" as Barnaby cries "No Popery."

Barnaby finds himself at the forefront of the destruction and chaos of the rioters and his position there is designed to be ironically appropriate. Virtually no one connected with the riots has any more idea than he as to why he is where he is. Barnaby clearly parodies Gordon himself, and both illustrate the uses to which simplicity and weakness and even madness may be put. They are both moral indicators of the state of society. Dickens' original idea, to have three Bedlamites lead the rioters, would have only made more obvious what is already clear. The rioters are emblematically represented by each of the leading characters in the destruction. Gordon is mad and his insanity takes the form of millennially inspired religious fanaticism. All will be well if only Catholics are erased or at least denied citizenship, though it is clear that mere denial of civil rights would not be the end of it. It is a path leading to religious genocide. It is the "one thing needful." Gashford uses this madness for power and destruction out of a kind of world-hatred in response to his own personal rejection and failure. Chester is involved through the background out of a long diseased personal hatred for Haredale. Hugh represents all the totally alienated, who having been called animals long enough become animals and learn only contempt and bitterness for men in society. Dennis is the upholder of bad laws and inhuman punishments and joins the riots out of a bad scheme to defend Protestant hanging and to deny Catholic alternatives like the stake. Simon Tappertit is the leader of the vain, jealous and ambitious, those who wish power at any cost because their merits seem unrewarded in the normal course of things. If Simon cannot by his charm win Dolly, then the country will have to be turned upside down to permit him the recourse of rape. The mob could hardly be more carefully analyzed than in this collection of its leaders. All have different personal motives which are momentarily submerged in a common and expedient cry, in this case, "No Popery." There is never any shortage of millennial panaceas behind which to rally all the hungry, the deluded, the mad, the sick, the lonely, the disinherited and disenfranchized. But there is also an element to the riots which is not so easily accounted for, a kind of frenzied attraction to upheaval and destruction that affects even the apparently normal and quiet citizen:

> Each tumult took shape and form from the circumstances of the moment; sober workmen, going home from their day's labour, were seen to cast down their baskets of tools and become rioters in an instant; mere boys on errands did the like. In a word, a moral plague ran through the city. The noise, and hurry, and excitement, had for hundreds and hundreds an attraction they had no firmness to resist. The contagion spread like a dread fever: an infectious madness, as yet not near its height, seized on new victims every hour, and society began to tremble at their ravings. (p. 403)

In our time one is forced to recall the mob rise of nazism; sadism, private grievances and frustration become authorized; and all the good, sober, patriotic burgers turn anarchy into totalitarianism. It is all in *Barnaby Rudge,* which could have been written a hundred years later than it was and have seemed incredibly appropriate. "The great mass never reasoned or thought at all, but were stimulated by their own headlong passions, by poverty, by ignorance, by the love of mischief, and the hope of plunder." (pp. 402-3) Dickens sees, however, that the majority are as much the victims of their new leaders as they were of their old conditions. The attitudes that produce or tolerate hunger and disease and human suffering are the same ones that will not hesitate to use these conditions for further exploitation of the mass of sufferers.

> "No Popery, brother!" cried the hangman.
> "No Property, brother!" responded Hugh.
> "Popery, Popery," said the secretary with his usual mildness.
> "It's all the same!" cried Dennis. "It's all right. Down with him, Muster Gashford. Down with everybody, down with everything! Hurrah for the Protestant religion!" (p. 288)

Dickens shows us glimpses of the individual aberrations that lie behind the facade of the mob.

As I have said above, however, it all begins and ends with Rudge and the murder of Reuben Haredale. What antidote is there to the horrors of racial bigotry, to the hatred and revenge, to the jealousy and lying? The answer must lie in the individual and his relation to himself. While Dickens has not yet begun the profound analysis of his later work as to what constitutes a strong and tranquil good nature and its attainment, he is perhaps more explicit here as to the signs of such a mind. Gabriel, the angel of the Annunciation, becomes here the human "angel" who presents for his creator the image and the philosophy of the heart, nor is he unaware of the charges against this image as one of vague benevolence or imprecise physiology. Chester, who is a clear forerunner of Pecksniff in the next novel, speaks for all those who have attacked Dickens on these grounds:

> "About to speak from your heart. Don't you know that the heart is an ingenious part of our formation—the centre of the blood-vessels and all that sort of thing—which has no more to do with what you say or think, than your knees have? How can you be so very vulgar and absurd? These anatomical allusions should be left to gentlemen of the medical profession. They are really not agreeable in society. You quite surprise me, Ned." (p. 243)

This statement comes in the chapter that sees Chester reject his son totally with instructions to the servant that henceforth he is never at home to "that gentleman." The chapter is accompanied by an illustration entitled "Mr. Chester's Diplomacy" which shows the father holding a symbolic nutcracker inquisitorially, while behind him hangs a huge painting of Abraham sacrificing Isaac, with a very obvious Ram waiting to sacrifice itself. It is a very nice point. For Edward there is no ram because for Chester there is no God. But it is perfectly clear that for Dickens the heart is the centre (Latin: cor), the true man, and that Dickens perfectly understands his term to be psychological in effect. The nearest concept to Dickens' use of "heart" is the Renaissance use of Right-Reason. Gabriel is "bluff, hale, hearty, and in a green old age: at peace with himself, and evidently disposed to be so with all the world." (p. 18) He is a man of courage, compassion, joy and constancy. He is not one of those of whom Dickens can say, in speaking of the changes that have occurred in the Maypole Inn, "God help the man whose heart ever changes with the world, as an old mansion when it becomes an inn!" (p. 78) Haredale says of Gabriel, " 'A better creature never lived. He reaps what he has sown—no more.' " (p. 605) And Dolly, who foreshadows the creation of Pet in *Little Dorrit* with her spoiled light head and light heart, has a better fate than her successor and seems to be made of the same stuff at heart as her father. After her suffering and the social trauma that produces reassessment and awakening, Dickens tells us that "She had found her heart at last. Never having known its worth till now, she had never known the worth of his," (p. 557) and a little later she herself reveals in almost identical words that she knows she has found herself: " 'You have taught me,' said Dolly, raising her pretty face to his, 'to know myself, and your worth; . . .' " (p. 602) To know one's heart is essential if one would look clearly into others'.

Gabriel remains unchanged through all adversity while Dolly Varden grows through adversity. Joe Willet is somehow softened through suffering and his loss of limb seems necessary to bring others to the awareness of his value. It is also true of Haredale that he is brought to confess, " 'I have turned *from* the world, and I pay the penalty.' " (p. 605) The penalty is a soured vision, a lonely exile, a festering self-pity and a barely repressed and finally murderous hatred. Haredale ends his life in the rigours of monastic repentance cut off from a world too evil for him to bear. Mrs. Varden is brought to realize the dangers and folly of playing games too earnestly. If the events of '80 produce individual revelations to those in the novel, they are also meant to challenge the assumptions of those who rely (both character and reader) on things being as they have always been. A trust in social order is ineffectual in producing order, it is a kind of repression by default. John Willet rules the Maypole as he rules his son, with unquestioning and blind dictatorial patronage. The inn is the pride of English hostelry, the best among the most treasured, unalterable and immoveable of English institutions:

> All bars are snug places, but the Maypole's was the very snuggest, cosiest, and completest bar, that ever the wit of man devised. Such amazing bottles in old oaken pigeon-holes; such gleaming tankards dangling from pegs at about the same inclination as thirsty men would hold them to their lips; such sturdy little Dutch kegs ranged in rows on shelves; so many lemons hanging in separate nets, and forming the fragrant grove already mentioned in this chronicle, suggestive, with goodly loaves of snowy sugar stowed away hard by, of punch, idealized beyond all mortal knowledge; such closets, such presses, such drawers full of pipes, such places for putting things away in hollow window-seats, all crammed to the throat with eatables, drinkables, or savory condiments; lastly, and to crown all, as typical of the immense resources of the establishment, and its defiances to all visitors to cut and come again, such a stupendous cheese! (p. 151)

How quickly is all this rendered into chaos by the riots:

> Yes. Here was the bar—the bar that the boldest never entered without special invitation—the sanctuary, the mystery, the hallowed ground: here it was, crammed with men, clubs, sticks, torches, pistols; filled with a deafening noise, oaths, shouts, screams, hootings; changed all at once into a bear-garden, a mad-house, an infernal temple: men darting in and out, by door and window, smashing the glass, turning the taps, drinking liquor out of China punchbowls, sitting astride of casks, smoking private and personal pipes, cutting down the sacred grove of lemons, hacking and hewing at the celebrated cheese, breaking open inviolable drawers, putting things in their pockets which didn't belong to them, dividing his own money before his own eyes, wantonly wasting, breaking, pulling down and tearing up: nothing quiet, nothing private: men everywhere—above, below, overhead, in the bedrooms, in the kitchen, in the yard, in the stables—clambering in at windows when there were doors wide open; dropping out of windows when the stairs were handy; leaping over the bannisters into chasms of passages: new faces and figures presenting themselves every instant—some yelling, some

> singing, some fighting, some breaking glass and crockery, some laying the dust with the liquor they couldn't drink, some ringing the bells till they pulled them down, others beating them with pokers till they beat them into fragments: more men still—more, more, more—swarming on like insects: noise, smoke, light, darkness, frolic, anger, laughter, groans, plunder, fear, and ruin! (p. 414)

The destruction here is not only of property. Gone also is the unshakeable belief that nothing can change the quiet rural peace and hospitality, the security and snugness of an English inn. Nothing stands between the representative Maypole and such destruction but trust and love. The riots occur first in the minds of men and, once they do, the ruin of house, home, family and public institution is as sure as the passage of night after day. John Willet is blind to the tenuous nature of peace and blind to the needs and virtues of Joe and blind to the smouldering passions of Hugh. His obtuseness results from the assumption that he and everything around him is fixed, permanent and final. He is

> . . . one of the most dogged and positive fellows in existence—always sure that what he thought or said or did was right, and holding it as a thing quite settled and ordained by the laws of nature and Providence, that anybody who said or did or thought otherwise must be inevitably and of necessity wrong. (p. 3)

It is not sufficient that men be aware of the suffering and injustice around them or of the needs and desires of others. It is first of all essential that they look into their own hearts and discover the truth about themselves (as Dolly Varden does) in order to attain the strength and constancy and stoic superiority to circumstance that characterize Gabriel. Gordon is blind to his own weakness and the falseness of Gashford; Tappertit is blinded by his vanity; John Willet is blinded by habit and comfort; Haredale is blinded by bitterness; Rudge is blind to the relief of confession and is led by the literally blind Stagg, whose suffering has bred no compassion and no bond of sympathy with others.

If Dickens is suggesting that the course of human history is determined by the outcome of the struggle between the psychologically, emotionally, humanly whole on the one hand and the spiritually halt and lame on the other, then Religion is the perfect vehicle for exposing the distinction. Puritan gloom and guilt is to

Dickens not merely a distorted response to God and man and man's place in an ordered universe. It is a sickness of the soul, a rationalization for an individual failure. It is not a dialectic but an anti-life posture to the world given a deluding veneer by ritual, dress, and rhetoric. The austere appearance of the Puritan is for Dickens a disguise for a meanness in the soul. At the comic end of the scale it takes the form of an ironic pretense that is meant to be a lie and yet emerges under scrutiny to be the truth: "'I hope I know my own unworthiness, and that I hate and despise myself and all my fellow-creatures as every practicable Christian should.'" (p. 105) This is the testament according to Miggs. Her real spite and bitterness are exposed much later in the novel and typically her frustrated spinsterdom includes the whole of humanity to justify her own ugliness. The more sinister aspect of what lies behind the dark, sober exterior of the Puritan is revealed in what we are told of the mad Gordon himself:

> It would be difficult to convey an adequate idea of the excited manner in which he gave these answers to the secretary's promptings; of the rapidity of his utterance, or the violence of his tone and gesture in which, struggling through his Puritan's demeanour, was something wild and ungovernable which broke through all restraint. (p. 270)

The exterior meekness characteristically reveals an inner fire, a zealous passion for changing everything into a pattern for the accommodation of the alienated individual. Men like Gordon would be God, for they are at odds with humanity itself and would change it. The mad driven impulse to be pure is the source of the most inhumane of all natures. The absurdity of the Puritan rationalization is revealed by the degree of drunkenness, violence and general excess of those who follow Gordon and wear the blue cockade. Such seemingly contradictory evil grows from the inability to recognize and come to terms with human weakness, the brotherhood of sin, that is part of our humanity. Coercion replaces persuasion and the first object of the rioters, who began by seeking to alter government legislation, is frequently the free liquor, the enemy of reason, obtained by force. Dickens' humanism sees the Puritan response to living as inimical to life and joy, that is, alienated from the earth and nature and humanity itself and consequently desirous of death:

> There were men who rushed up to the fire, and paddled in it with their hands as if in water; and others who were restrained by force from plunging in, to gratify their deadly longing. (p. 423)

These are the people naturally attracted to any destructive and self-annihilating enterprise. Gabriel, too, likes to drink but his drinking is a social celebration, as much at home, with "Toby," as abroad. Moreover, he eats and drinks without guilt, with what can only be described as Dickensian pleasure. This annunciation of life is essentially creative and is characterized by peace with himself and then brotherhood to all and includes a sense of reconciliation to earth and life itself. A man like Gabriel is really glad to be an aware part of the living universe. It is this element of pre-lapsarian harmony of man and nature that Barnaby illustrates in his five-year country residence where he roams free with the dogs and birds for companions. The peace of this period is "home."

> "Oh mother, mother, how mournful he will be when he scratches at the door, and finds it always shut!"
>
> There was such a sense of home in the thought, that though her own eyes overflowed she would not have obliterated the recollection of it, either from her own mind or from his, for the wealth of the whole wide world. (p. 354)

There is a great deal of concentration in this novel on images of home, or locations or places to which characters are compelled or from which they are driven. The Maypole and the Warren and the Golden Key and Chester's Inn and Stagg's cellar and Barnaby's various hiding places—even the attitudes to Newgate, to which many released victims return for want of other "homes"—all seem to suggest that the whole question of feeling at home in the world or destructively un-at-home or alienated in it, is a central concern in the novel and related in Dickens' mind to the passion of the Puritan response. Tolerance or intolerance seem to have to do with how much at home one feels oneself. The more tenuous one's hold on place, in the largest sense, the more hostile to others, seems to be the rule. The arrival of Stagg into the country idyll with his aura of the events of the past (Rudge) and his blindness to the present destroys the home that Barnaby has found. Stagg is the snake who enters the garden. Thereafter, the maypole itself, sign of hospitality and good cheer, is torn down and thrust in at the inn window as a reminder of Puritanism and that the restoration of maypoles, dances and theatre had been in effect for only a hundred years. The maypole is the symbol of Spring and life. The image of the rioters dying in their mad wallowings in the lake of liquid fire and fumes at Langdale's distillery recalls Milton's image of the devils in Hell, as Marcus rightly suggests,[5] but it is no casual allusion. The outcast angels of Heaven and the rioters of *Barnaby Rudge* are alienated from their natural worlds in precisely the same way. Dickens fully understands the causes of riot and destruction, the despair of society's outcasts; but death, not life, chaos, not order, is all that results from a social riot led by the banner of Puritanism, which is itself the religion of alienation. If Puritanism is the religion of alienation ("I hate and despise myself and all my fellow creatures") then the politics of alienation is Fascism ("Down with Popery"—"Down with Everything") and the two conspire to produce social chaos in the name of a new order. "Where is my daughter?" becomes the only anguished and angry cry of Gabriel as home, family and even Parliament itself are threatened. Books are characteristically burned on the bonfires along with canaries in cages. Destruction and death become ends and satisfactions in themselves as the terrible forces of despair gain authority. Hugh the centaur, Dennis the authorized murderer and Barnaby the disinherited are the natural leaders. Hugh, labelled as an animal and denied his humanity, returns to society its earned response.

> "He's quite a animal, sir," John whispered in his ear with dignity. "You'll excuse him, I'm sure. If he has any soul at all, sir, it must be such a very small one that it don't signify what he does or doesn't in that way. Good night, sir!" (p. 97)

Chester speaks of Haredale as an animal: " 'Pah! A very coarse animal, indeed!' said Mr. Chester, composing himself in the easy-chair again. 'A rough brute. Quite a human badger!' " (p. 95) Dennis reveals that murder will not be contained within the bounds of the law, for what is taught in the State by example will flourish on its own account. The hangman's cry, " 'Don't hang me here. It's murder,' " is the supreme indictment of capital punishment.

Barnaby Rudge marks one of the major advances in Dickens'

work. It indicates clearly that a good many of the counters that will be shifted and juggled and made the staple of later novels are already employed here. The spoiled daughter; the rejected son; murder as the ultimate alienation; water and its symbolic use in connection with identity; birth and rebirth; the forms of social and personal regeneration and their connection; the insistence that Christianity or Godliness is an accepting and loving joyful state of mind; the rejection of all dogma, doctrine, code and absolutism along with an abhorrence of gloom and despondency in religion; all these are materials or attitudes that *Barnaby Rudge* firmly establishes. There is not yet much emphasis on how one becomes a Gabriel rather than a Chester. Nor is there the kind of growth in character which later clearly shows Dickens' awareness of human possibility. Dolly falls far short of Bella Wilfer as a portrait, but not as a moral lesson. One day Dolly is thoughtless and the next she has arrived at self-realization and fulfillment, while Bella is visible to us proceeding through a gradual and exacting series of progressive stages of self-discovery. Bella's heart is much more hardly won than Dolly's. I cannot separate in Dickens' canon his growth of talent from his growth of perception. The moral convictions alter, or become clearer, only in that Dickens renders them more and more into detailed psychological terms. His writing is to become more and more concrete. The radical alteration of society occurs not through riot, or as we shall see later, not even through revolution, but through the conversion of the heart, through individual growth and understanding. Dickens would almost certainly agree with Blake that "Men are admitted into Heaven not because they have curbed and govern'd their Passions or have No Passions, but because they have Cultivated their Understandings."[6] The value of riot and revolution is that they may make such personal change possible, that they reveal what lies explosively just beneath the surface of an apparently peaceful world. What Dickens says of Mrs. Varden may apply to the larger situation of the body politic:

> . . . certain it is that minds, like bodies, will often fall into a pimpled ill-conditioned state from mere excess of comfort, and like them, are often successfully cured by remedies in themselves very nauseous and unpalatable. (p. 54)

The eruption of repressed fury and despair will show us the causes of violence, hatred and social corruption and disorder if we will but look for them, but the remedies lie within ourselves. The object of all experience, public and private, is to turn the "vinegar of misanthropy into purest milk of human kindness," (p. 612) otherwise suffering has been in vain.

[1]For instance, John P. DeCastro, *The Gordon Riots* (London: Oxford Univ. Press, 1926), and G. F. E. Rudé, "The Gordon Riots," *Transactions of the Royal Historical Society,* 5th series 6(1956):93-114.

[2]John Forster, *The Life of Charles Dickens,* Vol. 1 (London: Chapman and Hall, 1873), p. 217.

[3]See for instance the comments on *Barnaby Rudge* in John Butt and Kathleen Tillotson, *Dickens at Work* (London: Methuen, 1957).

[4]Genesis 6:11.

[5]*From PICKWICK to DOMBEY,* p. 210.

[6]William Blake, "A Vision of the Last Judgment," *Selected Poetry and Prose of William Blake* (New York: Modern Library, 1953), p. 398.

"LIVING IN A WALE"
MARTIN CHUZZLEWIT

It is man's fault if God is not able to do him good, for he gives to the just and to the unjust, but the unjust reject his gift.

WILLIAM BLAKE

•

The truth is that in 1917 there was nothing that a thinking and sensitive person could do, except to remain human, if possible.

GEORGE ORWELL

•

And, oh! ye Pharisees of the nineteen hundredth year of Christian Knowledge, who soundingly appeal to human nature, see first that it be human. Take heed it has not been transformed, during your slumber and the sleep of generations, into the nature of the Beasts.

MARTIN CHUZZLEWIT

•

On several occasions Mrs. Gamp speaks of life as a "Wale." She is punning on "vale" but she is also, in her linguistic innocence, punning on whale. Jonas is a variant of the name Jonah. Jonas, like Jonah, tries to run away from his fate by getting into a boat, in this case the Antwerp packet. Did Dickens have in mind the Book of Jonah when writing *Martin Chuzzlewit*, or can the Biblical story throw any light on the Dickens novel? What has the story of Jonah to do with Dickens' claim that

> My main object in this story was, to exhibit in a variety of aspects the commonest of all the vices: to show how Selfishness propagates itself; and to what a grim giant it may grow, from small beginnings.[1]

Barnaby Rudge was an investigation of the effects of evil on historic or linear time. By exploring the nature of past events Dickens hoped to be able to arrive at a clearer understanding of the individual attitudes, values and aberrations that lie behind them. Now Dickens turns from past exterior time to present interior space. This shift to analysis of individual vice is a major development. In his search for the sources and nature of vice, Dickens focuses all his attention on one particular human evil, Selfishness. He has told us what his novel is about. Pecksniff, as Anthony Chuzzlewit recognizes with grudging admiration, is the master hypocrite, but how is hypocrisy related to selfishness? The greed of Anthony, the meanness and brutality of Jonas and the pride and arrogance of the two Martins are all more easily related to selfishness. We need to discover how all these failings are related to the central evil and how America functions in the overriding theme of the novel.

What then, does Dickens mean by "Selfishness?" When a man is blind and indifferent to every interest in the world, except what he mistakenly believes to be his own, he is said to be selfish. Yet ironically, tragically often enough, this very interest, his own, which he values most, works to his own destruction, or the destruction of his real self. The selfish man is still in Dickens' work a given and the author makes no attempt to show us how or why he reached that condition, yet his characteristics are perfectly apprehended and presented in Pecksniff, the archetype of selfishness, who believes himself to be separate, different from and in opposition to all else. Because the selfish man sees no common interest or bond of humanity between himself and the rest of his world he is free from moral compunction, free to construct a false self, mask, rôle, or persona, and at pains to protect his real self from the encroachments of a hostile world. The false self is a created image or ego, presented to the world for two purposes. Behind it, the decaying real self appears to be protected, that is, it gives the illusion of a genuine defense, and it serves also to deceive a world which, because it is alien, must be exploited. A world which worships false images may readily be deceived by one more such image, as a fish, knowing nothing of the man wielding the rod, is deceived by a false fly which looks real. For those living in a world of false appearances only the false will appear to be real. This is what Pecksniff's hypocrisy means and how it is related to selfishness. For such a man then, the world is a discordant jungle in which creatures prey on each other and everyone is at odds. The aim is to be king of the jungle. The church organ, and the music it produces under the hands of Tom Pinch, is the central symbol of harmony in the novel, presented as a soothing contrast to the discord of the Pecksniff world. The novel moves towards resolution by reconciliation and acceptance, by love in short, and alienation, hostility and death must be overcome. The false self or ego is contrasted to the heart, hypocrisy is opposed to candour. Selfishness is afraid and leads to murder (or on a national level, war) and self-fulfillment leads to love and a symbolically happy marriage. There are, however, degrees of selfishness and the novel explores them all. Pecksniff never knows, after losing his daughters, his friends, his fortune, and all else, that he has destroyed his self, or that the world might be anything other than diametrically opposed to him. He is locked into his own perverted system. The two Martins are a different story.

Before proceeding to examine how they are saved, however, it is worthwhile looking at the story of Jonah and the whale.

> "Ah!" sighed Mrs. Gamp, as she meditated over the warm shilling's-worth, "what a blessed thing it is—living in a wale—to be contented! What a blessed thing it is to make sick people happy in their beds, and never mind one's self as long as one can do a service! I don't believe a finer cowcumber was ever grow'd. I'm sure I never see one!" (p. 413)

It might seem too far-fetched at this point to suggest that Mrs. Gamp's "cowcumber" is a comic reference to the gourd which gave Jonah so much comfort on the desert hill outside of Ninevah, but the broadness of such a joke is not out of the question. Of Sweedlepipe, and his fall from the carriage, Mrs. Gamp remarks that:

> "He was born into a wale," said Mrs. Gamp, with philosophical coolness; "and he lived in a wale; and he must take the consequences of sech a sitiwation." (p. 751)

Of Ruth and her naïve enquiry, Mrs. Gamp has this to say:

> "Which shows," said Mrs. Gamp, casting up her eyes, "what a little way you've travelled into this wale of life, my dear young creetur!" (p. 625)

And in case the reader has missed the pun Dickens has had the confusing Sairey (another Biblical pun) remark three or four lines before, in reference to the boat carrying Jonas and his wife,

> "And I wish it was in Jonadge's belly, I do," cried Mrs. Gamp; appearing to confound the prophet with the whale in this miraculous aspiration. (p. 624)

Jonas, like Jonah, fails to escape his fate, even though his God is only Tigg Montague, for he is called back from his attempted escape by sea before he can experience the storm, but he does experience a storm later, much like Jonah's, while on the journey to Pecksniff.

> The thunder rolled, the lightning flashed; the rain poured down like Heaven's wrath. Surrounded at one moment by intolerable light, and at the next by pitchy darkness, they still pressed forward on their journey. (p. 645)

It is not clear in the first two of the four chapters of the Book of Jonah why the prophet wishes to run away from God and his duty. What is clear is that nothing could be more deluded than to think that a journey over a sea could evade the Divinity or cross the universal border which He circumscribes. Only a man blind, asleep or desperate would venture such a thing. Jonah is asleep, deep inside the ship during the storm, dead to the reality of his situation. When he is cast overboard like a piece of jetsam he finds himself inside the whale. The whale is provided by God. It is part of a Divine plan and strangely enough it is only in there that Jonah seems to come awake and be freed from his desperate alienation from God. In the whale Jonah offers up his extraordinary prayer of reconciliation and acceptance:

> The water compassed me about, even to the soul: the depth closed me round about, the weeds were wrapped about my head.
>
> I went down to the bottoms of the mountains: the earth with her bars was about me for ever: yet hast thou brought up my life from corruption, O Lord my God.[2]

Jonah, at this point, is instantly freed. In other words, no sooner does he accept the "earth with her bars about me" than he is free. The whale then is the earth, the symbol of nature, the vale of tears of Sairey Gamp indeed, and only a reconciliation to it and therefore to one's humanity and mortality will make one free. The whale is a tyrant only to a victim, as for a tyrant to be a tyrant requires either a reluctant or a willing slave. The tyranny of nature which is the whale is also a saving grace when seen as human preserver. The whale is a boat, a protective womb, a place of harmony into which a man may be perfectly fitted. To accept the whale is to be free and, as Orwell says, we are all in the whale: "Get inside the whale —or rather, admit that you are inside the whale (for you *are,* of course)."[3] Satan is cast out of Heaven at the precise instant he refuses to accept Divine supremacy, and to return to it he has only to do what is impossible for him, accept the Divine order. Hell then would disappear. Oddly enough, Satan's rebellion against what appears tyranny to him renders him instantly a tyrant. Dickens tells us that Jonas too becomes a tyrant through his alienation:

> . . . for, conscious that there was nothing in his person, conduct, character, or accomplishments, to command respect, he was greedy of power, and was, in his heart, as much a tyrant as any laurelled conqueror on record. (p. 449)

But the essence of the Jonah story is its insistence on what is enduring. Jonah is called upon to perform the prophet's duty and cannot reconcile himself to God's change of heart or his own failure. He is recalcitrant and would prefer his own rightness to God's mercy. His is the sin of pride. Like all prophets or believers, he must accept the terrible burdens of meaning, order and salvation. It seems, in brief, easier to live in an alien universe opposed to God, than to accept the harmony of suffering and salvation in a Divine system. Nothing could be further from the truth in Dickens' moral world order. An intensive study of Selfishness and the Book of Jonah, which Northrop Frye calls "the most humourous book in the Bible,"[4] shows how close they are in *Martin Chuzzlewit.* Frye goes on in his analysis of Blake's vision:

> Any kind of imagination separated from its material or emanation becomes a Spectre of Selfhood, and when Tharmas falls and becomes separated from Enion he turns into the Spectre of Tharmas. As such, he is the direct perversion of everything he was in his former state. Whereas formerly he was the water of life in Beulah, the liquid imagination which is continually changing its shape, he is now the spirit of chaos of which the chief form in the fallen world is the sea, and which continually tries to break out of its confining rock to overwhelm

> life in ruin. The only link left between the unfallen and fallen Tharmas is the attraction which the moon, a primary Beulah Symbol, still has on the sea. The Spectre of Tharmas thus suggests the Biblical Leviathan, the water-monster who symbolizes the tyranny of the state of nature, and who is slain whenever new life is reborn.[5]

Thus Blake (or Frye) would seem to make the connection between the Spectre of Selfhood and the whale. Translated into personal and social terms the opening sentence of the above quotation seems to suggest that any projection of false image, any phony self or designed rôle divorced from the source of its reality produces a powerful Spectre, a monster of the mind, one characteristic of which is hypocrisy. This is what *Martin Chuzzlewit* is about when it presents versions of "Selfishness." This idea of the whale as symbol of our separated nature, falsely projected symbol of our self-alienation to which we must again, as in the Biblical tale, become reconciled, is strongly urged by D. H. Lawrence:

> And he is hunted, hunted, hunted by the maniacal fanaticism of our white mental consciousness. We want to hunt him down. To subject him to our will. And in this maniacal conscious hunt of ourselves we get dark races and pale to help us, red, yellow, and black, east and west, Quaker and fire-worshipper, we get them all to help us in this ghastly maniacal hunt which is our doom and our suicide.[6]

Nothing could be clearer evidence of the precision of Dickens' concept or intention than his making Pecksniff an architect who never builds anything. His "projections" and "elevations," mostly suggested for others to do, are all vain appearances that come to nothing. He makes an entire world out of window-dressing. And when he does receive credit for a building it is someone else's building. Who is Pecksniff, what is he, who knows him?

> "My dear," observed Mr. Pecksniff, with a placid leer, "a habit of self-examination, and the practice of—shall I say of virtue?"
>
> "Of hypocrisy," said Mary.
>
> "No, No," resumed Mr. Pecksniff, chafing the captive hand reproachfully, "of virtue—have enabled me to set such guards upon myself, that it is really difficult to ruffle me. It is a curious fact, but it is difficult, do you know, for any one to ruffle me. And did she think," said Mr. Pecksniff, with a playful tightening

of his grasp, "that *she* could! How little did she know his heart!" (p. 483)

So free is he from any constraints of reality that Pecksniff can say anything in his fixed rôle of righteousness. He pretends to garden, to dig and delve, in his country idyll (a parody of Eden); he pretends to be at one with nature, though we first see him blown over by the wind; he pretends to live the simplest of pure lives with his pretendedly ingenuous daughters. He is in fact the symbolic centre of Selfhood in the novel.

It is for this reason that Old Martin is saved by locating himself with Pecksniff, just as young Martin is saved by going to America. They choose precisely similar routes to salvation and they choose the only possible ones. Both go to their own Edens for their private experiences of the Fortunate Fall. The young, new man goes to the New World and the old man goes into the English countryside. Old Martin locates with Pecksniff in order to be at the source of deception. Either the architect is the best of men or he is totally false, but either way the desperate old man should be able to discover differences between people by witnessing contrasts from inside as it were. " 'Can you or anybody teach me to know who are my friends, and who my enemies?' " (p. 31) This is the cry from the bewildered mind and heart. Old Martin's mind, prior to his enlightenment, is like the room Tom Pinch is set to work in for his unknown benefactor. The following description is one of those images that strike the reader as a metaphor redolent of the theme of the novel.

> Dust was the only thing in the place that had any motion about it. When their conductor admitted the light freely, and lifting up the heavy window-sash, let in the summer air, he showed the mouldering furniture, discoloured wainscoting and ceiling, rusty stove, and ashy hearth, in all their inert neglect. Close to the door there stood a candlestick, with an extinguisher upon it: as if the last man who had been there had paused, after securing a retreat, to take a parting look at the dreariness he left behind, and then had shut out light and life together, and closed the place up like a tomb. (pp. 612-13)

Just as Tom sets the room to rights, clears out the dust and cobwebs, lets in the light and brings order to chaos, so he is Old Martin's "True Heart" who restores trust and charity to a mind shuttered off and rotting with cynicism and mistrust.

> "There is a kind of selfishness," said Martin: "I have learned it in my own experience of my own breast: which is constantly upon the watch for selfishness in others; and holding others at a distance by suspicions and distrusts, wonders why they don't approach, and don't confide, and calls that selfishness in them." (p. 804)

Old Martin learns very late, but not too late, what Pecksniff can never learn, that it is the distorted perception of the Selfhood that can "make life a desert by withering every flower that grew about me!" (p. 781) This is learnt in old England by an old man, nor is there anything new in the New World. Everyman, everywhere, must discover what young Martin discovers in Eden, U.S.A. Like his grandfather (indeed they are mirror images of each other), Martin is completely lacking in self-awareness. He knows that selfishness is a family failing but cannot see that the traits of his ancestors have any part in his own make-up. " 'All I have to do, you know, is to be very thankful that they haven't descended to me, and to be very careful that I don't contract 'em.' " (p. 94) He regards the family weakness as though it were measles and could somehow be caught from the outside. The resistance to the moral disease seems however to require self-knowledge rather than mere caution. His idea of harmonious friendship is finding some-one who will serve him without demur. " 'I am not at all the sort of fellow who could get on with everybody, and that's the point on which I had the greatest doubts. But they're quite relieved now. —Do me the favour to ring the bell, will you?' " (p. 75) No sooner does misfortune strike him, however, than Martin begins his journey to self-awareness, his discovery of human interdependence, and Dickens quickly begins to sow hints of this progress through the novel. " 'Help yourself,' said Martin, handing him the only knife.' " (p. 228) And again:

> Feeling (however disinclined he was, being weary) that it would be in bad taste, and not very gracious, to object that he was unintroduced, when this open-hearted gentleman was so ready to be his sponsor, Martin—for once in his life, at all events—sacrificed his own will and pleasure to the wishes of another, and consented with a fair grace. So travelling had done him that much good, already. (p. 284)

Just as the grandfather has Tom Pinch to awaken him, so Martin is provided with Tom's counterpart, Mark Tapley, whose good humour and selflessness are the accompaniment to Martin's change of heart. Martin reaches Eden still steeped in illusion, clinging to images of his own inevitable greatness and buried beneath the air-castles built from the transparent materials of self-importance.

> Poor Martin! For ever building castles in the air. For ever, in his very selfishness, forgetful of all but his own teeming hopes and sanguine plans. Swelling, at that instant, with the consciousness of patronising and most munificently rewarding Mark! (p. 352)

The Fall, the discovery of Good and Evil, is the discovery of the human condition, of mortality, of love, of frailty and of human weakness and strength. This at least is clearly what Dickens understands as indicated by his allegory in *Martin Chuzzlewit* and the American experience. Martin learns in America what his grandfather learns in England and what all men must learn everywhere. He falls from ignorance, from a false height into a real and existential despair and thence he rises through a reassessment of his own nature and condition and of his dependence on and relatedness to other human beings.

> Eden was a hard school to learn so hard a lesson in; but there were teachers in the swamp and thicket, and the pestilential air, who had a searching method of their own. (p. 525)

Mark is his model and it is fortunate for Mark that Martin falls sick first for he would otherwise want a nurse. Being near to death and far from home and devoid of any comforts save that of Mark's friendship, Martin falls. He loses his illusions, his images, his projections and in place of his shattered Selfhood he gains his self. "So low had Eden brought him down. So high had Eden raised him up." (p. 525) Dickens is fully aware that such a change does not take place in an instant. He knew what he was doing when he made his images of selfishness, knew how deeply they become wedded to the mind and with what difficulty they are sloughed off; he knew how self-knowledge is acquired, and he wishes his reader to share his awareness.

> It was long before he fixed the knowledge of himself so firmly in his mind that he could thoroughly discern the truth; but in the hideous solitude of that most hideous place, with Hope so far removed, Ambition quenched, and Death beside him rattling at

> the very door, reflection came, as in a plague-beleaguered town; and so he felt and knew the failing of his life, and saw distinctly what an ugly spot it was. (p. 525)

Martin returns worthy of Mary, the characteristic good angel to whom the hero aspires in his spiritual and picaresque quest.

Dickens presents America as a kind of national Pecksniff, or Spectre of Selfhood on a national scale. It is in this novel the image of a whole nation and people obsessed with a single image of itself, largely constructed out of rhetoric and entirely belied by experience and practice. It is as though Dickens, on thinking over and digesting his reactions to America as recorded in *American Notes,* had finally come to some philosophic conclusion as to the meaning of his impressions. America is, in my view, the "grim giant" of Dickens' preface. It is this sense of a vision of a national disease of the spirit that reminds one strongly of Swift and indeed Dickens mentions Swift as he has his "good" American discuss the rôle of satire in the New World.

> ". . . I believe no satirist could breathe this air. If another Juvenal or Swift could rise up among us tomorrow, he would be hunted down. If you have any knowledge of our literature, and can give me the name of any man, American born and bred, who has anatomised our follies as a people, and not as this or that party; and who has escaped the foulest and most brutal slander, the most inveterate hatred and intolerant pursuit; it will be a strange name in my ears, believe me. In some cases I could name to you, where a native writer has ventured on the most harmless and good-humoured illustrations of our vices or defects, it has been found necessary to announce, that in a second edition the passage has been expunged, or altered, or explained away, or patched into praise." (p. 276)

Satire is possible and tolerable only for a culture strong enough to doubt itself at some deep level. The very nature of the ego or Spectre precludes doubt, for doubt would indicate remnants or beginnings of self-awareness, and this in turn would weaken the image that was designed to obscure the doubt in the first place. It is a defense of defenses that precludes satire, for satire is designed to penetrate false images. Dickens himself decides to play the rôle of satirist, and the history of early American reaction to *Chuzzlewit* would seem to bear out the contentions in the above quotation. The violence in America that Dickens describes, the rhetoric, the images of patriotism, the flag and the eagle, the social rituals of levees and speech-making, the spitting and the slavery, all seem intimately related to the amoral, impenetrable, social indifference of Pecksniff and the avarice and homicidal, sadistic brutality of Jonas. Interestingly enough, Melville, an American, presents his symbolic analysis of America in terms of the story of the Book of Jonah also. The best in America, as elsewhere, is shown to be characterized by totally unpretentious candour, but such candour is all too rare.

> Martin stared at him for a moment, and burst into a hearty laugh; to which the negro, out of his natural good humour and desire to please, so heartily responded, that his teeth shone like a gleam of light. "You're the pleasantest fellow I have seen yet," said Martin, clapping him on the back, "and give me a better appetite than bitters." (p. 270)

Martin is not the first or last visitor to America to find the black man the best company there. It is precisely the lack of opportunity for social pretension and personal humbug that aids the black man in his retention of reality, a situation similar to that of Fagin in England. Mr. Bevan is Dickens' other concession to what the true American ought to be.

> There was a cordial candour in his manner, and an engaging confidence that it would not be abused; a manly bearing on his own part, and a simple reliance on the manly faith of a stranger; which Martin had never seen before. He linked his arm readily in that of the American gentleman, and they walked out together. (p. 277)

As Steven Marcus points out, Dickens indicates his awareness of the loss in America of the private self.

> He immediately understood, as Tocqueville had a few years before him, that a new language was being born in America; that Americans were losing the habit of speaking conversationally and spoke in private situations as if they were addressing a public meeting; . . .[7]

Everyone has a title, usually military, everything is done in public and at the wish of the public, conversation easily turns to rhetoric and bombast and the terrifying implication is that the Self may find it increasingly difficult to survive in face of Image-worship on such a scale.

What is required by Dickens' moral quest is the making of a new world from regenerated, realized selves. Fallen men must rise with a new awareness of their own rich humanity and with a new capacity for love. Mary waits for Martin and he returns and joins his equally new grandfather. Mary has her counterpart in Mrs. Lupin, who also waits for Mark Tapley to discover where his best interests really lie. Mark and Tom Pinch are not without their weaknesses and one of the signs of Dickens' mastery of his moral content here is his insistence that even goodness may be tainted and even dangerous when it is not fully aware. Mark is a far cry from Pecksniff, but he is not free from rôle-playing and while pride is nowhere more gently or lovingly treated by Dickens, Mark's is false pride nevertheless. Mark himself knows it is a weakness: " 'My constitution is, to be jolly; and my weakness is, to wish to find a credit in it.' " (p. 737) His desertion of Mrs. Lupin, rationalized as it is, remains a fear of comfort, a desire for suffering along strongly Puritan lines. His return to Mrs. Lupin is the result of his actual suffering in America and the consequent growth of the courage to love. Tom Pinch likewise must undergo a fall before he can be fully integrated into the regenerated society of Dickens' ending. Sylvère Monod calls Tom "simple-minded" but perhaps simple-souled is nearer to the truth. Tom's adult innocence is socially dangerous, a sort of Peter Pan horror, for he is deceived as to his sister's real condition by her kindness and deceived by Pecksniff's sanctimonious exterior and patronizing usage. His worship of Pecksniff leads him to be used so that, as Pecksniff's social tool and advertisement, he actually augments the influence and power of evil. It takes Tom a long time to understand fully that the Pecksniff he has created never existed. Being without pride Tom is able to reconcile himself to his own stupidity and suffer no guilt or other results of damaged self-image. His fall into experience is his salvation, for while his illusion is gone his gentleness and compassion and joy all remain; the image that originally deceived him was not an image of himself. Tom remains sexually alone because he can afford it more than anyone else at the end of the novel. Dickens wishes to present him as the whole man, married, in a sense, to everyone.

We have seen in earlier novels how Dickens was fascinated by the metaphoric social implications of theatrical rôle-playing. In

Martin Chuzzlewit he pursues this psychological concern with more penetration than before, probing more openly into the nature of the self, the sources of hypocrisy and the quality of a society that is built on a frozen rôle. What is necessary is what Frye describes (in Blake's work) as "the liquid imagination which is continually changing its shape," it is the "water of life." A modern psychologist suggests that this capacity for change, for flexibility and freedom, is the distinctive mark of the whole human being.

> . . . the distinctive thing about the human being is that he can one day be the romantic lover, another day the woodchopper, another day the painter. In a variety of ways the human being can select among many self-world relationships. The "self" is the capacity to see one's self in these many possibilities. This freedom with respect to [the] world . . . is the mark of the psychologically healthy person; to be rigidly confined to a specific "world," . . . is the mark of psychological disorder.[8]

Another modern psychologist describes the same phenomenon as being "game-free."[9] He advocates the "attainment of autonomy" and the "recovery of the capacities: awareness, spontaneity and intimacy." The word "recovery" suggests that we once had these capacities as children and have somehow lost them. But we did not lose them by accident. Is this not precisely what Dickens deals with?

> . . . a premature little woman of thirteen years old, who had already arrived at such a pitch of whalebone and education that she had nothing girlish about her: which was a source of great rejoicing to all her relations and friends. (p. 134)

The presence of children, or what is child-like, is a threat to the rôles or games or ego-images of a deadened world that resists coming to life. Jonas is a murderer and wishes to murder his father because he has been trained from birth in laissez-faire commercial ruthlessness.

> The education of Mr. Jones had been conducted from his cradle on the strictest principles of the main chance. The very first word he learnt to spell was "gain," and the second (when he got into two syllables), "money." But for two results, which were not clearly foreseen perhaps by his watchful parent in the beginning, his training may be said to have been unexceptionable. One of these flaws was, that having been long taught by

his father to over-reach everybody, he had imperceptibly acquired a love of over-reaching that venerable monitor himself. The other, that from his early habits of considering everything as a question of property, he had gradually come to look, with impatience, on his parent as a certain amount of personal estate, which had no right whatever to be going at large, but ought to be secured in that particular description of iron safe which is commonly called a coffin, and banked in the grave. (p. 119)

Charity Pecksniff likewise is mean, bitter and pretentious because she has been educated to be unreal. There are few images in Dickens' work more gruesome than the fireside performances of the Pecksniff family. Only courage, awareness, love and ultimately faith can alter the power of selfishness and the cycle of learned generational falsehood, as we see with increasing clarity in later novels. As Mark Tapley puts it,

> "In all the story-books as ever I read, sir, the people as looked backward was turned into stones," replied Mark; "and my opinion always was, that they brought it on themselves, and it served 'em right." (p. 297)

Dickens is here giving a moral interpretation of myth. The power of the past is to turn people into stone, to take away their freedom of movement. What we come to see more and more is this concentration on various forms of rigidity and imprisonment and the opposition to moral confinement in the freedom to choose. Morality as the power of choice is increasingly evident and emerges as the definition forged into being by the structure of the novels. The function of rôle, of self-image, of appearance, that is, the external shape of things, are set up against a quality of process, the power to alter or grow continuously, almost organically. This is the existential dimension to Dickens' moral quest. In *Martin Chuzzlewit* these qualities of rôle, appearance and death are sometimes explicitly linked. Mr. Mould buries according to the rule of appearance:

> "The beadle's son-in-law, eh?" said Mould. "Well! I'll do it if the beadle follows in his cocked hat; not else. We carry it off that way, by looking official, but it'll be low enough then. His cocked hat, mind!" (p. 403)

Mrs. Gamp brings people into the world by it and commerce is conducted on it. The Anglo-Bengalee is really Bullamy, the most desirable usher-doorman-footman in the insurance world by virtue of his appearance. Dickens becomes increasingly preoccupied with the dynamics of freedom and more and more self-assured in the images of "mind-forged mannacles." How can the iron grip of past and illusion and pride be broken? To be turned to stone or "recalled to life," is the heart of the moral dilemma.

There is something quite terrifying, almost horrific, in the degree to which Cherry and Merry, Charity and Mercy Pecksniff, represent their father in the world. The very idea of children, designed, conceived, named and trained as the emissaries and advertisements of their father's Selfhood would, were its presentation not veiled in a Dickensian covering of protective humour, be monstrous. There is, too, something extraordinary in the antithetical rôles of the faithful, silent Pinch and the loud false Pecksniff, especially as revealed in the ironies of the scene of Tom's dismissal. But Pecksniff has no monopoly on the novel's irony. Anthony is buried by his dutifully murderous son amidst universal admiration for the child's filial piety and devotion. As Anthony lived, so he dies, mourned by no one except Chuffey, whose grief is regarded as an entirely inappropriate, incomprehensible social embarrassment. Jonas is indeed the prophet of the novel, for his own conduct and fate warn the reader more clearly than any discourse that false appearance and false value lead to destruction, misery and chaos. It is interesting that it is the earliest of Dickens' critics who has most clearly seen the significance of the novel's moral implications.

> The elder Chuzzlewits are bad enough, but they bring their self-inflicted punishments; the Jonases and Tigg Montagues are execrable, but the law has its halter and its penal servitude; the Moulds and Gamps have plague-bearing breaths, from which sanitary wisdom may clear us; but from the sleek, smiling, crawling abomination of a Pecksniff, there is no help but self-help.[10]

There is no comment on the novel more penetrating than this last.

The complexity of the social scene grows in Dickens' work with every novel. The relations between individuals, their psychic make-up, and their personal perception on the one hand and the state of the community at large and of the nation itself on the other are seen with growing clarity to be intricately interwoven and mutually determinant. A nation valuing a Pecksniff is also one that values speed and efficiency more than people, "for steel and iron are of infinitely greater account, in this commonwealth, than flesh and blood." (p. 341) And in a country such as Dickens portrays, language may be designed precisely not to communicate, as is most obviously the case in America, though the same malady is found as surely at home.

> . . . for though lovers are remarkable for leaving a great deal unsaid on all occasions, and very properly desiring to come back and say it, they are remarkable also for a wonderful power of condensation; and can, in one way or other, give utterance to more language—eloquent language—in any given short space of time, than all the six hundred and fifty-eight members in the Commons House of Parliament of the United Kingdom of Great Britain and Ireland; who are strong lovers, no doubt, but of their country only, which makes all the difference; for in a passion of that kind (which is not always returned), it is the custom to use as many words as possible, and express nothing whatever. (p. 675)

We began with a whale, or "wale," and let us end with a dragon, for the Dragon Inn is where Dickens ends his novel. The joyous wedding party inside the Dragon finds itself in the friendliest, most comfortable place of all. Jonas, the "Griffin," is dead, but the friendly Dragon survives to shelter those who will accept love and permit trust and fidelity and compassion to pervade their vision. Dickens curiously indicates novels to come in *Martin Chuzzlewit.* There is a Pip in this novel, " 'Pip's our mutual friend,' " (p. 451) and young Martin clearly foreshadows the Pip of the later novel: " 'that I have been bred up from childhood with great expectations, and have always been taught to believe that I should be, one day, very rich.' " (p. 93) Certainly this work leads us squarely into the penetrating Dickens of the later psychological and moral complexity. We have moved from examining the past to the making of the present, and the present and the future are made by the quality of mind and heart of each human being in his encounter with his world. Dickens' moral view has now become more fully realized. Be aware of the past; live in the present; look to the future. It remains to explore further and probe deeper into the sources of failure and the means of realizing this delicate balance that can take one out of time and into the vortex of being. " '. . . a Werb is a word as signifies to be, to do, or to suffer (which is all the grammar, and enough too, as ever I wos taught); . . .' " (p. 733) To learn the "werb" is to live contented in the "wale."

[1]Preface to the Cheap Edition of *Martin Chuzzlewit*, 1849.

[2]Jonah 2:5-6.

[3]George Orwell, "Inside the Whale," *An Age Like This, 1920-1940 (The Collected Essays, Journalism and Letters of George Orwell, Vol. 1)*, (New York: Harcourt, Brace & World, 1968), p. 526.

[4]*Fearful Symmetry* (Boston: Beacon Press, 1947), p. 210.

[5]*Fearful Symmetry*, pp. 281-2.

[6]"Herman Melville's *Moby Dick*," *Studies in Classic American Literature* (New York: Viking, 1964), p. 160.

[7]*From PICKWICK to DOMBEY*, p. 219.

[8]Rollo May, "Contributions of Existential Psychotherapy," *Existence: a New Dimension in Psychiatry and Psychology*, ed. Rollo May, Ernest Angel and Henri F. Ellenberger (New York: Basic Books, 1958), p. 76.

[9]Eric Berne, M.D., *Games People Play* (London: Deutsch, 1966).

[10]John Forster, *The Life of Charles Dickens*, Vol. 2 (London: Chapman and Hall, 1873), p. 59.

"WHAT ELSE CAN I BE?"
A CHRISTMAS CAROL

"In every cry of every Man,
In every Infant's cry of fear,
In every voice, in every ban,
The mind-forg'd manacles I hear."

WILLIAM BLAKE

•

"I wear the chain I forged in life," replied the Ghost. "I made it link by link, and yard by yard; I girded it on of my own free will, and of my own free will I wore it."

A CHRISTMAS CAROL

•

Written during the period of *Martin Chuzzlewit*'s composition, *A Christmas Carol* represents in a simple metaphor the whole synthesis of Dickens' moral theory at this point in his career. Scrooge, like Old Martin Chuzzlewit, is the subject of conversion. It is true that conversion here is not much more than magical or symbolic. Indeed, by writing a fairy or ghost tale, Dickens deliberately avoids dealing with the question of psychological or spiritual growth. Nevertheless it is of paramount importance to an understanding of all Dickens' work to realize that he has settled on and clearly delineated his subject as conversion. As Johnson points out, in his brilliant essay on this novel, "Scrooge's conversion is more than the transformation of a single human being. It is a plea for society itself to undergo a change of heart."[1] Dickens has flirted with the conversion idea before in all his writing. Oliver pleads with Fagin and Nancy pleads with Sikes for conversion. Nicholas and Old Man Trent, the two Martins and Mrs. Varden are all subject to this moral pressure by their creator. Only now, however, do we see how clearly and totally is Dickens committed to this view.

Converted from what to what? *A Christmas Carol* gives the answer more precisely and more simply than anywhere else in Dickens—converted from closedness to openness, from frigidity to warmth, from isolation to brotherhood, from death to life. This is the meaning of Scrooge and Marley and this is the meaning of Christmas.

> Dickens is certain that the enjoyment most men are able to feel in the happiness of others can play a larger part than it does in the tenor of their lives. The sense of brotherhood, he feels, can be broadened to a deeper and more active concern for the welfare of all mankind. It is in this light that Dickens sees the Spirit of Christmas. So understood, as the distinguished scholar Professor Louis Cazamian rightly points out, his "philosophie de Noël" becomes the very core of his social thinking.[2]

Christmas comes to represent the recurring possibility, the residual touchstone event of time that symbolically offers us the evidence and experience of brotherhood and openness. It is Christmas all the time for the annual event is only ritual expression of ever-present spiritual possibility. Christmas takes place in the mind and the mind of the individual, Scrooge's mind, is Dickens' vehicle for his presentation of the Christmas Spirit.

Scrooge and Marley are one and the same. Dickens loves to see the inherent ironies in business forms or idioms of language and just as he plays with the idea of the firm's name, Dombey & Son, so he presents "Scrooge and Marley" as a single entity.

> Scrooge never painted out Old Marley's name. There it stood, years afterwards, above the warehouse door: Scrooge and Marley. (p. 8)

Marley is now dead and Dickens tells us how important it is for us to understand that fact: "There is no doubt that Marley was dead. This must be distinctly understood, or nothing wonderful can come of the story I am going to relate." (p. 7) If Hamlet's father had not been dead, Dickens tells us, the return of the ghost would lose its point. *Hamlet* also is a play about conversion and the allusion reinforces Dickens' subject—spiritual development and change initiated by confrontation with the past in the form of a ghost. Marley is dead as a "door-nail," which leads us smoothly to the door-knocker that becomes Marley himself. The door-knocker is the symbol of entrance, the link between cold outer world and domestic warmth. In view of Marley's subsequent rôle as the means by which Scrooge enters a new world it is entirely appropriate that he should first appear as a door-knocker. If Marley and Scrooge are one, or parts of the same, then Marley's being dead would suggest that part of Scrooge is dead. Scrooge does not, of course, know that he is dead. He thinks that life in others, his nephew for instance, is humbug, that is, pretense, cant, or delusion. Marley only discovered he had been dead in life after he was dead in death. The chains that Marley forged in life, the cash boxes that signify his spiritual bondage, he wears in death also, the only distinction being that now he knows he is chained. Scrooge is an old man and he sees Marley's ghost at Christmas and only after his interviews with his nephew and the collectors for charity. What happens subsequently suggests that Scrooge is not left undisturbed by these interviews. If Marley is part of Scrooge (or an image of him) and with his haunting brings Scrooge's past, present and future, it is not unreasonable to suppose that Scrooge is deeply troubled by his present life and wishes to alter his kinship to the Marley part of himself. It should be remembered that once there had been a Scrooge whom Scrooge wishes to become again. In other words, if the Marley of Marley-Scrooge can be laid to rest, Scrooge may be himself, which he is in the end, when he can say " 'I'm quite a baby.' " (p. 72) Scrooge finds that he is looking at himself in Marley. Of the chain Marley says " 'Is its pattern strange to *you*?' " (p. 19) and "Scrooge glanced about him on the floor, in the expectation of finding himself surrounded by some fifty or sixty fathoms of iron cable: but he could see nothing." (p. 19) It is only later that he comes to see everything. Chains and locks play an important part in *A Christmas Carol*. Scrooge lives in solitary confinement. He is "self-contained" and "solitary as an oyster." Like chains being dragged or unused doors which open reluctantly, he has a "grating voice." Even this changes, as we shall see. Scrooge imprisons himself: "Quite satisfied, he closed his door, and locked himself in; double-locked himself in, which was not his custom. Thus secured against surprise, he took off his cravat; . . ." (p. 16) He is attempting to lock out both his superstitious fear and Christmas itself. For Scrooge, Christmas is a particular trial and challenge. Christmas is seen by Dickens as a time

> . . . in the long calendar of the year, when men and women seem by one consent to open their shut-up hearts freely, and to think of people below them as if they really were fellow-passengers to the grave, and not another race of creatures bound on other journeys. (p. 10)

To Scrooge who shuns openness and contact and love it is therefore a time for being particularly careful to shut himself away. " 'I wish to be left alone' said Scrooge." The wearing of chains, a practice which seems antithetical to Christmas, is widespread as Scrooge sees when he looks at the many spirits flying round his house. "Every one of them wore chains like Marley's Ghost; some few (they might be guilty governments) were linked together; none were free." (p. 22)

Scrooge, "captive, bound, and double-ironed," sets about the task of freeing himself with the assistance of three time elements, the past, the present and the future. Up to this point, Scrooge has been dead to all three. He cannot remember the past, yet it is remembered easily once the process starts.

> "Remember it!" cried Scrooge with fervour; "I could walk it blindfold."
>
> "Strange to have forgotten it for so many years!" observed the Ghost. "Let us go on." (p. 26)

He does not live in the present—" 'It's not my business,' " (p. 12) and he has no thought for the future, " 'Tell me what man that was whom we saw lying dead?' " (p. 69) Scrooge must arrive at the point where he can say " 'I will live in the Past, the Present, and the Future.' " (p. 70) How may this be done?

The rôles of Marley, former partner, and of the three Christmas spirits seem naturally to us now to fall into the mode of psychotherapy and this is how the metaphor may make sense to the reader of today. In a perfectly regular pattern the therapy begins with the past and moves to the future. All through the process violent change and discomfort are experienced by the presentation of images of the subject to himself. Scrooge is taken back to his childhood and the beginnings of his compassion start with pity for the image of himself as a child. Only by self-compassion and self-forgiveness are we led to relations with others in whom we see ourselves. When Scrooge is asked by his first "guide" what bothers him he replies " 'Nothing,' . . . 'Nothing. There was a boy singing a Christmas Carol at my door last night. I should like to have given him something: that's all.' " (p. 28) The situation of Scrooge and the first Spirit reads strangely like an account of modern therapy, as the patient is forced to witness, with undisguised agony, the repressed images of a rejected past.

> "Spirit!" said Scrooge, "show me no more! Conduct me home. Why do you delight to torture me?"
>
> "One shadow more!" exclaimed the Ghost.
>
> "No more!" cried Scrooge. "No more. I don't wish to see it. Show me no more!"
>
> But the relentless Ghost pinioned him in both his arms, and forced him to observe what happened next. (p. 35)

The girlfriend, who knew Scrooge much better than he knew himself, predicted that Scrooge would wipe out the memory of her. She even knew why Scrooge gave her up. " 'You fear the world too much,' she answered, gently." (p. 34) It is fear then that has made Scrooge close himself off, fear of the suffering and change that is life itself. From this point of view one might regard *A Christmas Carol*, in spite of all its supernatural imagery and religious overtones, as the most existential of parables. No wonder that many contemporary religionists regarded Dickens as a pagan thinker, for his love of holly and mistletoe and hot punch is one with his belief in immediate sensual, earthly rewards of spiritual conversion and brotherly love. Dickens continually reshapes Christian terms into a humanist mythology.

A knowledge of the past produces remorse and perhaps self-pity and a more general awareness of the self, but it is not enough. Understanding, hope, faith and love must be added to produce the second element of the courage to be. Scrooge must confront the general social consequences of his personal (and representative) frigid imprisonment. On two occasions the Spirit of Christmas Present quotes Scrooge's own words back at him. Scrooge has taken refuge in the present behind a shield of cant. " 'Man,' said the Ghost, 'if man you be in heart, not adamant, forbear that wicked cant until you have discovered What the surplus is, and Where it is.' " (p. 47) When he sees Ignorance and Want, that powerful piece of allegory of the boy and girl who will generate together the destruction of man and the world, he is again forced to hear his own words " 'Are there no prisons? Are there no workhouses?' " Scrooge must learn to look upon Cratchit, not as a unit of economy, whose private circumstances are, for his employer, a happily-kept secret, but as a human being who does not cease to be human because he comes to work for Scrooge. When Scrooge sees the first Spirit his bed-curtains have to be torn aside for him. When the second Spirit comes Scrooge opens his curtains himself. For the last Spirit Scrooge does not even have to return to his bed, his therapist's couch. He meets it out in the world. There remains only one element wanting to complete his awakening.

The overriding image of the chapter "Last of the Spirits" is that of death itself. What gives point to the life of compassion is the recognition that we are all "fellow passengers to the grave." After the fact of our birth, the inevitability of our death is what binds us together.

> Oh cold, cold, rigid, dreadful Death, set up thine altar here, and dress it with such terrors as thou hast at thy command: for this is thy dominion! But of the loved, revered, and honoured head, thou canst not turn one hair to thy dread purposes, or make one feature odious. It is not that the hand is heavy and will fall down when released; it is not that the heart and pulse are still; but that the hand WAS open, generous, and true; the heart brave, warm, and tender; and the pulse a man's. Strike, Shadow, strike! And see his good deeds springing from the wound, to sow the world with life immortal! (pp. 64-65)

Scrooge must confront his own mortality. His great difficulty in recognizing his own death is his fear of stripping off the final veil, his last refuge from life. Everyone will die but Scrooge. If Scrooge cannot die, then it matters not what he does in life. But the Ghost is "relentless" and pulls back the unspeakable shroud that covers one's own face. Scrooge can come alive only when he sees that he is dead. How, Scrooge asks, can he "have his fate reversed?" His desperate appeal that it should be reversed is its reversion. Scrooge is a new man already.

When Scrooge is reborn he is the centre of all time, he lives in eternity for he is no longer the prisoner of time. " 'I will live in the Past, the Present, and the Future!' " (p. 71) His tears and his laughter are now free and so is his imagination. Now he can see what was invisible before.

> He went to church, and walked about the streets, and watch-

> ed the people hurrying to and fro, and patted children on the head, and questioned beggars, and looked down into the kitchens of houses, and up to the windows, and found that everything could yield him pleasure. He had never dreamed that any walk—that anything—could give him so much happiness. In the afternoon he turned his steps towards his nephew's house. (p. 74)

The world is transformed precisely in proportion to the transformation of Scrooge's perception. It is the same world, but it is completely different also. Even Scrooge's grating voice is now altered: "'Hallo!' growled Scrooge, in his accustomed voice, as near as he could feign it." (p. 75) *A Christmas Carol* begins with the knocker and ends with it. "'I shall love it, as long as I live!' cried Scrooge, patting it with his hand. 'I scarcely ever looked at it before.'" (p. 73) Now indeed the knocker will represent a link, not a barrier, between Scrooge and the world.

Scrooge has had two allies all along in his agony of isolation, repression and fear. His nephew, Fred, and Bob Cratchit represent the salving spirit of Christmas. They have never abandoned hope and faith. They have waited for Scrooge, never giving up, so that they provide a natural point of resort and friendship when Scrooge is ready for them. Their patience with the intolerable old miser is indeed superhuman, but Dickens, I suppose, is demanding a humanity much larger and stronger than we normally think possible. Any sensitive reader of Dickens will share the anger and understand the irony expressed by Edgar Johnson at the end of the following quotation:

> Dickens, however, leaves his surface action so entirely clear and the behavior of his characters so plain that they do not puzzle us into groping for gnomic meanings. Scrooge is a miser, his nephew a warmhearted fellow, Bob Cratchit a poor clerk—what could be simpler? If there is a touch of oddity in the details, that is merely Dickens's well-known comic grotesquerie; if Scrooge's change of heart is sharp and antithetical, that is only Dickens's melodramatic sentimentality. Surely all the world knows that Dickens is never profound?[3]

Dickens is so profoundly radical perhaps that readers have preferred not to notice the challenges to our humanity in his work. His is above all a humanistic vision. "What Dickens has at heart is not any economic conception like Marx's labor theory of value, but a feeling of the human value of human beings."[4] The prisons and workhouses are made in the mind of Scrooge and only there will they be unmade. As far as Scrooge is concerned, the ghost of Marley is now laid to rest forever, for Jacob turns out to be a dear and living friend after all, and like his Biblical namesake, he has brought a ladder, up which Scrooge may climb to Heaven. In terms of the moral of Scrooge's own conversion Marley is saved as he saves Scrooge, for he comes alive in Scrooge's grateful memory. Scrooge's mind is the burial place and the resurrection place for Marley and the only possible place for such events. Dickens can now move on to a book-length story of conversion of a scope and insight not before attempted in the English novel. The move from the warehouse of "Scrooge and Marley" to the firm of "Dombey and Son" is a smooth and natural one.

[1]Johnson, *Charles Dickens*, Vol. 1, p. 487.

[2]Johnson, p. 484.

[3]Johnson, p. 489.

[4]Johnson, p. 486.

"A METAPHYSICAL SORT OF THING" DOMBEY AND SON

I consider that the majority of adults (including myself) are or have been, more or less, in a post-hypnotic trance, induced in early infancy: we remain in this state until—when we dead awaken, as Ibsen makes one of his characters say, we shall find that we have never lived.

RONALD D. LAING

•

"We go on taking everything for granted, and so we go on, until whatever we do, good, bad, or indifferent, we do from habit. Habit is all I shall have to report, when I am called upon to plead to my conscience, on my deathbed. 'Habit,' says I; 'I was deaf, dumb, blind, and paralytic, to a million things, from habit.' 'Very businesslike indeed, Mr. What's-your-name,' says Conscience, 'but it won't do here!' "

DOMBEY AND SON

•

If Scrooge requires four ineffable therapists to bring him to his regeneration, Dombey brings us a step nearer psychological realism by requiring only one human therapist. This is how Julian Moynahan describes Florence in his excellent, albeit caustic essay:

> In *Dombey and Son* Florence assumes the role of the therapist and suffers the hostility that neurotics of this sort [Dombey] are ready to vent on anyone willing to challenge their essential isolation.[1]

Dombey and Son is about Dombey. Florence is his better angel. Where Pecksniff was complete, incorrigible and not even a fractionally changed morality figure from first to last, Dombey is seen at every point in a state of process. He is clearly a character in tension not just suffering from a conflict between himself and the world and his having to be in it, but tormented also by one or another of the conflicting but possible responses within himself towards the world. Unlike Pecksniff, who is all of a piece and competes with the world, Dombey has not really found a satisfactory way to be in the world at all. Pecksniff is blind but undoubting, Dombey tries doubtingly not to see. Dombey feels incomplete until he has Paul, is then frustrated by Paul's slowness in growing up to be Dombey again, then loses Paul and acquires Edith who in turn fails to meet his abstract design. This process of undermining is the method Dickens chooses for exposing Dombey's failure to realize himself.

In his later works, from *David Copperfield* on, Dickens more and more concentrates on showing characters moving through stages of spiritual or emotional or psychological growth, rather than undergoing dramatic changes. He moves away from conversion to expansion. Characters do not shift from blindness to sight but from obscurity to clearer perception. They end their fictional careers at the beginning of something. This is already observable in *Dombey and Son.* It is for this reason that critics of the twentieth century are happier working with the "psychological realism" of the later work, what they call the dark novels, rather than the morality-play atmosphere of the earlier works. Dickens himself was obviously anxious to explore the "how" of moral growth and thus his own career anticipates the tendencies of the twentieth-century reader. But although *Dombey and Son* indicates what is to come in later novels, for nothing happens to Dombey that is not suggested as inherent in his characterization, it remains a conversion novel and thus fits into the group it composes with *Martin Chuzzlewit* and *A Christmas Carol.* We are aware that Dombey struggles and suffers, there is plenty of evidence for that, but he is so successful at being his own worst enemy that his *felix culpa* at the end (along with its inevitable symbolic critical illness) can only be regarded as more reminiscent of St. Paul (whose name Dombey has) than of the progress of, say, Christian Pilgrim or of Pip's progress. Not only is there no reason to doubt Dickens' intention as related by Forster, but the wording suggests just how seminal that intention was to the whole conception of the novel.

> Though his proposed new "book in shilling numbers" had been mentioned to me three months before he quitted England, he knew little himself at that time or when he left excepting the fact, then also named, that it was to do with Pride what its predecessor had done with Selfishness.[2]

Dickens pursues the idea of making his central theme a vice, in this case pride, and once again it will repay us to look carefully at what the vice means. Pride, an exaggerated regard for self, is much like hypocrisy and selfishness in that it requires an image to be carefully maintained. In this case the image is one of eminent wealth, power, social importance and superiority and unimpeachable respectability. This entire structure of self-image is described in the novel as a house, both a domestic and a business house, and it is designed to keep Dombey separated from the world. Dombey's name is the same as the name of the house. Dombey and the house are interchangeable. Florence recognizes changes in the domestic life and in her father's state of mind as changes in the house. It goes into mourning and has its furniture and pictures covered up; it gets redecorated and refurnished and starts all over again at the remarriage; it becomes a more private, lonely and isolated place as Dombey withdraws into himself. Although Dombey did not invent the design, although he inherited it he is nonetheless responsible for reinforcing and perpetuating it. He himself is part of somebody else's design and his upbringing has had as its sole objective his preparation for being the foundation of the house. The key to the house is the reader's understanding of the novel itself. It is a design to which emotion and feeling and love and impulse are inimical. Dombey, like Scrooge, presumably "fears the world too much." This kind of frozen living-death is a protection against life itself. In his dealings with the Toodles Dombey uses money to keep them off, to professionalize them, and to control them.

> "Oh, of course," said Mr. Dombey. "I desire to make it a question of wages, altogether. . . . When you go away from here, you will have concluded what is a mere matter of bargain and sale, hiring and letting: and will stay away. The child will cease to remember you; and you will cease, if you please, to remember the child." (p. 16)

Later, when the grieving Dombey is accosted by Toodle and his commiserations, he denies any possible human exchange between them and is nonplussed when commerce will not serve to define their relationship, for they are "related" through Paul in spite of Dombey's denial.

> "Your wife wants money, I suppose," said Mr. Dombey, putting his hand in his pocket, and speaking (but that he always did) haughtily.
>
> "No thank'ee Sir," returned Toodle, "I can't say she does. *I* don't."
>
> Mr. Dombey was stopped short now in his turn: and awkwardly: with his hand in his pocket. (p. 278)

It is precisely because of Dombey's inability to understand human complexity that he fails. Money, because of its neutrality, becomes the medium of non-communication. It keeps people at a distance and in their place. It depersonalizes people and relations. It is an incomprehensible language, which is why there is no satisfactory answer to Paul's question, "What is money?" It is a language that extends to the description of people, to Florence herself, only to describe them falsely. "In the capital of the House's name and dignity, such a child was merely a piece of base coin that couldn't be invested—a bad Boy—nothing more." (p. 3) But Dombey is human and he consists of desires and hopes and fears that are kept silent only at a great cost and with great effort. "Strong mental agitation and disturbance was no novelty to him, even before his late sufferings. It never is, to obstinate and sullen natures; for they struggle hard to be such." (p. 842) As one critic points out, the novel can be described as "the contest for Mr. Dombey's soul,"[3] and as such reminds one very much of those James novels in which various embodied forces contend for a human spirit. Here, however, the only combatants are Florence and Dombey themselves and I would suggest that Florence represents in herself that female element (which romantically idealized in Dickens' work means everything gentle, regenerative and good) missing or repressed in Dombey. I shall return to this later.

Dombey, like Scrooge, is a closed up, sealed off, remote and chilly figure, and to the spiritually incarcerated quality of the latter Dombey adds a pretension and stiffness and formality without parallel. Yet Dombey is not principally the representative of the world of business; this is not primarily a "socio-economic" novel, as one critic suggests.[4] Dombey is not proud and unapproachable because he is a successful businessman. He is a proud, arrogant, stubborn man who happens to be in business, and he would be the same if he were a physician, like those who wait upon his dying wife, or if he were anything else. His public rôle is merely an aid to his private isolation, his self-importance and social power assist him in sustaining his separateness from everybody and everything. Dombey is a frigid man and Dickens persistently uses the language of cold temperatures to describe him, sometimes comically and sometimes seriously in what are almost psychoanalytic terms, so that the following reads like the description of a patient from the cases of Kraft-Ebbing or Havelock Ellis. I have italicized those phrases which reveal Dickens interpreting the mind of his character.

> In the course of these remarks, delivered with great majesty and grandeur, Mr. Dombey had *truly revealed* the *secret feelings* of his breast. An indescribable *distrust* of anybody stepping in between himself and his son; a haughty *dread* of having any rival or partner in the boy's respect and deference; a sharp *misgiving,* recently acquired, that he was not infallible in his power of bending and binding human wills; as sharp a *jealousy* of any second check or cross; these were, *at that time,* the *master keys* of his soul. In all his life, he had never made a friend. His cold and distant nature had neither sought one, nor found one. And now when that nature concentrated its whole force so strongly on a partial scheme of parental interest and ambition, it seemed as if its icy current, instead of being released by this influence, and running clear and free, had thawed for but an instant to admit its burden, and then frozen with it into one unyielding block. (p. 47, my italics)

Dombey's attitudes towards people are described in degrees of coldness. When Miss Tox waves goodbye, we are told that "Mr. Dombey received this parting salutation very coldly—very coldly even for him—. . . ." (p. 277) When Dombey befriends the Major his emotional thermometer rises slightly: "Mr. Dombey, in his friendlessness, inclined to the Major. It cannot be said that he warmed towards him, but he thawed a little." (p. 272) Nor does the frozen quality of Dombey confine itself to his person and personality alone but it extends outward like an infection from himself until he seems to blight nature itself.

> He stood in his library to receive the company, as hard and cold as the weather; and when he looked out through the glass room, at the trees in the little garden, their brown and yellow leaves came fluttering down, as if he blighted them. (p. 52)

Inside his room he is more like an unfeeling object than a human being, so completely has he reified his self into the sterile image of an impenetrably idealized concept—"Dombey and Son."

> The stiff and stark fire-irons appeared to claim a nearer relationship than anything else there to Mr. Dombey, with his buttoned coat, his white cravat, his heavy gold watch-chain, and his creaking boots. (p. 52)

Julian Moynahan entitles his essay on this novel "Firmness versus Wetness," thereby indicating his awareness of the implications of the unyielding Dombey and the melting Florence, but one might go further in explaining the imagery of ice and thaw, for instance in the pun on Florence's name, "Flo." Firmness and wetness are ice and water, sterility and fertility, or death and life. We have a clue here to Dickens' dependence on tears as symbolic of the open and moveable state of the feeling and living heart. Dombey, however, in spite of his daughter's wealth of love and feeling and warmth, can freeze even Flo.

> If anything had frightened her, it was the face he turned upon her. The glowing love within the breast of his young daughter froze before it, and she stood and looked at him as if stricken into stone. (p. 256)

When Paul is being christened, that is given his father's name, the place reflects the world which the child is about to inherit officially.

> Little Paul might have asked with Hamlet "into my grave?" so chill and earthy was the place. The tall shrouded pulpit and reading desk; the dreary perspective of empty pews stretching away under the galleries, and empty benches mounting to the roof and lost in the shadow of the great grim organ; the dusty matting and cold stone slabs; the grisly free seats in the aisles; and the damp corner by the bell-rope, where the black trestles used for funerals were stowed away, along with some shovels and baskets, and a coil or two of deadly-looking rope; the strange, unusual, uncomfortable smell, and the cadaverous light; were all in unison. It was a cold and dismal scene. (p. 55)

The celebration at home following this event is no warmer.

> There was a toothache in everything. The wine was so bitter cold that it forced a little scream from Miss Tox, which she had great difficulty in turning into a "Hem!" The veal had come from such an airy pantry, that the first taste of it had struck a sensation as of cold lead to Mr. Chick's extremities. Mr. Dombey alone remained unmoved. He might have been hung up for sale at a Russian fair as a specimen of a frozen gentleman. (p. 57)

Mr. Dombey is in his natural milieu and cold is to him what heat is to Satan. This quality of frozen stasis persists and is reflected in everything connected with Dombey even up to the time of the destruction of his "House."

> Presiding, therefore, with his accustomed dignity, and not at all reflecting on his wife by any warmth or hilarity of his own, he performed his share of the honours of the table with a cool satisfaction; and the installation dinner, though not regarded downstairs as a great success, or very promising beginning, passed off, above, in a sufficiently polite, genteel, and frosty manner. (p. 501)

We can only speculate as to why Dombey is a "specimen of frozen gentleman," but we have a good deal of evidence to assist us in making some meaningful assumptions as to the kind of world such a "species" would produce. *Dombey and Son* is the name of the business "House" and of the novel. The fact that "Dombey and Son" is a "Firm" further extends the imagery of the unyielding father and his self-conception. The novel is the world of Dombey and although we have nothing here like a Jamesian interior projection of Dombey's mind or "point of view," the exterior images and the language and metaphor of the novel no less faithfully reflect the aura and quality of a world emanating from the mind of the protagonist. We are told that "A.D. had no concern with anno Domini, but stood for anno Dombei—and Son, . . ." (p. 2) and that "Those three words conveyed the one idea of Mr. Dombey's life." (p. 2) Dickens indeed reveals his belief that the world one lives in is a projection of the state of mind which perceives it.

> So, pursuing the one course of thought, he had the one relentless monster still before him. All things looked black, and cold, and deadly upon him, and he on them. He found a likeness to his misfortune everywhere. (p. 282)

Dombey is not just mourning the past but distorting the present.

His own design for the world has been completely altered, for had Florence died his scheme would have been flawless. As it is, he is left with the error, the daughter, and has lost the necessary ingredient, the son. This lack of accord between his own schemes and images and the events of life produces the diseased images of the world proceeding from his own mind.

> Because he knew full well, in his own breast, as he stood there, tingeing the scene of transition before him with the morbid colours of his own mind, and making it a ruin and a picture of decay, instead of hopeful change, and promise of better things, that life had quite as much to do with his complainings as death. One child was gone, and one child left. Why was the object of his hope removed instead of her? (p. 282)

In the period when the dynastic dream still seems viable we find that Paul, as yet, is nothing, though one day he might become in his turn "Dombey and Son," as Dombey did. Paul's function in the novel is to help explain Dombey. In the mind of Dombey, Paul has no reality, no individuality. He is merely essential to make Dombey into "Dombey and Son." The world Paul inhabits, a "Dombey and Son" world, is one that has no place in it for children because it is created by adult self-images. Mrs. Pipchin is a practitioner or specialist in "the study and treatment of infancy." (p. 97) Doctor Blimber is another such specialist.

> "Shall we make a man of him?" repeated the Doctor.
> "I had rather be a child," replied Paul.
> "Indeed!" said the Doctor. "Why?" (p. 145)

Dombey is impatient, like the other parents of children at Blimber's, for his child to pass through the unpleasant waiting period of childhood, and Blimber's is an institution specializing in the acceleration of the whole process. Dombey

> had settled, within himself, that the child must necessarily pass through a certain routine of minor maladies, and that the sooner he did so the better. If he could have bought him off, or provided a substitute, as in the case of an unlucky drawing for the militia, he would have been glad to do so on liberal terms. But as this was not feasible, he merely wondered, in his haughty manner, now and then, what Nature meant by it. . . . (p. 90)

Had Paul lived, what sort of man would he have been? The answer to this question is complicated by the presence of his sister. She is thoroughly inimical to the whole image and scheme of dynastic succession in Dombey's mind. The period of Paul's existence is a struggle for his soul, but it is only a minor reflection of the larger struggle of the entire book, the struggle between the forces represented by Florence, the flowing life-principle as against Dombey and Dombey's father, whose presence is felt in the novel though he himself is absent.

> "He will be christened Paul, my—Mrs. Dombey—of course."
> She feebly echoed, "Of course," or rather expressed it by the motion of her lips, and closed her eyes again.
> "His father's name, Mrs. Dombey, and his grandfather's! I wish his grandfather were alive this day!" And again he said "Dom-bey and Son," in exactly the same tone as before. (pp. 1-2)

His grandfather is of course alive in Dombey himself and Mrs. Dombey's unspoken but clearly implied hope for some break in the pattern is groundless. Having played out her rôle in Dombey's design she dies. So overpowering is Dombey's energy for his design that those who project their own images (like Edith and Florence), rather than accepting the ones conceived for them by Dombey, must be rejected to form worlds of their own. Edith and Florence come to appear to Dombey as the embodiment of two responses to which he is most bitterly opposed. The one is loving, demanding, seeking to soften him; the other is cold, proud, opposed to him and like himself. In answer to either figure he is forced back upon himself, he is challenged, and out of this challenge comes the hatred resulting from the discomfort he is caused. Dickens has come to see that for him and his time the Devil has become a totally internalized aberration of personality, a distorting, a tyrannous, crippling possessor of the mind. This is the new demonology, with its psychological dimension.

> It was not in the nature of things that a man of Mr. Dombey's mood, opposed to such a spirit as he had raised against himself, should be softened in the imperious asperity of his temper; or that the cold hard armour of pride in which he lived encased, should be made more flexible by constant collision with haughty scorn and defiance. It is the curse of such a nature—it is a main part of the heavy retribution on itself it bears within itself—that while deference and concession swell its evil qualities, and are the food it grows upon, resistance and a questioning of its

> exacting claims, foster it too, no less. The evil that is in it finds equally its means of growth and propagation in opposites. It draws support and life from sweets and bitters; bowed down before, or unacknowledged, it still enslaves the breast in which it has its throne; and, worshipped or rejected, is as hard a master as the Devil in dark fables. (p. 560)

We see in the planning of Paul's career the image of Dombey's own. Bereft of childhood, existing only as the object of someone else's scheme, denied his own character, his own Self so to speak, Paul, had he lived and were there no Florence, would have become another Dombey—a reflection of the past—an inheritor of a self-image, an idealized and falsified self as substitute for what was lost and damaged. This is presumably what happened to the father. I must at this point elicit the aid of a modern psychoanalyst, who, in describing the alienation of personality, produces an account that seems strangely applicable to Dombey.

> The alienated patient is not born alienated, nor does he choose alienation. Lacking genuine acceptance, love, and concern for his individuality in childhood, he experiences basic anxiety. Early he begins to move away from his self, which seems not good enough to be loved. He moves away from what he is, what he feels, what he wants. If one is not loved for what one is, one can at least be safe—safe perhaps by being very good and perfect and being loved for it, or by being very strong and being admired or feared for it, or by learning not to feel, not to want, not to care. Therefore, one has to free oneself from any need for others, which means first their love and affection, and, later on, in many instances, sex. Why feel, why want, if there is no response? So the person puts all his efforts into becoming what he *should* be. Later, he idealizes his self-effacement as goodness, his aggression as strength, his withdrawal as freedom. Instead of developing in the direction of increasing freedom, self-expression, and self-realization, he moves toward safety, self-elimination, and self-idealization.[5]

The fly in Dombey's ointment is Florence. She is a mistake and not part of the abstract design.

Florence loves Paul as Paul. She is in this sense his surrogate mother and he clings to her with a desperation born of his desire to keep a grip on his own reality and value as fostered by her.

> Upon the Doctor's door-steps one day, Paul stood with a fluttering heart, and with his small right hand in his father's.

> His other hand was locked in that of Florence. How tight the tiny pressure of that one; and how loose and cold the other! (p. 143)

Florence is Paul's only link with the world of love, joy, compassion and his deepest feelings.

> When they all drew a little away, that Paul might see her; and when he saw her sitting there all alone, so young, and good, and beautiful, and kind to him; and heard her thrilling voice, so natural and sweet, and *such a golden link between him and all his life's love and happiness,* rising out of the silence; he turned his face away, and hid his tears. (p. 201, my italics)

Moreover, Dickens never lets us forget the social implications of the rôle of Florence. While Dombey has money and the social power bestowed by it, Paul's question "What is money?" hangs in the air throughout the novel and is answered only in the person of Florence, for it is she only who makes sense out of what to do with it, who translates it into something human. In the scene in which Walter asks for financial aid, Dombey provides the means for aid and Florence the compassion that motivates Paul to kindness.

Florence works against Dombey's scheme of things by introducing elements into his world that are in opposition to it, as warmth is destructive to ice, and she troubles Dombey in himself at various levels. Her power appears to be unthinkably greater than his when it comes to personal relationships. "It seemed his fate to be ever proud and powerful; ever humbled and powerless where he would be most strong." (p. 561) Florence is closer to Paul, she wins the love of Walter, she rouses the loyalty of Susan Nipper and this produces another enemy for Dombey, and she can then win the affection and therefore the devotion of Edith.

> As she sat down by the side of Florence, she stooped and kissed her hand. He hardly knew his wife. She was so changed. It was not merely that her smile was new to him—though that he had never seen; but her manner, the tone of her voice, the light of her eyes, the interest, and confidence, and winning wish to please, expressed in all—this was not Edith. (p. 504)

Florence, then, forces upon Dombey's awareness the difference between his and her effect upon people and the true sense of his own isolation. "Girls," as Dombey says, "have nothing to do with

Dombey and Son" and Dombey is devoid of what might be called the Florence-element. Until he acquires it (or releases it) he is to remain frozen and isolated. He suffers acutely all along from his own frigidity and from the isolation it produces. He is well aware of the difference between Paul's response to him and to Florence, for instance when they part at Blimber's.

> If Mr. Dombey in his insolence of wealth, had ever made an enemy, hard to appease and cruelly vindictive in his hate, even such an enemy might have received the pang that wrung his proud heart then, as compensation for his injury.
>
> He bent down over his boy, and kissed him. If his sight were dimmed as he did so, by something that for a moment blurred the little face, and made it indistinct to him, his mental vision may have been, for that short time, the clearer perhaps. (p. 149)

The struggle, Dickens tells us, inside such a person is a titanic one. Dombey wants to admit Florence and what she represents into his life but has built his armour out of deep need and at great cost and it is not easily shed. Because of Florence's challenge he cannot be indifferent to her. She must either be admitted or be totally denied. At one point he softens:

> There are yielding moments in the lives of the sternest and harshest men, though such men often keep their secret well. . . . Some passing thought that he had had a happy home within his reach—had had a household spirit bending at his feet—had overlooked it in his stiff-necked sullen arrogance, and wandered away and lost himself, may have engendered them. . . . But as he looked, he softened to her, more and more. As he looked, she became blended with the child he had loved, and he could hardly separate the two. (p. 503)

Then all his pride and fear return as Edith, the image of himself, reappears. I have above used the term alienation and have quoted a psychologist on the subject but it should be noted that it is a term Dickens himself employs.

> In his sullen and unwholesome brooding, the unhappy man, with a dull perception of his alienation from all hearts, and a vague yearning for what he had all his life repelled, made a distorted picture of his rights and wrongs, and justified himself with it against her. The worthier she promised to be of him, the greater claim he was disposed to ante-date upon her duty and

> submission? When had she ever shown him duty and submission? Did she grace his life—or Edith's? Had her attractions been manifested first to him—or Edith? Why, he and she had never been, from her birth, like father and child! They had always been estranged. She had crossed him every way and everywhere. She was leagued against him now. Her very beauty softened natures that were obdurate to him, and insulted him with an unnatural triumph. (p. 561)

The full irony of "unnatural" depends on our understanding of Dombey's attempt to invert all that is natural in himself and his relationship. Finally, the thing that Dombey fears most, his hatred of Florence, becomes a reality.

> It may have been that in all this there were mutterings of an awakened feeling in his breast, however selfishly aroused by his position of disadvantage, in comparison with what she might have made his life. But he silenced the distant thunder with the rolling of his sea of pride. He would bear nothing but his pride. And in his pride, a heap of inconsistency, and misery, and self-inflicted torment, he hated her. (p. 562)

There is a great deal more in this novel on the subject of Dombey and Florence, for Dickens has worked out the nature of this relationship and its psychological dynamics with care. In the symbolic structure of the novel a whole human being is presented as ideally being made up of the male and female principles. The male is active, aggressive, commercial, and powerful, and represents a kind of material social force. The female is embodied ideally in Florence and brings love, regeneration, gentleness and warmth to the human scene. Dombey is devoid of Florence and must come to incorporate her. Miss Tox's celebrated comment, eagerly embraced by all the critics, is not so simple-minded a commentary on the moral of the novel as it seems.

> "And so Dombey and Son, as I observed upon a certain sad occasion," said Miss Tox, winding up a host of recollections, "is indeed a daughter, Polly, after all." (p. 845)

This is true not only for Dombey individually but for society at large. Power, commerce and respectability without warmth, compassion and fellow-feeling produce disastrous consequences.

If Florence, Flo, represents the moving, flexible life-force of love and acceptance, then the sea used persistently as it is, comes to represent the nature of living and the flux of life and change that speaks to Paul. Dombey's firmness is not softened by Paul's death. Yet death is part of life and the sea is symbol of that tragic, accepting awareness of life and death that gives Dickens' writing its supreme stature.

> "There's perils and dangers on the deep, my beauty," said the Captain; "and over many a brave ship, and many and many a bould heart, the secret waters has closed up, and never told no tales. But there's escapes upon the deep, too, and sometimes one man out of a score, —ah! maybe out of a hundred, pretty, —has been saved by the mercy of God, and come home after being given over for dead, and told of all hands lost." (p. 690)

This is a religious allegory. Few are saved but the salvation of some gives faith to the many. The sea takes away and the sea restores. Paul in his dying offers Dombey another son, whom he rejects at first, although acceptance is finally inescapable if Dombey would become human. "Remember Walter" is the clue. The ship, "The Son and Heir," seems to be brilliantly named by Dickens though it is not so easy to say why until one realizes that its going down into the sea is Paul's death and that Walter's resurrection, phoenix-like from the wreck, is the restoration of a son to Dombey. Walter is reborn from the sea in classical fashion, the sea is his element as it is the element of the world of the Wooden Midshipman and the circle therein. Cuttle and Gills both have names indicative of their being at home in this element. They acquire to themselves all those characters in the novel who can, as Conrad's Stein puts it, learn to swim with the current, or be "in the destructive element immerse." There are those in other words who have the love and acceptance of life and its conditions to live meaningfully. Florence, Toots, Polly, all come into the Midshipman's orbit. First Walter, then Florence, Flo, and then both together form the hub of this constellation. When Walter returns to the sea it is with Florence as his wife.

Those who are not for the worst aspects of Dombey are against him, but ironically his real enemies are those who help sustain his image of himself and this they always do for their own purposes. That Dickens in his minor characters is thinking in terms almost allegorical is made clear by his instructions concerning the illustrations to Hâblot Knight Browne: "I want to make the Major, who is the incarnation of selfishness and small revenge, a kind of comic Mephistophelian power in the book," and of Mrs. Skewton, "the mother affects cordiality and heart, and is the essence of sordid calculation."[6] The words "incarnation" and "essence" suggest how strongly Dickens is conscious of an abstract moral design behind the plot of his novel. The Major and Edith's mother are diabolic in their manipulation of others' weaknesses. So is Carker, who has discovered precisely how to feed Dombey's pride by a system of esteem coupled with persistent self-denigration. Once again it is clear that Dickens' conception of his characters' behaviour is incomparably thorough and consistent. The very fears and inadequacies that make Dombey what he is also require continual reassurance and submission from those around him. He cannot brook opposition or tolerate disagreement. His sense of his self is so weak that in spite of his appearance of self-reliance he is chronically dependent on the flattery and attendance of others. This further explains his dependence on Paul, to complete himself, and his desire for a second wife, again to fill out the image of himself and help sustain it. Dr. Weiss has noted this phenomenon also in the alienated person.

> This explains the existence of what I call *"echo phenomenon"* in the alienated patient. His own inner voice often is so weak and unconvincing that he hardly hears it. A pertinent statement, a creative idea, a promising plan on which he has been working for weeks remains unreal and meaningless to him until, with much hesitation, he expresses it to another person. When, however, "the other," whom he experiences as an insider of life, repeats his statement, his idea, or his plan, this echo suddenly sounds real and convincing to him, while his own—usually much better—formulation of the same thought remains unreal. In his inner experience he does not count. He does not exist as an individual on his own.[7]

It is only after Dombey is totally stripped of every fragment of sustenance for his ego that his regeneration can take place. Florence, Edith, Carker, money, power, prestige and flattery are all removed. Being so humbled and emptied Dombey is free to start from scratch. Carker is one of the two arch-enemies raised by Dombey's blind indifference and superiority.

> "You may imagine how regardless of me, how obtuse to the possibility of my having any individual sentiment or opinion he is, when he tells me, openly, that I am so employed." (p. 628)

Carker's sense of his own worthlessness is much more real than the ironies of his self-contempt before Dombey would suggest. How else can we explain the depth of his hatred for his brother except on the grounds of his own inadequacy, a feeling confirmed for him by his sister's rejection of him in favour of their socially worthless brother. Unlike Dombey, Carker cannot find refuge in an image, and hatred and hostility become therefore his prime motivation. To humble the proud Dombey and Edith will increase Carker's sense of his own importance. Edith, too, pits herself against Dombey and strangely enough she is in a situation closely akin to Carker's, a fact which he instantly recognizes. Edith's self-contempt is a much more explicit thing than Carker's. Her opposition to Dombey takes the form of her insisting on the terms of buying and selling that he himself has used to govern his dealings with people. She will give no more than her bond calls for and Dombey is hoist, one might say, with his own deadly petard. Edith has always been led to regard herself as an object of trade and her beauty as a saleable commodity which makes it hateful to herself. Alice is the more explicit parallel case. This situation, the reification of children and people generally, which the network of similarities in the novel is meant to emphasize, is only an elaborate extension of what we saw in *The Old Curiosity Shop*. There are states of mind in which people see not other people, whole and individual, but objects that serve to augment a projected image of oneself. From the most basic greeds of Mrs. Brown to the hideous social pretensions of Mrs. Skewton up to the dynastic dreams of Dombey we trace the same pattern. Even such a minor figure and story as Rob the Grinder's is created to fulfill Dickens' moral purposes in the novel. Rob also exists to satisfy Dombey's sense of his own importance—Rob is literally an "object" of charity and his being made into a Grinder without regard to his circumstances, personality or wishes turns him first into a martyr and goes a long way to turning him into a social outcast and delinquent.

> His social existence had been more like that of an early Christian, than an innocent child of the nineteenth century. He had been stoned in the streets. He had been overthrown into gutters; bespattered with mud; violently flattened against posts. Entire strangers to his person had lifted his yellow cap off his head and

> cast it to the winds. His legs had not only undergone verbal criticisms and revilings, but had been handled and pinched. That very morning, he had received a perfectly unsolicited black eye on his way to the Grinders' establishment, and had been punished for it by the master: a superannuated old Grinder of savage disposition, who had been appointed schoolmaster because he didn't know anything, and wasn't fit for anything, and for whose cruel cane all chubby little boys had a perfect fascination. (p. 68)

In this regard it is interesting to see that Mr. Morfin is the only person connected with Dombey who remains uncompromised and unaffected by him, and Dickens explains this to us very clearly by pointing out that Mr. Morfin has managed to remain true to himself, all along.

> He had treated Mr. Dombey with due respect and deference through many years, but he had never disguised his natural character, or meanly truckled to him, or pampered his master passion for the advancement of his own purposes. He had, therefore, no self-disrespect to avenge; no long-tightened springs to release with a quick recoil. (p. 816)

But it is also Mr. Morfin whose remarks on habit head this chapter, for he realizes that the danger of habit and use is universal and of real moral consequence. We are blinded by habit and demoralized by custom and only re-examination of oneself and one's relation to others provides any safeguard against moral inertia. Dombey might, from Morfin's point of view, be said to be caught in the grip of the habit of generations of idealized and deadly unquestioning self-image making. Narcissus first gazed at himself with surprise, then from habit. The worship of idols becomes habit, even when the idol is a false version of oneself. A political (or religious) belief quickly becomes mere habit. It is an interesting and rather frightening version of human and social affairs.

Finally we are faced with a novel in which the author can write,

> Breathe the polluted air, foul with every impurity that is poisonous to health and life; and have every sense, conferred upon our race for its delight and happiness, offended, sickened and disgusted, and made a channel by which misery and death alone can enter. Vainly attempt to think of any simple plant, or flower, or wholesome weed, that, set in this foetid bed, could

> have its natural growth, or put its little leaves off to the sun as GOD designed it. And then, calling up some ghastly child, with stunted form and wicked face, hold forth on its unnatural sinfulness, and lament its being, so early, far away from Heaven —but think a little of its having been conceived, and born and bred, in Hell! (p. 647)

We must ask ourselves how such a phenomenally bitter and angry piece of writing comes to appear in an apparently totally controlled and even genteel study of family relations. We have, I hope, already answered this question. Dickens' radicalism sees that the social Hell which he everywhere describes or suggests, the workhouse, the disease, the hunger, the foul and poisonous and polluted air and water, these things have their origin in the heart and mind of man. No matter which way one turns in seeking terms in which to discuss Dickens' moral perspective one ends with a humanism rooted in love and compassion, the source of psychic wholeness and of social integration. Dickens' Christianity becomes very clearly this kind of humanism and Christ becomes the ideal man of love and human sympathy.

> Harriet complied and read—read the eternal book for all the weary and the heavy-laden; for all the wretched, fallen, and neglected of this earth—read the blessed history, in which the blind lame palsied beggar, the criminal, the woman stained with shame, the shunned of all our dainty clay, has each a portion, that no human pride, indifference, or sophistry, through all the ages that this world shall last, can take away, or by the thousandth atom of a grain reduce—read the ministry of Him who, through the round of human life, and all its hopes and griefs, from birth to death, from infancy to age, had sweet compassion for, and interest in, its every scene and stage, its every suffering and sorrow. (pp. 826-27)

The consequence of Harriet nursing Alice follows an exchange of some interest much earlier.

> "Heaven help you and forgive you!" was the gentle answer.
>
> "Ah! Heaven help me and forgive me!" she returned, nodding her head at the fire. "If man would help some of us a little more, God would forgive us all the sooner perhaps." (p. 482)

Dombey is part of a dehumanized world, dehumanized by the failure of people to perceive the continuum between us and not-us. Dombey is the victim of a system of values and a view that truncates the human spirit and quality, that pays no regard to what it is like to be: the passions, needs and aspirations of individuals are somehow not seen. Instead, the disturbing language of commerce or barter or the characteristics of things rather than people signify the nature of a world gone awry. It is for this reason that people so often appear as things in Dickens, for people come to see themselves and others in terms of the most confining images. Dickens becomes increasingly interested in how such a situation develops. If a person like Dombey (as hinted by Paul's training) is the victim of his parents and society, how can he break this cycle of horror? It is with seeking both the causes and solutions of these aberrations from humanity that Dickens' work becomes increasingly preoccupied. Whatever the difficulties of escaping the determination of one's outlook and character, Dickens never will allow us or himself to lose faith in the possibility of redemption. Rob's comment, " 'But it's never too late for a—' [Indi—] '—widdle, . . . to mend; . . .' " (p. 846) might stand as the moral of *Dombey and Son*. Our dealings with the firm of Dombey and Son have, in explanation of its full original title, been then "Wholesale," the general social situation, "Retail," the exemplifying particular case, and for "Exportation," that the reader may take its moral implications to heart.

[1]"Dealings with the Firm of Dombey and Son: Firmness versus Wetness," *Dickens and the Twentieth Century*, p. 124.

[2]Forster, Vol. 2, p. 309.

[3]Kathleen Tillotson, *"Dombey and Son," Novels of the Eighteen-Forties* (London: Oxford Univ. Press, 1961), p. 171.

[4]While Julian Moynahan does not actually call the novel itself "socio-economic," he does make the following comment:

> Dombey moves from hardness through debility to a maundering, guilt-ridden submission to feminine softness. A Victorian patriarchy of stiff and tyrannical men of affairs surrenders to a matriarchy of weeping mothers and daughters. Translated into socio-economic terms this would mean that the control of railroads, shipping lines and investment houses would pass under the control of softies like Morfin, adepts in guilt like Carker the Junior, milky young men like Walter Gay. ("Firmness vs. Wetness," p. 130)

But surely this is a fanciful distortion of the novel? Dombey is not an efficient business tycoon, a wise employer or a rational man and it is his lack of sentiment, fellow-feeling and his self-deception that permit the

"House" (and the marriage) to collapse. Surely any business or family with Walter at its head will stand on firmer, not weaker, foundations. Dombey is not as tough as he looks, from the start. That is the central point.

[5]Frederick A. Weiss, "Self-Alienation: Dynamics and Therapy," *Man Alone*, ed. Eric and Mary Josephson (New York: Dell, 1962), p. 466.

[6]David C. Thomson, pp. 68-9.

[7]Weiss, p. 467.

"THE DISCIPLINED HEART"
DAVID COPPERFIELD

And now, O Friend! this history is brought
To its appointed close: the discipline
And consummation of the Poet's mind
In everything that stood most prominent
Have faithfully been pictured; we have reach'd
The time (which was our object from the first)
When we may, not presumptuously, I hope,
Suppose my powers so far confirmed, and such
My knowledge, as to make me capable
Of building up a work that should endure.

WILLIAM WORDSWORTH

•

The Man who does not know The Beginning never can know the End of Art.

WILLIAM BLAKE

•

"Ha! ha! ha! What a refreshing set of humbugs we are, to be sure, ain't we, my sweet child?"

DAVID COPPERFIELD

•

Dickens' growing awareness that the nature of society depends on the moral quality of individuals comes to its first full development in the structure of *David Copperfield*. It is the first of his novels recounted entirely in the first person. One might say that Dickens has now most completely moved his emphasis from the anatomy of society to the autonomy of self. This is not to say that either of these subjects ever totally excludes the other. But we have seen Dickens' growing concentration on individual psychology and the increasing intensity and realism with which the self is presented. It is fair, I believe, to say that *Bleak House* and *Hard Times* revert to the anatomy of society more forthrightly, but that even in these novels and most certainly in all the others written after 1850, the principal narrative objective will be to try to realize ways in which the self can develop into an autonomous and fully realized whole. *David Copperfield* is preparation for this task in a number of ways. It is an exercise in personal exorcism and an attempt at depth psychology. It is a form of autobiography because Dickens must use the case he knows best. At the same time, before taking an even harder look at other minds and hearts the author must be on some secure terms with his own. It is therefore both practice and practise, both therapy and case history.

As one critic has pointed out, *David Copperfield* is to Dickens what *Portrait of the Artist* is to Joyce, "the end is a completed portrait of the artist as a young man."[1] I am even more impressed with the parallel to Wordsworth's *Prelude*, "The Growth of a Poet's Mind," for we are encountering here not nearly so much distance as Joyce aims for. The first-person narrative is used here in an attempt to order experience in such a way as to arrive at some conviction and estimate of what that experience has produced and for what purpose. It seeks to impose meaning on event. The stronger the moral purpose, the greater the necessity for the creation of this personal, exploratory myth found in Dickens and Wordsworth, so that the general can be based with assurance on the particular. It is of course no more than accident that *David Copperfield* and the *Prelude* both appeared in 1850, just as it is coincidence that David says " 'I sought out Nature, never sought in vain . . .' " and Wordsworth says "Nature never did betray the heart that loved her." Nor can one make too much of the fact that the "I" figures of both works make perambulatory trips in Switzerland in their search for influences, though similarities may lead us to an increased awareness of Dickens' purpose in *David Copperfield*. In Dickens we find this:

> As the endurance of my childish days had done its part to make me what I was, so greater calamities would nerve me on, to be yet better than I was; and so, as they had taught me, would I teach others. (p. 815)

In Wordsworth occurs this:

> The last and later portions of this gift
> Have been prepared, not with the buoyant spirits . . .
> Prophets of Nature, we to them will speak
> A lasting inspiration, sanctified
> By reason, blest by faith: what we have loved
> Others will love, and we will teach them how.[2]

It is a commonplace fallacy of criticism to regard such works as Joyce's *Portrait, The Prelude* and *David Copperfield,* and *Sons and Lovers* as autobiographies. Rather their subject is art and they illustrate in themselves how art is made; their purpose is moral and they present the reader a paradigm of the quest for meaning in personal experience and the need to establish the relation of the "I" to the world. The "I" is metaphoric, and microcosmic, it is every personal vision, and the quest is universal. To give order to experience is to turn passive into active. It is to move from the chapter "I am Born" to "I make another Beginning." To make metaphor is to make sense. To make art is to give meaning to the past and purpose to the present. *David Copperfield* is the exemplary tale of how art is made, why it is necessary and what purpose it serves. In the Dickens canon it marks the point at which the most intense moral conviction coincides with the most uncompromising rendering of individual experience. The result is not only a portrait of what it means to be an artist but also of what it means to be a whole man.

The principal metaphor of this novel is drowning. Survival in life, being able to swim, becomes here spiritual survival as well. David is born with a caul, a proof against drowning, and it stands him in good stead, which is why he begins with this fact when he tells the story as an adult. Steerforth drowns, returning to the scene of the crime, and unwittingly causes Ham to drown. Martha tries to drown herself. Emily's father drowned and little David wonders whether the dead father has any power to call Emily into the sea also.

> But there have been times since, in my manhood, many times there have been, when I have thought, Is it possible, among the possibilities of hidden things, that in the sudden rashness of the child and her wild look so far off, there was any mercifull attraction of her into danger, any tempting her towards him permitted on the part of her dead father, that her life might have a chance of ending that day? (p. 36)

This element of "rashness," that is tempted not only to its own destruction but encompasses the destruction of others, is seen most clearly in Steerforth, first in his treatment of poor Mr. Mell. Later we learn of his treatment of Rosa, at whom he once threw a hammer, and finally we witness his seduction of Emily. It is also echoed in Jack Maldon, one more of Dickens' idle and thoughtless young men, who wants to make of Annie what Steerforth made of Emily and who says, " 'When a plunge is to be made into the water, it's of no use lingering on the bank, . . .' " (p. 231) which brings us back to drowning. Dickens quite consciously extends this theme from the literal to the metaphorical. After his mother dies David "thought of the sea that had risen, since I last heard those sounds, and drowned my happy home, . . ." (p. 143) and Barkis, we are told, goes out with the tide. When David falls in love with Dora we are given a description of his feelings:

> . . . I was steeped in Dora. I was not merely over head and ears in love with her, but I was saturated through and through. Enough love might have been wrung out of me, metaphorically speaking, to drown anybody in. (p. 474)

But David is lucky, and whether it is the caul, or whether it is the artist's mind blending compassion and wisdom with understanding and the strength for honest self-exploration, he does not drown. David's is the story of the Self as moral survivor. One must be master of the element one lives in, and the element, life, is destructive. The metaphor points up the necessity of learning to use the current or fighting it and sinking, using great forces which can be directed or controlled only by disciplined submission. It is an idea we have seen in the Midshipman world of *Dombey* and one that becomes insistent in the canon. One of the most interesting features of the character of David as it emerges in his reconstruction of his experience is the absence of any bitterness or resentment in the recital of recalled suffering and grief. David is like to "drown" after Dora's death but Agnes' letter is the life-line thrown to him while he is abroad. It is her calmness, her assurance, her constancy that soothes and reconciles his spirit. She is the model of the swimmer, but more of Agnes later. Why should one need a caul? What threats exist, what storms can come besides the storms of nature like the one that drowns the rival lovers at Yarmouth?

Being born to parents, or step-parents, or guardians or simply into an adult world, is the primary great barrier in the way of self-discovery, for the tendency of the adult is to use or shape or bend the child to fit an image or a purpose in the adult mind. From Oliver to Paul Dombey, we have squarely placed before us the child's struggle to exist in some terms other than those imposed on it by the adult. R. D. Laing describes this as family "politics."

> Projection . . . is usually unknown to the people who are involved. Different mappings are usually going on, simultaneously.
>
> Pure projection is not enough. Having become images of ghostly relations under the operation of projection, we have to be *induced* to *embody* them in our own lives: to enact, unbeknown to ourselves, a shadow play, as images, of images of images . . . of the dead, who have in their turn embodied and enacted such dramas projected upon them, and induced in them, by those before them. . . . It is my impression that we receive most of our earliest and most lasting instructions in the form of attributions. We are told that such and such is the case. One is, say, told that one *is* a good or a bad boy or girl, not only instructed *to be* a good or bad boy or girl. One may be subject to both, but if one *is* (this or that), it is not necessary to be told to be what one has already been "given to understand" one is.[3]

The same awareness in Dickens is not a social complaint or a moral stricture; it is an awareness that this is one of the moral difficulties to existence itself, a disposition natural in the adult, and one necessary to be overcome by the child growing into fully self-realized humanity. The number of orphans in *David Copperfield* has been well remarked. Emily, Rosa, Dora, David and Ham have all lost both parents before the novel's end and Agnes, Steerforth, and Uriah are blessed with only one parent. It is not easy to explain to everyone's satisfaction Dickens' predilection for orphans. However, it is clear that he finds the orphan-situation best suited to his presentation of the dynamics of moral growth. The parentless child is both freer and more in urgent need of becoming, as it were, his own parents. He is less protected, more exposed to a variety of accidents and can be shown as more independent, individual, more suitable as moral protagonist. This is as true for Tom Jones as it is for David Copperfield. From Dickens' point of view the issues are made clearer and the conflicts are more readily focused by the absence of one or both parents. In addition to all this the orphan provides for the novelist a kind of metaphoric short-cut, for what are we all but orphans, in the long run? David's love for and dependency on his mother, Clara Copperfield, is given a sharp jolt on the appearance of the Murdstones, with their incestuous-like tyranny over unsuspecting widows and children. David's mother has her own independent desires that take no account of David at all, as revealed by the cruel irony of her remark to her son after he has responded to being savagely and unjustly beaten by biting Murdstone. " 'Oh, Davy!' she said. 'That you could hurt any one I love!' " (p. 61) Indeed, Mrs. Copperfield reminds us of Mrs. Nickleby, not only because she is "pettish, wilful" but because she is blind to the realities of others. It is not surprising that David turns more and more to other attachments, to Emily and to Peggotty, whose name, strangely enough, is the same as his mother's, Clara. The absence of a strong kind father is felt not only by David, who, like Pip later, speaks of

> . . . my first childish associations with his white gravestone in the churchyard, and of the indefinable compassion I used to feel for it lying out alone there in the dark night, . . . (p. 2)

but also by Steerforth, " 'David, I wish to God I had had a judicious father these last twenty years!' " (p. 322), and again, " 'but I tell you, my good fellow, once more, that it would have been well for me (and for more than me) if I had had a steadfast and judicious father!' " (p. 322) Steerforth has something worse than a weak, vain mother like Clara Copperfield. He has a possessive and doting mother, and it is a strange irony that Murdstone, by forcing David into independence and self-reliance, assists him to self-realization and a self-control that Steerforth never attains. The dangers facing the lonely, frightened orphan do not consist merely of the crime and violence and hardship that once sufficed Dickens in his presentation of Oliver. True, there is now Murdstone and Grinby and very little to eat, but worse, there is the despair or the anger or bitterness that might distort character and pervert a life, or there is malaise or there is fantasy. The books that play so large a rôle in keeping David's spirits and imagination alive and hopeful can also become the only reality.

> . . . I fitted my old books to my altered life, and made stories for myself, out of the streets, and out of men and women; and

> how some main points in the character I shall unconsciously develop, I suppose, in writing my life, were gradually forming all this while. (p. 168)

David the child is not free from certain kinds of illusion as David the story-teller clearly sees. His marriage to Dora is an act of blindness, of the undisciplined heart, as is his dependence on Steerforth, who blinds him with his lustre as Murdstone dazzled his mother. David's passage through many identities in his search for the truth about himself and his relation to his world is symbolized by his changing names, given to him by others. David is Brooks of Sheffield, Trot, Daisy, Doady, to mention only some of them. It is only at the end that he is, even as far away as in Australia, "David Copperfield Esq., the Eminent author." To realize this destiny David has had to understand and confront his experience fully and honestly and to recognize the worth of Agnes, who is his better Angel, a part of himself that must be brought to fruition. That this is achieved is evidenced by the telling of the tale itself.

There is something almost terrifying about the honesty with which the "I" of the story lays bare the truth about the past. There is the description of David's response to news of his mother's death, his grief mixed with pride at his distinction and his bathing in the sympathies received. There is his drunken spree and his meeting with Agnes in the theatre. There is Dora's death and her painful insistence that it is better so. These brutal insistencies on the truth are close to a psychoanalysis of painful self-truths.

There are those rare individuals that survive through strength, courage, talent and luck or those that survive through the goodness and strength of others and their capacity to respond to it and there are those who survive by their own innate faith and goodness like Daniel Peggoty.

> "But water ('specially when 'tis salt) comes nat'ral to me; and friends is dear, and I am heer. —Which is verse," said Mr. Peggotty, surprised to find it out, "though I hadn't such intentions." (p. 867)

Mr. Peggotty is more of a poet, in the spirit of the whole novel, than he realizes. If I am right about this novel, Daniel's remark takes on a new profundity, for becoming the artist and the whole man are one, and to be a poet without "such intentions" becomes comic evidence of natural goodness. Then there are those who survive by drowning others. Heep and Littimer trade on appearances, the very appearances that have proved such a danger to David all along. Humility and respectability may be part of a universal system of deception. Heep has no self and therefore no morality. We are told that Heep writhes "himself into the silence like a conger-eel." Like Milton's serpent, who proceeds "In tangles, and made intricate seem straight / To mischief swift," so Dickens' human serpent is

> "such an incarnate hypocrite, that whatever object he pursues, he must pursue crookedly. It's his only compensation for the outward restraints he puts upon himself." (p. 778)

The guile that works for Heep, where sophistry and appearance work for Satan, takes the form of humility and respectability so valued in the world that, as Eve hears what pleases her most, so society finds in Heep its own flattery. Heep and Littimer find that their modes of behaviour work quite well.

> " 'Be umble, Uriah,' says father to me, 'and you'll get on. It was what was always being dinned into you and me at school; it's what goes down best. Be umble,' says father, 'and you'll do!' And really it ain't done bad!"
>
> It was the first time it had ever occurred to me, that this detestable cant of false humility might have originated out of the Heep family. I had seen the harvest, but had never thought of the seed. (p. 575)

In fact, such a system works quite well, for what we have here is the confessed parable of a society programming people to feed back to it images of its own false values. This is how the model prison functions as a self-generating system. It explains what it wants and teaches what it will accept and since it will accept what is very easily mirrored back to it, the mutual and totally false admiration-society is able to proceed forever. The prison only reflects, only exists by virtue of, the society outside. The distance between Murdstone and Steerforth and their impact on others, and the prison image at the end is not as great as might at first appear. Only real honesty and self-knowledge and the proper uses of suffering, love and compassion, even for oneself in the past (perhaps first for oneself) are the only remedy. Here indeed David and Traddles are apart from Heep and able to visit the prison, unmoved almost, looking at these creatures as though they were of another planet, or in a zoo.

David discovers himself finally when he discovers the worth of Agnes and his love for her. It is a strange achievement that this entire, long and agonizing quest should end at home. It is a story of the heroics of the hearth. Strange that the great quest novels should end in this way. Ulysses, after fighting all the hazards of the known and unknown world, becomes the great prototype of hearth-finders and returns to Penelope. Tom Jones wins Sophia, Greek wisdom and a human wife at once, after nearly losing his life. David's search is in a sense a striving for perfect ordinariness, the quiet fulfillment of a totally human peace in hearth, home and family. If this goal seems to be ideally middle-class and Victorian it must also be seen as classical and religious in its implications. Constancy and faith have been hardly won. Agnes, the lamb of God (and the name of Oliver's mother) is "pointing upwards" to a better self and an order, within which one must find one's peace on earth. It is almost perfectly Stoical in its values, and one had need be a Stoic, so unpredictable and irrational are the events of life and the impulses of self. King Charles' head and the donkeys on the lawn are ever present to remind us that the world will not be shaped by any order we would impose on it. One of the clearest signs of Stoic humanism is in Ham's echo from *Hamlet*, the high point of Renaissance Stoicism. Hamlet's "If it be now, 'tis not to come; if it be not to come, it will be now," etc. becomes Ham's "if my time is come, 'tis come. If 'tan't, I'll bide it," just before his selfless death, which like Hamlet's, is in contrast with the death of a treacherous rival.[4]

Some men are lawyers, like Traddles, and some are artists like David, but regardless of one's rôle in life, to know oneself and to be earnest are the primary requirements for fulfilling one's destiny well.

> The man who reviews his own life, as I do mine, in going on here, from page to page, had need to have been a good man indeed, if he would be spared the sharp consciousness of many talents neglected, many opportunities wasted, many erratic and perverted feelings constantly at war within his breast, and defeating him. I do not hold one natural gift, I dare say, that I have not abused. My meaning simply is, that whatever I have tried to

> do in life, I have tried with all my heart to do well; that whatever I have devoted myself to, I have devoted myself to completely; that in great aims and in small, I have always been thoroughly in earnest. (p. 606)

[1]John Jones, *"David Copperfield," Dickens and the Twentieth Century,* p. 136.

[2]*The Prelude* (1850), Bk. 14, lines 415-16, 444-7.

[3]*The Politics of the Family* (Massey Lectures, 1968), (Toronto: Canadian Broadcasting Corp., 1969), p. 11.

[4]This allusion to *Hamlet* should not be surprising. I have tried to show earlier how Dickens made use of the play (*Nicholas Nickleby*). In my view, no other work of literature had so powerful an influence or was so continuously present to Dickens. Marley's ghost causes a reference to Hamlet's father. Little Paul's christening produces a reference to Hamlet's melancholy. References to *Hamlet* are continuous through the letters. In *David Copperfield* we have "Hamlet's aunt," Mrs. Waterbrook (p. 371) and in *Bleak House* we find significant mention of Yorick. *Great Expectations* produces one of the most memorable performances of *Hamlet* ever recorded, that of Mr. Wopsle, and I suspect that the gravedigger scene from the play might be the seed from which the whole theme and structure of *Our Mutual Friend* grows.

"FOR GOD'S SAKE LOOK AT THIS!" BLEAK HOUSE

To hinder another is not an act; it is the contrary; it is a restraint on action both in ourselves and in the person hinder'd, for he who hinders another omits his own duty at the same time.

Murder is Hindering Another.

Theft is Hindering Another.

Backbiting, Undermining, Circumventing, and whatever is Negative is Vice.

WILLIAM BLAKE

•

Hamlet. Why may not that be the skull of a lawyer? Where be his quiddits now, his quillets, his cases, his tenures, and his tricks? Why does he suffer this rude knave now to knock him about the sconce with a dirty shovel, and will not tell him of his action of battery? Hum! This fellow might be in's time a great buyer of land, with his statutes, his recognizances, his fines, his double vouchers, his recoveries. Is this the fine of his fines, and the recovery of his recoveries, to have his fine pate full of fine dirt? Will his vouchers vouch him no more of his purchases, and double ones too, than the length and breadth of a pair of indentures? The very conveyances of his lands will scarcely lie in this box; and must th' inheritor himself have no more, ha?

Hor. Not a jot more, my lord.

Hamlet. Is not parchment made of sheepskins?

Hor. Ay, my lord, and of calveskins too.

Hamlet. They are sheep and calves which seek out assurance in that.

WILLIAM SHAKESPEARE

•

Trust in nothing but in Providence and your own efforts.

BLEAK HOUSE

•

Bleak House is distinguished in two clear respects by the maturity and skill and fictional control that characterize the growth in Dickens' stature. In the first place the structure and design of the novel clearly reflect the concern with the two points of view, the "objective" nature of society and the subjective quest of the "I" for an existential redemption. Esther, seemingly orphaned like David before her, confronts the world and presents her history in a personal narrative. Yet while she pursues her own course, the world goes on in its accustomed ways and here the omniscient author, not Esther, shapes its appearance. Secondly, and of paramount importance, is the increasing presence in the fiction, clearly discernible here, of Dickens' growing sense of a universal framework beyond both the "they" and the "I." The traces of Christian faith that appear all through the novels are no longer merely insisted on. The sense of universal Divine order is wrought into the very fabric, structure and diction of the later novels. The moral quest leads more and more to a vision of fulfillment in harmony, peace and reconciliation of man and his world. The garden of the endings becomes less the happy ending of fairy-tale and more the natural outcome earned through meaningful and unavoidable human suffering. Marriage thus becomes gradually but firmly and with increasing purpose substituted for guardianship and filial dependence. God as Father and Christ as Son merge in the human protagonist. Outside both Esther and Chancery is a world waiting to be discovered, a world created anew by virtue of its continual rediscovery. If this is an accurate way of describing what we may feel in reading the later novels, and of accounting for the emotive power and profundity of vision that produce this reaction, it is also necessary to explain how Dickens is able to render the vision into fiction. It should not be surprising, if I am right, to see that Dickens turns more and more to history, tradition and myth for his authority and moral support, and to re-interpreting ancient myths to make new ones. What is the treatment of Chancery here but the making of a new myth? Dickens must have felt, or believed and thence discovered, that if his perception of man's situation was true, universal and timeless, then that situation had always been the same and the lessons of myth and metaphor were timeless also and so applicable to the present. The great images of his cultural tradition were necessary for his time and must be restated.

It is for this reason that the two opening chapters of *Bleak House* present not only two mythological stages of the world's history, but also their moral application to the present state of society. Chapter 1 presents us with images of prehistory; we are in the early verses of Genesis, "as if the waters had but newly retired from the face of the earth." In the world of London's fog and mud, where the Lord High Chancellor is "at the very heart of the fog," Dickens tells us that "it would not be wonderful to meet a Megalosaurus, forty feet long or so." This monstrous or "elephantine lizard" finds its equivalent in the nineteenth-century not-yet-ordered world described here in Jarndyce versus Jarndyce which "still drags its dreary length before the court." The monsters that in prehistory were forty feet long are now Chancery suits forty years long. Chancery, then, is the centre of one of the novel's principal loci. When we turn to Chesney Wold we are in a setting where the waters have returned to the earth. "It is a deadened world," ruled by "Dedlocks," and it is "not so unlike the court of Chancery." Both are worlds of the past filled with "oversleeping Rip Van Winkles" but they may be awakened like "sleeping beauties" who, we are asked to recall by the allusion, were awakened by a kiss, the symbol of love and union. "The waters are out." The park is inundated and has become a lake and the trees are islands, the bridges washed away. What is the state of mind for which the "Flood" in Lincolnshire is an appropriate setting? It is a world in which the people are separated from their Earth, from other people and from themselves, "and cannot hear the rushing of larger worlds and cannot see them circle round the sun." In short it is an alienated world unable to see its place in a larger scheme of things. Dickens' growing insistence on the Stoic necessity of man's discovery of his place in a universal harmony is clearly seen in these two opening chapters. Lady Dedlock, having first betrayed and then suppressed her love and the truth, must suppress all feeling as far as possible. For her, living this grotesquely distorted life of emotional self-mutilation, the world becomes an intolerable place. Lady Dedlock is "Loved to death" in this deadened world. We are told later, quite explicitly, that

> Weariness of soul lies before her, as it lies behind—her Ariel has put a girdle of it round the whole earth, and it cannot be

> unclasped—but the imperfect remedy is always to fly, from the last place where it has been experienced. (p. 154)

A world becomes a prison when we violate our own natures and deny our common humanity and the capacity for love. Our world, "which has its limits too (as your Highness shall find when you have made a tour of it, and are come to the brink of the void beyond)," seems too small when its inhabitants refuse to function within its designed limits. This theme is to be fully explored in *Little Dorrit*. Thus we have a picture of fog and mud and flood, a world of sleep and death where the sufferings of many are linked to the betrayal of the individual self. To be "In Chancery" and to be "In Fashion," the titles of chapters 1 and 2, are both states of mind, conditions of perception, as though one were to speak of being "in a state" or "in a trance." What alternative, what antidote is there to these conditions? What will clear the fog and dry up the waters? Of course, the sun.

Esther Summerson, as the pun of her name suggests, is the embodiment of the love and compassion and humility that bring meaning and order out of chaos. Esther's first name recalls not merely the sun that rises in the east but the Old Testament woman who is the saviour of her people. She is the "I" of the novel because only in the perception of the "I" and in the fulfillment and realization of the individual soul can meaning be discovered in all else. Late in the novel Jarndyce tells Esther, " 'You can be nothing better than yourself; . . .' " (p. 608) and when Esther is talking to Richard and hears him say in a moment of rare honesty and self-knowledge, " 'I—I don't like to represent myself in this litigious, contentious, doubting character, to a confiding girl like Ada,' " (pp. 527-28) she says to him that he is "more like himself." When we first encounter Esther she is in a Puritan setting. If the opening two chapters, with their richness of allusion, are allegory, then the third chapter would fit precisely into it. The aunt is like an inhabitant of Babel. One of the possible responses to the Creation, the Fall and the Flood is the devising of a system of guilt, punishment and repression. If God is seen as righteous, vengeful and dangerous one may devise a kind of behavioural ledger of debit and credit. This not only appears to protect (while in fact increasing the sense of isolation) but justifies a good deal of self-indulgence. The outer form and severity of manner somehow permit the kind of gorging compensation that we see when Mr. Chadband eats. Esther's own good nature converts all this guilt into a drive towards expiation through love rather than through suffering. Her character and career cannot be traced to the benefits arising from the code of her "godmother" (superbly ironic term), but rather to her native ability (as a love-child?) for dispelling not only mud and fog and flood and the wind that is in the east, but also the gloom that was part of her upbringing. Esther, moreover, like Oliver with his Brownlow and Maylies, is lucky in being adopted by Jarndyce. But then Jarndyce is lucky in discovering Esther. Chancery and its locales, its parody in Krook's Court, the chambers of Tulkinghorn and Vholes, constitute the first locus; Chesney Wold is the second; and wherever Esther is, primarily in Bleak House, is the third. None of these places is fixed, of course. Richard and Gridley carry Chancery with them everywhere, they are "In Chancery" and it is in them. So Lady Dedlock carries her anguish everywhere and her husband bears his dignity as a tortoise does its shell, around him in all places and at all times. So Jo carries Tom-all-Alone's with him and literally spreads it, in the form of smallpox, to those he meets even far away.

Esther transforms Bleak House and causes it to proliferate, as we see in the second Bleak House established at the novel's close. She brings order, symbolized by her keys and accounts, and love. Jarndyce is a good man whose hyper-sensitivity to suffering in others is his only flaw. As the Stoics say, the man who suffers by sympathy exactly as the sufferer does becomes of little use to the sufferer. Jarndyce's link with the philanthropists suggests his inability actually to look at the evils he abhors. He has hardly confronted the little Jellybys any more than has Mrs. Jellyby herself. It is Esther who first exposes their plight, sent there as his emissary. It is after Esther's arrival that Jo is brought to Bleak House itself and housed in the stable, like Christ, and it is after Esther's influence is felt that Jarndyce visits the Neckett children and is able to say "for God's sake look at this!" If Bleak House, with its unpromising name and its "growlery," can be transformed into a place of light and love, it is primarily because its owner has resolutely remained outside the orbit of Chancery and all it signifies. There is no doubt that Chancery and its workings are evil in themselves. Nothing can excuse it. Yet, by the same token, nothing can obscure the illusions and the greeds and disputes that drive people to place their reliance on Chancery and help to sustain it. Richard is the classical case in point. He and Vholes together present in small the whole nature of Chancery. A goodnatured, improvident man places his faith in riches and in the Court's capacity to satisfy this desire. By this reliance the court is sustained, Vholes is given further employment and hope turns to despair. The victim is willing and becomes prey to the life-devouring predator.

> I never shall forget those two seated side by side in the lantern's light; Richard, all flush and fire and laughter, with the reins in his hand; Mr. Vholes, quite still, black-gloved, and buttoned up, looking at him as if he were looking at his prey and charming it. (p. 535)

Vholes is a vampire.

> So slow, so eager, so bloodless and gaunt, I felt as if Richard were wasting away beneath the eyes of this adviser, and there were something of the Vampire in him. (p. 820)

He is sustained by the blood of others. The desk in Vholes' office is a coffin. "Mr. Vholes gives it a rap, and it sounds as hollow as a coffin," (p. 551) and the lawyer is always to be found there. It is this desk, or what it symbolizes, that does indeed become the emblematic burial place of Richard, who not only moves next door to Vholes but dies having given up his life-force, his energy, to sustain his lawyer and counsellor. Richard exchanges Jarndyce for Vholes. If Richard is the pathetic but obvious case, Gridley, though less obvious, is equally pathetic and no less clearly analyzed by Dickens. Gridley is an innocent victim of Chancery, or is he? Certainly he is more sinned against than sinning, but the story he tells of the origins of the case is of crucial significance to our understanding of Chancery's rôle.

> "After my mother's death, all was to come to me, except a legacy of three hundred pounds that I was then to pay my brother. My mother died. My brother, some time afterwards, claimed his legacy. I, and some of my relations, said that he had had a part of it already, in board and lodging, and some other things. Now mind! That was the question, and nothing else. No one disputed the will; no one disputed anything but whether part of that three hundred pounds had been already paid or not. To settle that question, my brother filing a bill, I was obliged to go into this accursed Chancery; . . ." (p. 214)

What would Jarndyce have done? Paid the three hundred pounds, of course. We must recall the warning of the opening chapter: "Suffer any wrong that can be done you, rather than come here!" (p. 3) The Gridley family squabble does after all seem, at best, ungenerous. Chancery exists because even families cannot be united. Little hope then exists for the larger family of man. Chancery is the living sign of man's fruitless dependence on law in general. The institutions that are designed to substitute for our hearts and minds are certain to disappoint and punish us as they can only exaggerate and reflect back upon us the meanness of spirit and the falsity of the values that gave birth to them in the first place. Dickens loathes Chancery as a manifest social evil but he goes far beyond this satire to examine the attitudes and perceptions that lie behind it. There will always be Smallweeds and Vholeses and Richards but the reader is invited to choose an alternative perception that excludes the existence of Chancery. Let it consume itself, as it must, and burn up with its own noxious vapours as Krook does. Jarndyce will not even visit Chancery. It is a warning that unheeded almost destroys George.

Vampirism and parasitism and litigation are some of the forms that appear in response to the fact of life, the existence of man in the world. They are self-generating and like Lady Dedlock's journeyings to escape herself they are "fruitless." So also is Deportment, a comic version of the parasite's devices. So also is Philanthropy. Chancery is really much more closely linked to the later Circumlocution Office and Mr. Merdle than one might suppose. Dickens is becoming more and more insistent on the destructive nature of abstract speculation and empty forces. The Jellybys and the Pardiggles engage in activities designed to take them out of the world. The neglected Jellyby children do not embody for us the lesson that charity begins at home. They symptomize the results of a system for making home invisible. They are part of a world of unreality made unreal deliberately by "utopic philanthropy." Like those used by the government of Laputa, these systems for looking far off free the gazers from the difficult engagement in Life. The suffering they overlook and the suffering they cause are likewise untroubling. Everything must be kept vague and general.

. . . the only genuine mission, of both man and woman, was to

> be always moving declaratory resolutions about things in general at public meetings. (p. 422)

Dickens engages in some complex metaphysical speculation in regard to Jobling and Guppy.

> That very popular trust in flat things coming round! Not in their being beaten round, or worked round, but in their "coming" round! As though a lunatic should trust in the world's "coming" triangular!
>
> "I had confident expectations that things would come round and be all square," says Mr. Jobling, with some vagueness of expression, and perhaps of meaning, too. "But I was disappointed. They never did." (p. 278)

The disappointment is and must be universal in such expectations. The king of Borrioboola-Gha, instead of cooperating, sells the settlers for rum. The court of Chancery eats up its cases in costs. Tom-all-Alone's survives because it is more painful to contemplate than distant and invisible Africa. The cross on top of St. Paul's Cathedral is so high above Jo that it remains for him a distant mystery and like Swift's floating island is remote from the earth itself.

> And there he sits, munching and gnawing, and looking up at the great Cross on the summit of St. Paul's Cathedral, glittering above a red and violet-tinted cloud of smoke. From the boy's face one might suppose that sacred emblem to be, in his eyes, the crowning confusion of the great, confused city; so golden, so high up, so far out of his reach. (p. 271)

In such a world it is not surprising that Mr. Jellyby should find consolation in the hard present reality of walls, not the "walls of words" that are made in Chancery, but actual walls of lath and plaster.

> Her father released her, took out his pocket-handkerchief, and sat down on the stairs with his head against the wall. I hope he found some consolation in walls. I almost think he did. (p. 424)

The places in *Bleak House* constitute a series of linked and alternative microcosms. Bleak House itself is complicated, with its odd rooms and passages and angles and attics and cellars, yet it may be lived in and ordered and understood through love and compassion, just as the world itself may be. There is Jarndyce in Chancery but the man himself follows his own and separate course. The worlds of the novel may not be reconciled until Judgement Day. Vholes, like Dodson and Fogg and a host of others before him, survives. Conversation Kenge will have ample room for building new walls of words. Smallweeds will continue to be born devoid of childhood. Skimpoles will abound and Richards will succumb and Chanceries of one sort or another will be made by and for those who want them. Not until the great Seal is opened and the apocalypse is realized will Miss Flite's birds all fly free forever and all human conflict be resolved. When that happens the square will be made round and the crooked made straight. Then there will be no more marks left by disease on the faces of the good and beautiful. But waiting for the world to change and putting our trust in the Day of Judgement is to kill the present. The consequences of such a system of rationalization are the cruellest imaginable. The idea that one day all may be well produces the ugliest of *laissez-faire* results. Richard lives in the future. Woodcourt lives and works in the present. The one sustains Vholes, the other comforts the poor and sick. Those who have the love and compassion are enabled to see the qualities in others and can penetrate appearances, as Esther does with Caddy and Jo, and Woodcourt does with Esther. Love and gratitude produce responsibility, and Skimpole recognizes clearly his opposite in Esther.

> "You appear to me to be the very touchstone of responsibility. When I see you, my dear Miss Summerson, intent upon the perfect working of the whole little orderly system of which you are the centre, I feel inclined to say to myself—in fact I do say to myself, very often—*that's* responsibility!" (p. 531)

Esther comes to be a sun to others because of her own assurance that she is part of an ordered universe in which her rôle has meaning.

> I had never been a beauty, and had never thought myself one; but I had been very different from this. It was all gone now. *Heaven was so good to me, that I could let it go with a few not bitter tears,* and could stand there arranging my hair for the night quite thankfully. (p. 504, my italics)

There is almost an outrageous courage, a wilful assertion of meaning in Dickens' creation of this character, a woman, who can lose her looks and speak of "that little loss of mine." (p. 507)

> When I saw the strength of the weak little hand, and how its touch could heal my darling's heart, and raise up hope within her, I felt a new sense of the goodness and the tenderness of God. (p. 877)

Goodness is discovered by Esther in exactly those images that could evoke bitterness from one more cynical than herself.

The scope of Dickens' perspective in this novel is best seen by reference to a passage that closely resembles the speech from *Hamlet* that heads this chapter. Returning from an abortive trip to England, Hamlet is a changed man and has a kind of Stoic calm that causes him to reflect on the meaning of life and the necessity for moral conduct in terms that transcend the political. If death brings all to the grave it must matter more, not less, how one lives. To put our trust in wealth and land and crowns seems absurd. We need a higher code and faith so that quality may be brought to our actions. This kind of perspective is found in *Bleak House*. Compare the following passage where "Little Swills . . . like a very Yorick . . ." (p. 443) entertains at the Sol's Arms, while the lawyers labour like industrious bees vainly to ensure against death, to the passage from Shakespeare cited as an epigraph above.

> In dirty upper casements, here and there, hazy little patches of candlelight reveal where some wise draughtsman and conveyancer yet toils for the entanglement of real estate in meshes of sheep-skin, in the average ratio of about a dozen of sheep to an acre of land. Over which bee-like industry, these benefactors of their species linger yet, though office-hours be past; that they may give, for every day, some good account at last. (p. 443)

Dickens calls upon the allusion to reinforce his work with the full significance of Hamlet's discovery of values and duties and integrity which transcend his discovery of death, even his own.

To speak in terms of suffering, self-knowledge and redemption when we come to *Bleak House* is not in any sense strange. What is Bleak House itself but an image of the world? What order and meaning and joy can be brought to it, if not from the sympathies of its occupants, out of perceptions arising from an unobscured vision of the here and now, unfogged by evasion, illusion or rationalization, unmuddied by "compound interest," untroubled by doubts as to the design of the whole? Only such perceptions can discover in the world those beauties and those joys that we have wished to find there all along.

"AW A MUDDLE"
HARD TIMES

Our own cities are our own animal factories; families, schools, churches are the slaughterhouses of our children; colleges and other places are the kitchens. As adults in marriages and business, we eat the product.

RONALD D. LAING

•

No man is an island, entire of itself; every man is a piece of the continent, a part of the main.

JOHN DONNE

•

"Now, you see, Tom," said Mr. Harthouse in conclusion, himself tossing over a rose or two, as a contribution to the island, which was always drifting to the wall as if it wanted to become a part of the mainland: "every man is selfish in everything he does, and I am exactly like the rest of my fellow-creatures."

HARD TIMES

•

There is a passage in *Hard Times* where Tom Gradgrind, sitting disconsolately outside Bounderby's country house, tormented by guilt, frightened by his debts and generally miserable, absent-mindedly plucks roses from a bush and tears them up, throwing the crushed petals into the ornamental pond. It is a clear reference back to the dialogue in the first chapter where Sissy Jupe learns that flowers are somehow alien from human affairs and are not to be used as a subject of fancy.

"So you would carpet your room—or your husband's room, if you were a grown woman, and had a husband—with representations of flowers, would you?" said the gentleman. "Why would you?"

"If you please, Sir, I am very fond of flowers," returned the girl.

"And is that why you would put tables and chairs upon them, and have people walking over them with heavy boots?"

"It wouldn't hurt them, Sir. They wouldn't crush and wither, if you please, Sir. They would be the pictures of what was very pretty and pleasant, and I would fancy—"

"Ay, ay, ay! But you mustn't fancy," cried the gentleman, quite elated by coming so happily to his point. "That's it! You are never to fancy." (p. 7)

But the flower-killers turn out to be the fact-people, the literalists, rather than the fanciful and naïve who would weave flowers in carpets.

The passage in which Tom and Harthouse tear up roses is remarkable for me in another regard, for I read it as a clear allusion to Donne's famous "Meditation XVII," wherein the poet explores the theme of man's brotherhood, his unity with all mankind. "Any Man's death diminishes me because I am involved in mankind, and therefore never send to know for whom the bell tolls: it tolls for thee." If Dickens knew this passage, how the words must have rung in his mind! But even if this is not direct allusion, and I have no external evidence to substantiate my suspicion, the Donne images provide us with precisely the viewpoint from which *Hard Times* is written and against which Utilitarianism is satirized and exposed. For Utilitarianism has its roots in the assumption of the separateness of men.

That which, with Adam Smith, is political economy, becomes extended under Bentham's treatment until it practically includes the whole of ethics. He starts from the conception that the race consists of isolated individuals, every one of whom is eagerly striving to get the greatest possible number of goods at the least possible cost.[1]

It is not until we get to John Stuart Mill that nineteenth-century philosophy catches up with Dickens, for Mill's great liberal mind could no more be blind to a generous impulse in humanity than could Dickens'.

While Bentham—at any rate in practice—starts from the egoistic interest as the universal motive, Stuart Mill was convinced

> of the reality of disinterested feelings. . . . The moral feeling causes us to strive to produce happiness even when this happiness is not our own.[2]

It seems then that Donne's (and Dickens') point of view is antithetical to Bentham's, and *Hard Times* is totally dedicated to pursuing to its monstrous, logical conclusion the consequences of a philosophy of self-interest carried into practice.

But *Hard Times* is more than that. Perhaps this anti-Bentham theme is indeed only secondary. For if Utilitarianism was the contemporary form that social and political philosophy was taking, and if Dickens was horrified at this particular form of rationalism, he nevertheless sees beyond this form to the nature of "ism" itself. Whether it is scientism, Catholicism, Puritanism, fascism or Communism, the horrors of absolutism generally were clear to Dickens and he knew that any system that reduces humanity to convenient terms and seeks to make man fit the abstract pattern is disastrous. Dickens' reassurance to Charles Knight's concern that the novelist would regard him as "a cold-hearted political economist" illustrates my point, "My satire is against those who see *figures and averages, and nothing else*—the representatives of the wickedest and most enormous vice of this time— . . . Bah! What have you to do with these?"[3] It is this liberal and humane impulse to cry out against absolutism, against systems for the reduction of man in any form, that underlies *Hard Times.* It is this that explains the rejected title for the novel, "Black and White;" it is this that explains the connection in the novel between fact, self-interest, and rationalism, and their consequences. *Hard Times for These Times* is, as its punning title suggests, the kind of contemporary analysis of trends and attitudes that is Dickens' nearest approach to Huxley's *Brave New World,* Orwell's *1984,* and particularly *Gulliver's Travels* and its third and fourth books. Dickens' penetration in perceiving the sterility of a world that results in pushing rationalism into "The One Thing Needful" (Chapter 1) makes nonsense of the kind of carping criticism that has argued about the accuracy of the portraiture or the fineness of Dickens' understanding of Utilitarianism. *Hard Times* is not a school philosophy text. The novelist is fully aware that the fine points of philosophic argument are swept away in the broad political and social applications of any philosophy, and he rightly attacks its main thrusts, its spirit, its inherent dangers, in broad satiric strokes. Dickens sees the need to attack the hydra-heads of absolutism not with a scalpel but with a blunt instrument. My metaphor echoes what is in the novel itself, where the "ogre" at the blackboard is

> . . . a monster in a lecturing castle, with Heaven knows how many heads manipulated into one, taking childhood captive, and dragging it into gloomy statistical dens by the hair. (p. 9)

This ogre is not any teacher in the novel, it is The Teacher of Fact Incarnate, conceptualized in a figure of speech. It is in this satiric spirit that we find Coketown to be the perfect city of Fact, the physical expression of a mind whose imaginative faculty has almost died and of a spirit which, like Bounderby's, is "perfectly devoid of sentiment." (p. 14)

> You saw nothing in Coketown but what was severely workful. If the members of a religious persuasion built a chapel there—as the members of eighteen religious persuasions had done—they make it a pious warehouse of red brick, with sometimes (but this is only in highly ornamental examples) a bell in a birdcage on the top of it. The solitary exception was the New Church; a stuccoed edifice with a square steeple over the door, terminating in four short pinnacles like florid wooden legs. All the public inscriptions in the town were painted alike, in severe characters of black and white. The jail might have been the infirmary, the infirmary might have been the jail, the town-hall might have been either, or both, or anything else, for anything that appeared to the contrary in the graces of their construction. Fact, fact, fact, everywhere in the material aspect of the town; fact, fact, fact, everywhere in the immaterial. The M'Choakumchild school was all fact, and the school of design was all fact, and the relations between master and man were all fact, and everything was fact between the lying-in hospital and the cemetery, and what you couldn't state in figures, or show to be purchaseable in the cheapest market and saleable in the dearest, was not, and never should be, world without end, Amen. (pp. 22-23)

This ends as a prayer to a concept raised into an absolute Divinity. It is the worst form of idolatry. The speaker, who is the first personage encountered in the novel, is likewise built to a pattern. Gradgrind is the fitting inhabitant of such a place.

> The speaker's obstinate carriage, square coat, square legs, square shoulders, —nay, his very neckcloth, trained to take him by

> the throat with an unaccommodating grasp, like a stubborn fact, as it was, —all helped the emphasis. (p. 1)

This is the kind of satire we find in Kafka's *Castle,* where the ministry is obscured by its impenetrable maze of forgotten but immoveable forms and where God is made invisible by theology. In Coketown there are no men, only "hands," no horses, only Graminivorous Quadrupeds, no children, only numbers, all alike, all reduced to a single false formula. The idea of fact comes indeed to replace God, as we see in the cry, "Fact forbid!" Gradgrind himself is the perfect illustration of Dickens' concern. It is not so much that he is a bad man as that he is a mistaken man. Indeed, Gradgrind has all along intended to improve the human lot, and Dickens is not ungenerous in his presentation.

> In gauging fathomless deeps with his little mean excise-rod, and in staggering over the universe with his rusty stiff-legged compasses, he had meant to do great things. (p. 222)

Yet this same man has managed to produce the corruption of Tom and the suffering of Louisa and all by a failure of understanding, or perhaps the repression of his own imagination.

> As he now leaned back in his chair, and bent his deep-set eyes upon her in his turn, perhaps he might have seen one wavering moment in her, when she was impelled to throw herself upon his breast, and give him the pent-up confidences of her heart. But, to see it, he must have overleaped at a bound the artificial barriers he had for many years been erecting, between himself and all those subtle essences of humanity which will elude the utmost cunning of algebra until the last trumpet ever to be sounded shall blow even algebra to wreck. (pp. 99-100)

He has been wedded to a system and thus abdicated his sympathies, his perception, his heart. It is a form of self-blinding. Gradgrind represents the dangers of doctrine, dogma and absolutism, in this case Rationalism, in education, yet education by definition is resistant to the evils of its forms, for, except in a totalitarian state (and even there education for the State is to some extent self-defeating) education is the most disinterested form of social activity. It is always, relatively speaking, liberating and for this reason Dickens places much value and emphasis on it. It is Gradgrind's inevitable involvement with others (his pupils, his government, his constituents) that keeps his tenuous thread of sympathy unbroken and permits his redemption.

Carried into the realm of economy, however, the horrors of absolutist self-interest have no limit. Here it is Bounderby who is the archetype of the self-made business man, all head and no heart, though his lust for Louisa is irrational enough and but thinly disguised. "'Here I am, Mrs. Gradgrind, anyhow, and nobody to thank for my being here, but myself.'" (p. 15) Not only is this an impossibility and is proved to be moreover a lie but the very idea, placed under the microscope as it is throughout the novel and its course of events, is conceptually horrific. It is a glimpse at the absurdity and the non-human monstrosity of self-isolation, traced back to the mad illusion of self-conception. It is of course a fantasy. Bounderby and Gradgrind go together as a barely veiled allegory of Political Economy and Literalist Education and their first real disagreement, the beginning of division, is seen with Sissy Jupe's disposition. Girl No. 20 evokes sympathy from Gradgrind but none from Bounderby. Strangely enough, both of these embodiments of systems of rationalism inevitably betray their attitudes as largely humbug, for Gradgrind's view of man is a form of patently false perception and Bounderby's tale of his origins is a fairy story.

One of the first and principal losses in the world of absolute system is the dignity of the individual. The man who would seek to retain his own integrity, follow his own convictions, make his own judgements and try to perceive the truth is necessarily destroyed. The man who makes private promises and tries to keep them in spite of public pressures on him to abandon himself to a cause is crushed. Stephen, whose name is not accidentally that of the first Christian martyr, is just such a man. In his efforts to follow a complex rôle, to endure the suffering of domestic misery and simultaneously foster the love-relationship with Rachel, Stephen chooses the private life. The rhetoric of Slackbridge is professional and designed to produce a unity in the workers, "one united power," that leaves no room for personal decision or private allegiance. Caught on the one side, between his imprisonment in the stereotype of the "hands," created by Bounderby to justify his exploitation of the workers, and on the other by the Union's relentless demand for membership and public profession, Stephen is not merely cast out, he is used as scapegoat both by Tom Gradgrind and by Slackbridge, the two halves of the social vise that crushes him. His subsequent death from the accident at Old Hell Shaft, where others have died before, we are told, is the final martyrdom of the innocent. The obsolete mine shaft, left uncovered, is the relic of past industrialism that still kills in the present. Like his Biblical namesake, Stephen is no silent sufferer. He makes two great speeches in the novel, first to Bounderby and again to the union meeting. The parallel to the story of Stephen the martyr is very close.

> And they stirred up the people, and the elders, and the scribes, and came upon him, and caught him, and brought him to the council,
>
> And set up false witnesses, which said, This man ceaseth not to speak blasphemous words against this holy place, and the law.[4]

Slackbridge's ability to stir up the people at the Tribunal and his charges against Stephen as a traitor recall these events clearly. The Biblical Stephen's righteous eloquence could hardly have been uttered by the lowly Stephen Blackpool, but it might well represent the anger of Dickens himself as he regards the totalitarian forces ruling in a heartless industrial wasteland.

> Ye stiffnecked and uncircumcised in heart and ears, ye do always resist the Holy Ghost: your fathers did, so do ye.
>
> Which of the prophets have not your fathers persecuted? and they have slain them which shewed before of the coming of the Just One; of whom ye have been now the betrayers and murderers:
>
> Who have received the law by the disposition of angels, and have not kept it.
>
> When they heard these things, they were cut to the heart, and they gnashed on him with their teeth.[5]

Stephen and Rachel represent the reality of totally disinterested love in the novel, uncompromised even by the satisfactions of sexual intimacy. The modern reader is likely to be as frustrated as the characters themselves in reading of this self-denial, yet how can Stephen and Rachel win? Any yielding to temptation would only confirm the prejudices already operating against them.

As the world of loveless, unfeeling, utilitarian political economy is linked with the forces of education by Fact, so the small world of Stephen's and Rachel's love is linked to the circus-world by Mystery, its opposite. Love and the Circus have in common the elements of fancy and feeling and the magic of inexplicable human achievements. Sleary's circus is the image of a society as a family where interdependence is assumed as an essential characteristic to the survival of both the individual and the whole. Thus we see again the contrast between the elaborate, theoretical pretensions of the world of Fact and Ego, which in spite of its systematic thoroughness fails, and the totally non-theoretical but eminently practical artists, which Dickens counterpoints with elaborate, explicit irony. Each circus performer, in his expertise, respects the skill of the others and finds his place in an harmonious group with a common purpose.

> The father of one of the families was in the habit of balancing the father of another of the families on the top of a great pole; the father of a third family often made a pyramid of both those fathers, with Master Kidderminster for the apex, and himself for the base; all the fathers could dance upon rolling casks, stand upon bottles, catch knives and balls, twirl hand-basins, ride upon anything, jump over everything, and stick at nothing. (p. 35)

Sleary himself is all in-betweens, neither one thing nor another, and thus the antithesis of the rigid absoluteness of square Coketown fact.

> . . . a stout man as already mentioned, with one fixed eye, and one loose eye, a voice (if it can be called so) like the efforts of a broken old pair of bellows, a flabby surface, and a muddled head which was never sober and never drunk. (p. 35)

This should be contrasted with the earlier description of Gradgrind. By the end of the novel, Tom and his father become dependent on the Circus and its mysterious powers. The element of mystery, of magic, or miracle, of gravity and reason defied, where dogs do tricks and horses dance, is a world that cannot be comprehended in the language of political economy. The horse which dances defeats Bitzer because it is outside the realm of his experience, for it was Bitzer we remember who first defined for us a horse, a definition that takes no account of that reality which includes a horse's capacity for learning to dance. Bitzer's name suggests the collection of bits and pieces of information of which he is composed. He has no coherent view of himself or the world and is thus rendered helpless. It is this partial version of the truth, distorted into the whole truth, that defeats Gradgrind through Louisa and defeats Bounderby through his mother's devotion, of which the latter failed to take sufficient account. Love indeed turns out to be the greatest of all the undefinable mysteries which, being no less present because the authorities refuse to see it, upsets the best laid plans of those who cannot reckon with it, whose system excludes it. This is the great moral lesson that Sleary teaches Gradgrind, the teacher. Even Sleary's lisp seems functional as contrast to the precise diction in which precise fact gains authority.

> "It theemth to prethent two thingth to a perthon, don't it, Thquire?" said Mr. Sleary, musing as he looked down into the depths of his brandy and water: "one, that there ith a love in the world, not all Thelf-interetht after all, but thomething very different; t'other, that it hath a way of ith own of calculating or not calculating, whith thomehow or another ith at leatht ath hard to give a name to, ath the wayth of the dogth ith!"
>
> Mr. Gradgrind looked out of window, and made no reply. Mr. Sleary emptied his glass and recalled the ladies. (pp. 292-93)

Gradgrind's final silence is testimony to his submission to forces and mysteries far beyond his pathetic definitions, for just before this he has persistently applied empty labels of "instinct" and "scent" to explain the dog's behaviour, to all of which Sleary has answered " 'I'm bletht if I know what to call it.' " Love works to give Stephen his courage and strength to withstand almost intolerable social pressure. Love gives Sissy the power to shame Harthouse and exile him. Louisa's love for Tom brings him to a softened repentance. The titles of the three books, "Sowing," "Reaping," "Garnering," apply as much to the gentle and loving characters as to those who harvest nothing but thorns. Dickens finally invites the reader to an awareness that he can make the kind of world he lives in rather as Dickens has made his fiction, by choosing to perceive the whole human complexity and not electing for any version of man that destructively fragments and insults the mysteries of his nature. Not only will the absolute system produce endless suffering but it will be defeated in any case.

Hard Times is not any real departure from certain of those attitudes which we have traced from the start. Indeed one might go back to "Sunday under Three Heads" to find the first evidence of Dickens' awareness that Sunday prohibitions grow from a narrow, rigid, inhumane orthodoxy much akin to the kind of absolutist doctrine under attack in this novel. The kind of theory that produced the Poor Law and the attitudes behind the Workhouse System for discouraging indigence within the Parishes, and which Dickens exposed in *Oliver Twist,* seem very like Coketown-philosophies. Bounderby might easily be a member of the Poorhouse Board of the earlier novel without any alteration of his character. *Hard Times* does in fact seem to revert to the style of the early work and fit more naturally with the pseudo-allegorical social analysis of *Oliver Twist* and *Nicholas Nickleby* than with the character-exploration and the psychology and self-searching of *Chuzzlewit* and *Dombey* and *David.* One can explain this reversion only by theorizing that Dickens was driven by a real urgency to castigate certain trends in social thought that seemed at the time acutely dangerous. How else can one explain the almost short-hand quality of this novel, tossed off in a few months, conveying as it does the force of a polemical essay in the simple clarity of its structure. It is a time-out for Dickens, an aside in the main drive of his personal quest for a redemptive understanding of the human process. As one critic has pointed out, perhaps no novel of Dickens' has roused so much opposition and hostility as this one.

> *Hard Times* has, since the moment it appeared, attracted an unusually heavy and sustained barrage of polemical fire. Nothing more clearly indicates the problematical relationship between the world of this novel and the world of an individual reader than the claims, made seventy-five years apart, that Dickens understood neither utilitarian economics nor labor organizers.[6]

This is doubtless due in part to an attachment, almost a cultural attachment, on the part of the audience to the systems and values under attack in the book. We are hypnotized by facts, philosophies, systems, dogma, statistics and "political economy." We are Utilitarians and it is hard to acquire enough detachment to see the dangers in our disposition. Furthermore, as Monroe Engel rightly points out, the novel itself is not redeemed by the lightness and fancy and humour it advocates. It is totally serious, it is concentrated diatribe, and it invites a debate rather than a satiric laugh at the objects of its anger.

> Curiously enough, *Hard Times* grants a scant measure of the very quality for which it argues, imaginative pleasure. Its seriousness is so scrupulous, plain, and insistent that the reader moves along with simple, too rarely surprised consent. . . .[7]

Nevertheless the main outlines of Dickens' vision are still perceptible. It is through Stephen that we see Dickens insisting on a human purpose and meaning in an order greater than that available through economic theory or indeed through any form of rationalism. The local mysteries, the love of a dog for its master and its journeying home, the love of a man for an unobtainable woman, point to mysteries of a larger scale. It is only the sense of our common mortality and our common humility, enforced by our presence in a universal mystery, that produces the compassion necessary to an altered social order. Stephen, in his agony, looks up to see a star that leads him, he believes, to his Saviour.

> "Often as I coom to myseln, and found it shinin on me down there in my trouble, I thowt it were the star as guided to Our Saviour's home. I awmust think it be the very star!" . . . The star had shown him where to find the God of the poor; and through humility, and sorrow, and forgiveness, he had gone to his Redeemer's rest. (p. 274)

We cannot but be reminded of the Biblical Stephen's death, when he, in his agony, finds his God through his awareness of his own destruction by a world gone mad, a world that looks upward so rarely that it covers the earth with Old Hell Shafts, a world that sees no link between the lowly dog and the moving star, that sees no place for itself in a system beyond man's making, that is blind to the design of a universe that incorporates man. It is this blindness that leads to the making of false systems and crippling designs that must prove disastrous by their ignorance.

> But he, being full of the Holy Ghost, looked up steadfastly into heaven, and saw the glory of God and Jesus standing on the right hand of God, . . .
>
> And they stoned Stephen, calling upon God, and saying, Lord Jesus, receive my spirit.
>
> And he kneeled down, and cried with a loud voice, Lord, lay not this sin to their charge. And when he had said this, he fell asleep.[8]

The sun itself can be corrupted by those who cannot see their place in a larger design than they are capable of making.

> So does the eye of Heaven itself become an evil eye, when incapable or sordid hands are interposed between it and the things it looks upon to bless. (p. 112)

This passing observation, dropped into the midst of the description of a Coketown world, becomes the source and centre of the entire novel to which we now turn our attention.

[1]Harald Höffding, *A History of Modern Philosophy: A Sketch of the History of Philosophy from the Close of the Renaissance to Our Own Day,* Vol. 2, trans. B. E. Meyer (New York: Dover, 1955), p. 367.

[2]Höffding, p. 419, p. 418.

[3]Charles Knight, *Passages of a Working Life* (1873 ed.), Vol. 3, pp. 187-8.

[4]Acts 6:12-13.

[5]Acts 7:51-54.

[6]Paul E. Gray, "Introduction," *Twentieth Century Interpretations of HARD TIMES* (Englewood Cliffs, N.J.: Prentice-Hall, 1969), p. 9.

[7]Engel, *The Maturity of Dickens,* p. 172.

[8]Acts 7:55, 59-60.

"WHAT'S YOUR MORAL GAME?" LITTLE DORRIT

Lying is against the rules: children are not supposed to lie to their parents, and they are supposed to believe their parents if or when their parents lie to them. Yet parents may feel guilty to tell the truth, are often embarrassed by it, and may even come to believe their own lies: this can become diabolical.

RONALD D. LAING

•

Hamlet. . . . What have you, my good friends, deserved at the hands of Fortune that she sends you to prison hither?
Guil. Prison, my lord?
Hamlet. Denmark's a prison.
Ros. Then is the world one.
Hamlet. A goodly one; in which there are many confines, wards, and dungeons, Denmark being one o' th' worst.
Ros. We think not so, my lord.
Hamlet. Why, then 'tis none to you; for there is nothing either good or bad but thinking makes it so. To me it is a prison.

WILLIAM SHAKESPEARE

•

"The world has narrowed to these dimensions."

LITTLE DORRIT

•

William Blake's "Songs of Innocence" and "Songs of Experience" present "two contrary states of the human soul," each essentialized, and each embodied in a central image or set of images. In the one case, we find Innocence; the image is of the lamb, or the child as lamb, totally trusting, passive, gentle, pure and joyous and located in a world which cares well for it and prizes the above qualities; in the other case the image is of the earth imprisoned and in chains, all the colours change (e.g. from white and green to grey and red) and children find themselves in a totally strange and hostile world. The poem which introduces "Experience" presents a dialogue between the "Holy Word" (both God's and the Poet's, which are the same) and the "lapsed soul." Let me quote the first two stanzas of each speaker:

"O Earth, O Earth, return!
Arise from out the dewy grass;
Night is worn,
And the morn,
Rises from the slumberous mass.

"Turn away no more;
Why wilt thou turn away?
The starry floor,
The Wat'ry shore,
Is giv'n thee till the break of day."

EARTH'S ANSWER

Earth rais'd up her head
From the darkness dread & drear.
Her light fled,
Stony dread!
And her locks cover'd with grey despair.

"Prison'd on wat'ry shore,
Starry Jealousy does keep my den:
Cold and hoar,
Weeping o'er,
I hear the father of the ancient men.[1]

What has happened to Earth here we would describe today as alienation. Earth has come to feel itself out of place and victimized; it sees itself as imprisoned by forces which Earth has chosen to regard as inimical and which it may even have created itself, and which are therefore within Earth's control. We have then two states, one in which the will is unrestrained, an innocence terrifying because it takes no account whatever of pain and mortality; the other a totally inhibited will that is locked into its self-made delusion, the conviction that redemption and joy are denied it by what is outside, what is projected. "Innocence" without "Experience" becomes solipsism and "Experience" without "Innocence" becomes despair. It is somehow necessary to bring together these "contrary states," to achieve a perception that can reconcile them and ultimately transcend them by that perception, to acquire a vision that

> Joy and Woe are woven fine,
> A clothing for the Soul divine,

as Blake says, for only such a unifying vision heals the wound of our separateness and harmonizes us with the world. Such a vision would produce that concentricity of a human being bringing himself to a common axis with the turning world, as though clay were to centre itself on the potter's wheel. The spiritual power to which Blake's vision aspires and towards which Dickens' later work tends is not unlike the Satori or enlightenment of Zen, or the ataraxia or internal peace of Stoicism. This is surely the note on which *Little Dorrit* ends, with the hero and heroine like an island of stillness in a tempestuous sea. The achievement of *Little Dorrit* is this power to convey to the reader a sense of ever-narrowing focus on spiritual truth and discovery in the midst of apparent turmoil and chaos. All of Dickens' creative energy becomes absorbed in this necessity to convey individual moral redemption. The theme becomes not how to destroy the probably indestructible Circumlocution Office and the other forms of social madness, but how to Be, in spite of them.

It seems not to be possible to read criticism of *Little Dorrit* that does not deal with or at least mention prisons and families, as J. C. Reid rightly points out.[2] Especially since Lionel Trilling's brilliant essay, prisons have been found everywhere. Hillis Miller has pushed this reading furthest by saying, that in this novel the world is a prison and that prison is here a state of mind. But Miller fails to reconcile these two impressions of the novel. Dickens is either saying that the world is by its nature a prison, so it doesn't matter what one's state of mind is, which would be a despairing point of view, or he is saying it is a prison because we see it as one. What Dickens is certainly not doing is elaborating a contradiction, that the world is a prison by its nature with man as its inmate by his nature, while at the same time man is imprisoned merely (or not merely but totally, tragically if one prefers) by his state of mind. Miller's confusion, or blurring of his brilliant insights, illustrates how far we still are (in spite of all the prisons and families and images discovered and listed) from really having a sense of the whole novel, of its unity and the cohesion of its moral vision. I cannot help thinking that the reason for this difficulty lies in the unwillingness, even at this advanced stage of Dickens criticism, to trust the intelligence and respect the profundity of Dickens' vision. Even Hillis Miller's superb book is not free from some patronizing quality that seems strangely traditional on this subject.

My own view is that by the time Dickens writes *Little Dorrit* he has pushed his search for the sources and nature of evil and suffering to the point where he is looking for the element common to all aberration and self-delusion and he is coming to a frankly religious answer. It is of Dickens' mind at work in this novel that Lionel Trilling says,

> It is an imagination under the dominion of a great articulated idea, a moral idea which tends to find its full development in a religious experience.[3]

Little Dorrit's initials, A.D., stand just as surely for Anno Domini as they do not in *Dombey and Son*, where they stand for "Anno Dombei—and Son." Amy, whose name means love, is as much a Christ-child as a prison-child (she is quite designedly both) and it is John Baptist Cavelletto whose name and nature signal to the reader the coming of A.D. in the novel. To discover the significance of Amy Dorrit we must first see the world from which Arthur Clennam comes, try to discover the link between all the inhabitants of that world, and try to perceive the relation between the worlds ruled by Mrs. Clennam, Merdle, Casby and Dorrit.

I

Book I of *Little Dorrit* is called "Poverty" and Book II is called "Riches." Poverty and riches are, like prisons, the result of kinds of perception. Poverty is the problem, riches is the answer; both terms are used ironically. The poverty of the first book is not merely financial and the riches of the second book turn out not to be financial at all. "Poverty" begins in Marseilles, which is chosen by Dickens because it contains a greater variety of races and peoples than any other place he knows. It serves well, therefore, as a terrestrial microcosm, rather in the manner of the "Pequod," the ship captained by Ahab in *Moby Dick*. This microcosm intention is made quite explicit by Dickens.

> Hindoos, Russians, Chinese, Spaniards, Portuguese, Englishmen, Frenchmen, Genoese, Neopolitans, Venetians, Greeks, Turks, descendants from all the builders of Babel, come to trade at Marseilles, . . . (p. 1)

I shall return to Babel in a moment. Just as "Poverty" and "Riches" are ironically contrasted, so are "Sun and Shadow," the title of the opening chapter. All through the novel sun and shadow become ways of speaking about world-distorting myopia or liberating focus. Sun and shadow seem mutually exclusive but we shall see that they are not, just as "Fellow Travellers," the opening title of the second Book, seems to suggest companions but actually describes those who may be invisible to each other. In *A Christmas Carol* Dickens speaks of Christmas as a time

> . . . in the long calendar of the year, when men and women seem by one consent to open their shut-up hearts freely, and to think of people below them as if they really were fellow-passengers to the grave, and not another race of creatures bound on other journeys. (*A Christmas Carol*, p. 10)

The opening chapter of Book II suggests that riches have not produced that awareness, but rather have obscured it.

> Up here in the clouds, everything was seen through cloud, and seemed dissolving into cloud. The breath of the men was cloud, the breath of the mules was cloud, the lights were encircled by cloud, speakers close at hand were not seen for cloud, though their voices and all other sounds were surprisingly clear. Of the cloudy line of mules hastily tied to rings in the wall, one would bite another, or kick another, and then the whole mist would be disturbed: with men diving into it, and cries of men and beasts coming out of it, and no bystander discerning what was wrong. (p. 433)

It is an image of a world in chaos because of a blindness induced by being up in the clouds. Riches have placed these fellow-travellers at the top of a pinnacle crowned by a monastery, a tourist attraction, yet their acquisition of the means to travel seems to have placed them not nearer to but further from heaven. This brings us back to the Babel of the opening chapter, for Babel was likewise designed to get men off the earth and up to Heaven. Babel is one of the great mythological landmarks of alienation. Its origin lies in the desire of men to be gods, in their mistrust of God and their dislike of the earth and their own humanity, and in the consequent desire for other worlds. The punishment inflicted by God is most perfectly designed to fit the crime and follows naturally and inevitably from it. Having become alienated first from God and then from the Earth, man's next step, as long as the process is not reversed, is to become alienated from his fellow. This is why the common language ceases to be a bond and becomes a series of barriers.

As Marseilles lies "burning in the sun" we see in the opening chapter a Babel-like world. Men can no longer speak to each other, can no longer see each other and are out of tune with their world. It is an image of opposites, of war between the planets, in which the earth regards itself as victimized by the sun; we have gone from flood to fire. Man hides away. Like the earth in Blake's poem, this earth regards itself as "prisoned on a watery shore." Only one figure in this scene seems odd and his presence there is our clue to Dickens' dissociation from the images of Marseilles and its Babel-like imprisonment. John Baptist Cavalletto, like his Biblical counterpart and namesake, is the sign of an alternative and the signal of something else to come in the novel. In effect the prison contains two antithetical inmates, Rigaud, the devil, and John the Baptist. It is not an allegory pursued very far by Dickens, but it is clear enough to provide a suggestive framework for the novel. That Rigaud is a human devil has been widely noticed by readers. He is ubiquitous throughout and always appears to serve those whose veiled purposes have need of him. He continually changes his name yet is always easily recognized. He collects secrets and gains his power through the moral weakness of his victims. His evil appears to be connected with his absolute isolation and his complete self-justification, unresponsive to any code of common humanity or sympathy. " 'It is my humour to . . .' " etc. He is contrasted to his companion in every way. Cavalletto is reconciled to his world and his prison and so seems not to be in prison at all. He is tanned brown by the sun while Rigaud has hands that are "unusually white," except for the grime on them. Cavalletto is not a victim of time—" 'I can wake when I will, I can sleep when I will. It's all the same.' " (p. 3)—and yet he seems perfectly aware of his place in the temporal and spatial scheme of things: " 'I always know what the hour is, and where I am.' " (p. 4)[4] Finally, while Rigaud is all rôle (the "gentleman," the gallant who loves the ladies and murders them) Cavalletto remains entirely himself, rôle-free and in this respect more like Little Dorrit than anyone else in the novel. It is fitting that one so free of the demonic himself should know the devil so well and be able to find him at the last when no one else knows where he is.

II

Satan strives to be God and rule Heaven only to find that he is in Hell. Eve and Adam wish for the wisdom and immortality of gods and thus bring about the victory of death and their exclusion from the non-prison of Eden. Babel is built to guarantee the unity and safety of men and make them as gods and it produces precisely the converse effect—weakening and separating man from man. Jonah tries to run away from God and be free from duty and responsibility and finds himself inside the whale, at the bottoms of the mountains, and conceives that "earth with her bars was about me for ever." (Jonah 2:6) The paradox seems very persistent in myth and literature. The earth and our humanity may seem imprisoning, but in our attempt to escape them we confirm misconception or create new prisons. We are caught in a multiple bind if we regard our condition as cosmically imprisoning. Such a vision is naturally intolerable and men will seek ways to escape it, but of course, since this view of one's situation originated from within oneself it is impossible to escape it after one has projected such a scheme outside, objectified it. We think it comes from out there, but it comes from in here. It can be changed only in here. Every escape venture merely confirms the sense of confinement and victimization. Our prisons become increasingly complex and inescapable, as though one were to be more and more entangled in one's own knitting by a struggle to escape, all the while convinced that some invisible "Thing" or force is winding us around. This

"Thing," this monster of our own making, is called Nobody (a figure very similar in concept to Blake's Nobodaddy) and is the reason for the original title to *Little Dorrit*. The knitting analogy breaks down when one realizes that the true horror of this irony lies, as I have said, in there being no skein of wool at all—the tangle we are in is pure fantasy. Believing we are punished or victimized, we punish or victimize ourselves and thus confirm our original error. This is why Miss Wade is included as a clear case-history of paranoia. It explains Mrs. Clennam and her particular God created by her to punish her and thus justify her to herself. We wish to be gods because we cannot be human. We cannot be human as long as we wish to be gods. We are continuously cast out of Eden because we cannot accept the terms of our tenancy. Yet we learn what those terms are only by being expelled. The Fall is a metaphor defining our uniqueness. We learn the value of our humanity by our suffering in trying to be something else—if we will learn. This is what Arthur must do and does. Amy and Arthur, like Milton's Adam and Eve, go into the world hand in hand. Innocence and Experience marry to produce as a unity a new order of peace and harmony that can enter the "usual uproar" yet remain apart from its vanity because it is finally reconciled to its humanity.

It is strange that the full import of Dickens' original title has escaped the critics. Consider the following account of "Nobody" from Dickens' "Nobody, Somebody and Everybody" in *Household Words*,

> The power of Nobody is becoming so enormous in England, and he alone is responsible for so many proceedings, both in the way of commission and omission; he has so much to answer for, and is so constantly called to account; that a few remarks upon him may not be ill-timed.[5]

Dickens goes on to illustrate some characteristic social horrors of stupidity and incompetence, attributable to Nobody. Now this Nobody that Dickens has capitalized is not simply an ironic equivalent to Not Anybody. Nobody is a positive, dynamic phantasm that acquires a terrible life and force of its own from the minds of millions of projectors. Nobody is a public figure. Nobody comes to acquire a life of its own and remains the central concept of the novel in spite of Dickens' change of title.

> "[*Little Dorrit*] has a pleasanter sound in my ears, and . . . is equally applicable to the same story."[6]

"Equally" but not more so, for everything in *Little Dorrit* is infected by the living presence of Nobody. What form does this emanation take? Nobody is every Scheme, every Design, every Office, Plan, Air Castle, Form, Jargon, Formula behind which men shelter to protect themselves from the challenge of freedom, behind which they sustain their illusion of being victimized and imprisoned by forces beyond their control, behind which they screen themselves from the God who spoke to Jonah. Nobody may be the system projected by the psychotic like Miss Wade, in which case Nobody becomes Everybody, an identical projection since it too makes the Ego the only persecuted reality. Nobody may be the Past, as it is for Arthur, who excuses his lack of will or courage by this account, or it may be Society, which "forces" people to act in the way that they have decided that they wish to act, as in the case of Mrs. Merdle and Mrs. Gowan. Dickens has incorporated virtually every kind of rationalization into his satire. He has omitted none of the major forms that Nobody assumes: Government and the Barnacles, who merely play out the rôles assigned by a projected System; art as practised by Gowan; paranoia as practised by Miss Wade and Tattycoram who are the victims of "Social Prejudice" (orphans or bastards, illustrating a nineteenth-century minority group syndrome); Puritan religion as practised by Mrs. Clennam; Finance in the Merdles; Society in the Dorrits and Mrs. Merdle (who are intimately related by attitude even before the marriage of Fanny and Sparkler); National Chauvinism as practised by Bleeding Heart Yard, and so on and on and on. All of these constructed frameworks are prisons designed to protect. *Little Dorrit* is not the first novel in which Dickens explores this phenomenon and reveals his fascination with the idea of people retiring voluntarily to a prison from which they have been freed. In *Nicholas Nickleby* many of the freed children return to Squeer's school, and in *Barnaby Rudge* the prisoners return to the gutted Newgate. For Dickens these are merely extreme examples, syntheses, of the human desire for various forms of confinement and the abhorrence of and incapacity for freedom. Dickens deliberately puns on the word "form" in a dialogue which takes place in the Marshalsea Prison after Clennam has been incarcerated there:

> "No doubt there's a certain form to be kept up that it's for something else, but it's only a form. Why, good Heaven, we are nothing but forms! Think what a lot of our forms you have gone through. And you have never got any nearer to an end?"
> "Never," said Clennam. (p. 736)

The paper is only the outward and visible sign of the Circumlocution Office, whose purpose is to prevent things being done ("How not to do it") and it is only fitting therefore that the paper forms should serve to preserve the inactive rigidity of the larger form, the institution itself. The same is true of the form of debate in Parliament when the Office is defended. It is a vast, distracting, protecting game played on a national scale but emanating, as suggested above, from a human racial characteristic, a cosmic game that species play. Dickens knows that if the Circumlocution Office seems to victimize and frustrate, it also serves a widespread wish for it to non-function as it does. On the same grounds the men who are respected are those who are closed, so to speak, encased in form. "All buttoned-up men are weighty. All buttoned-up men are believed in." (pp. 565-66) This link between form, prison and respectability is thoroughly explored. Mrs. General not only has a military name but regards existence as requiring conduct along regimented lines. Her system of manners and language is explicitly protective and the following quotation is framed in language that illustrates its content, the alliteration reminding the listener of a dictionary, the words following each other like uniformed soldiers in procession, with Mrs. General in command:

> "A truly refined mind will seem to be ignorant of the existence of anything that is not perfectly proper, placid, and pleasant." (p. 477)

Mrs. Merdle is a form, a shape, and has been purchased to display jewels like a store-window dummy.

> It was not a bosom to repose upon, but it was a capital bosom to hang jewels upon. Mr. Merdle wanted something to hang jewels upon, and he bought it for the purpose. (p. 247)

To find the woman behind this form would be next to impossible. She agrees to be what Edith Dombey would not be:

> The very diamonds—a marriage gift—that rose and fell impatiently upon her bosom, seemed to pant to break the chain

> that clasped them round her neck, and roll down on the floor where she might tread upon them. (*Dombey and Son*, p. 563)

Mr. Merdle, like his wife, like Nobody and like the fortunes he controls, is simply not there.

> Let Mrs. Merdle announce, with all her might, that she was at Home ever so many nights in a season, she could not announce more widely and unmistakably than Mr. Merdle did that he was never at home. (p. 398)

And this is true of his usual guests, who are not people but forms or rôles or sets of characteristic gestures or words or labels like Bishop or Bar. Such a system of evasion, withdrawal and protection prevails from the noble Bar to the humble and lowly Rugg who is likewise a connoisseur of prisons.

> "This is an extensive affair of yours; and your remaining here where a man can come for a pound or two, is remarked upon, as not in keeping. It is *not* in keeping." (p. 740)

The prison-pun on the phrase "in keeping" illustrates the growing complexity of Dickens' language. It seems a fantastically, albeit unwittingly, cruel remark to make to one in Arthur Clennam's state of mind and is deliberately meant to grate on the reader. The Bleeding Heart Yarders can be infected by Merdle fever because they are no freer from the escape-syndrome, from moral escapades, than anyone in a higher social group. It is thus that they can be taken in by Casby, who is a miniature Merdle in himself and his own person rather than in his accoutrements or in a wife, and of whom Pancks can say, as though to express an aphorism for the entire novel, " 'You're one of a lot of impostors that are the worst lot of all the lots to be met with.' " (p. 800) Yet Pancks himself is not free from the worship of a shadow and it is only after he has himself been sheared by Merdle that he develops the courage of sufficient anger and frustration to expose Casby, an act not so much of castration, as Trilling suggests, as of revelation, of comic humiliation, and though the effect is certainly to make him impotent, it is an impotence produced by stripping away false appearance. Even Arthur is subject to the delusion of speculation. He is deluded by the evidence of abstration, as Pancks is hypnotized by his mathematical reckoning. Abstract reasoning may thus be seen to make one blind; it is employed to reinforce one's withdrawal from reality. It becomes one more elected imprisoning system. It is only the last evidence of Arthur's characteristic blindness. Only Doyce, who is to the world of business what Amy is to the family and society, is free from all these widespread delusions, and even he was not always so. Once Doyce thought he could penetrate the system of confusion, the maze of the Circumlocution Office. He realized, however, that he was augmenting the bureaucracy by illustrating its efficiency in prevention and was being used by it rather than vice-versa. The result was rapidly becoming his own destruction. Doyce is a practical man, a creator, an artist, a man at home with his tools and his work, who in the midst of his designs seems to reflect the larger designs of his Creator.

> His dismissal of himself from his description, was hardly less remarkable. He never said, I discovered this adaptation or invented that combination; but showed the whole thing as if the Divine artificer had made it, and he had happened to find it. So modest he was about it, such a pleasant touch of respect was mingled with his quiet admiration of it, and so calmly convinced he was that it was established on irrefragable laws. (p. 516)

Doyce is the antithesis of the alienated, he has no place in Babel, is thoroughly at home all the time (unlike Merdle) and rather than wanting to be a god he experiences a kind of joy in his humility in the face of "irrefragable laws." So different is he from those who have created the Babel-world of England that he must go to some virtually fairy-tale place where they value

> . . . practical men, who could make the men and means their ingenuity perceived to be wanted, out of the best materials they could find at hand; and who were as bold and fertile in the adaptation of such materials to their purpose, as in the conception of their purpose itself. (p. 672)

Doyce is the only man to speak categorically against "speculating," for he knows that it kills the present in its hopes of a future and distracts from the reality of action under one's human control, which is why the creative hand is mentioned in this quotation:

> "If I have a prejudice connected with money and money figures," continued Doyce, laying that plastic workman's thumb of his on the lappel of his partner's coat, "it is against speculating." (p. 673)

If money, Society and bureaucracy may be used to distract man from and confirm man in an erroneous view of his relation to the Cosmos, and in doing so become new prisons which may then again be attributed to Nobody, Religion would seem to be ideally suited to similar purposes. Perhaps more simply than in the other systems, Religion is able to take a false view of man in the world and create false images which are then worshipped as the truth to reinforce the original lie. Dickens explains this clearly.

> Verily, verily, travellers have seen many monstrous idols in many countries; but no human eyes have ever seen more daring, gross, and shocking images of the Divine nature, than we creatures of the dust make in our own likenesses, of our own bad passsions. (p. 775)

That Mrs. Clennam has the capacity to design sets of imprisoning conditions and responses is seen with penetration and admiration, appropriately enough, by Rigaud, himself an expert in perceiving evil and rationalization.

> "Thereupon full of anger, full of jealousy, full of vengeance, she forms—see you, madame!—a scheme of retribution, the weight of which she ingeniously forces her crushed husband to bear himself, as well as execute upon her enemy. What superior intelligence!" (p. 773)

Again the words "form" and "scheme." Mrs. Clennam is the forerunner of her logical extension in Miss Havisham, the supreme archetype of self-incarcerated and demonic pride, the totally alienated who having made herself a god proceeds to war with all mankind because one failed to worship her. Mrs. Clennam likewise cannot contemplate her inadequacies and having failed to be a woman must become a god, for she is indeed the god of retribution that she has made and her disguise is very thin.

> "And so, a graceless orphan, training to be a singing girl, carries it, by that Frederick Dorrit's agency, against me, and I am humbled and deceived!—Not I, that is to say," she added quickly, as colour flushed into her face; "a greater than I. What am I?" (p. 779)

The god which she makes is like the one made by those at Babel, projected from a mind miserable with itself and its limitation, unwilling to accept the condition of its humanity and needing a tyrant to justify its misery and mistrust. It is the disease of Satan, who, living in Heaven itself, would see God as tyrant. It is a form of idolatry, for idols are gods that man can make.

> Yet, gone those more than forty years, and come this Nemesis now looking her in the face, she still abided by her old impiety —still reversed the order of Creation, and breathed her own breath into a clay image of her Creator. (p. 775)

There is a good deal of irony in Dickens' portrait of Mrs. Clennam and her self-punishment, from his describing her luxurious "invalid regimen of oysters and partridges" to the deliberate echo of Mrs. General, " 'I am also shut up from the knowledge of some things that I may prefer to avoid knowing,' " (p. 184) for one of the incidental "benefits" of her system is a safe alienation from this world and its continuous challenges. It would be a mistake to think that Mrs. Clennam is unusual or even really differentiated from much less dramatic or powerful figures in the novel. Dickens wishes us to understand, not her peculiarity, but her typicality.

> Thus was she always balancing her bargain with the Majesty of heaven, posting up the entries to her credit, strictly keeping her set-off, and claiming her due. She was only remarkable in this, for the force and emphasis with which she did it. Thousands upon thousands do it, *according to their varying manner*, every day. (p. 50, my italics)

Like Mrs. Clennam, Mr. Dorrit cannot resist playing the rôle of a very minor and pathetic sort of god. He reminds me a great deal of Little Nell's grandfather. Blinded by self-delusion, compensating himself for suffering which he had no small part in producing (there are hints that his concluding crash with Merdle was foreshadowed by careless dealings which put him into the Marshalsea), he has a wonderful knack for hurting, even ruining, those he loves.

> Nothing would have been wanting to the perfection of his character as a fraternal guide, philosopher, and friend, if he had only steered his brother clear of ruin, instead of bringing it upon him. (p. 222)

His treatment of Amy is fully exposed by Dickens and requires no documentation here. He makes whole worlds of unreality which he then presides over like a benevolent, whimsical or tyrannical dictator, as the mood takes him, from old Nandy and the whole Marshalsea to the Alpine inn and the great tombs of houses in Italy with their retinues of servants. Dickens reveals how powerful is the capacity for self-delusion, how strong the unreal can be:

> Not a fortified town that they passed in all their journey was as strong, not a Cathedral summit was as high, as Mr. Dorrit's castle. Neither the Saone nor the Rhone sped with the swiftness of that peerless building; nor was the Mediterranean deeper than its foundations; nor were the distant landscapes on the Cornice road, nor the hills and bay of Genoa the Superb, more beautiful. Mr. Dorrit and his matchless castle were disembarked among the dirty white houses and dirtier felons of Civita Vecchia, and there scrambled on to Rome as they could, through the filth that festered on the way. (p. 636)

It should now be clear that the construction of imprisoning worlds is closely related to the existence of the festering filth that goes unnoticed under our feet as we take shelter in constructions which we falsely believe protect us. It is Mr. Dorrit's self-delusion which finally exposes him. Failing to realize that the past is part of ourselves, that we are not gods to alter the nature of time and space willy-nilly, and that we cannot " 'sweep it off the face of the earth and begin afresh,' " (p. 479) he cannot accommodate a part of himself and his experience that will not be repressed and finally emerges to overwhelm him.

There are many other forms of imprisoning self-delusion stemming from an alienated perception in *Little Dorrit*, including the comic version (Bleeding Heart Yard and Meagles) and romantic love (Flora and young John Chivery). The central case as a case is of course Miss Wade's. She suffers from what today we would popularly call paranoia. In clinical psychology paranoia actually refers to the systematic quality of the victim's delusion and since it is most frequently applied to delusions of persecution we always use it to refer to that. What I have been describing all through this chapter is really such a paranoia. It may stem from anything, or rather be constructed on any chosen base: being jilted, being imprisoned for debt, having one's "merits" ignored (Gowan), being patronized (Fanny) or simply being born after Adam and Eve and therefore being human, the almost universal case. Or it might be being born illegitimate or orphaned, a sort of exposed and unprotected form of being born into the world, which is used as the initial justification of paranoid fear and hostility. That such a fear and torment are akin to or conducive to a death-wish is illustrated by Fanny's continually wishing herself dead. Not only is death the only reconciliation with nature available to such a mind but it is also the only appealing answer to a world made intolerable by one's sense of misplacement in it. It is in this reading that Merdle's suicide is explained. The classic case of this kind in English literature is Edmund (*King Lear*) who projects a god who will "stand up for bastards." The case here is Miss Wade, and her paler reflection in Tattycoram, who serves to fill out the picture and who is shown in a state of such turmoil that her case appears almost pathological.

> The visitor stood looking at her with a strange attentive smile. It was wonderful to see the fury of the contest in the girl, and the bodily struggle she made as if she were rent by the Demons of old. (p. 26)

It would not be surprising to discover that "The History of a Self-Tormentor" is the first thorough clinical account of a paranoiac in English. Miss Wade only explicitly accentuates what has been clear all along. What is Mrs. Clennam but a self-tormentor, or Merdle, or even Arthur in a sense? But the terrifying Miss Wade is the extreme illustration. She is so locked into her system that all things conspire to substantiate her diseased and anguished loathing of everybody. It is a self-fulfilling perception of an alien world. The distance from Babel to Miss Wade's apartment is but a step. The Other, sinister and hostile, be it a god or one's fellow-man, can never be accepted.

If Miss Wade uses her birth to shut herself up in a prison of fear and hate, Arthur may be said to use his past.

> There was the dreary Sunday of his childhood, when he sat with his hands before him, scared out of his senses by a horrible tract which commenced business with the poor child by asking him in its title, why he was going to Perdition?—a piece of curiosity that he really in a frock and drawers was not in a condition to satisfy—and which, for the further attraction of his infant mind, had a parenthesis in every other line with some such hiccupping reference as 2 Ep. Thess. c. iii. v. 6 & 7. There was the sleepy Sunday of his boyhood, when, like a military deserter, he was marched to chapel by a picquet of teachers three times a day, morally handcuffed to another boy; and when

> he would willingly have bartered two meals of indigestible sermon for another ounce or two of inferior mutton at his scanty dinner in the flesh. There was the interminable Sunday of his nonage; when his mother, stern of face and unrelenting of heart, would sit all day behind a bible—bound, like her own construction of it, in the hardest, barest, and straitest boards, with one dinted ornament on the cover like the drag of a chain, and a wrathful sprinkling of red upon the edges of the leaves—as if it, of all books! were a fortification against sweetness of temper, natural affection, and gentle intercourse. There was the resentful Sunday of a little later, when he sat glowering and glooming through the tardy length of the day, with a sullen sense of injury in his heart, and no more real knowledge of the beneficent history of the New Testament, than if he had been bred among idolaters. There was a legion of Sundays, all days of unserviceable bitterness and mortification, slowly passing before him. (pp. 29-30)

This superb passage, famed for its evocation of the English Sundays that million of readers recognized, is the way in which Clennam now sees his past, decades later, as he drifts almost purposelessly back to "home." Unable now to act, unmarried and unable to bridge his deep loneliness, Arthur explains himself as having no will, and excuses his frozen middle-age with something akin to self-pity.

> "I have no will. That is to say," he coloured a little, "next to none that I can put in action now. Trained by main force; broken, not bent; heavily ironed with an object on which I was never consulted and which was never mine; shipped away to the other end of the world before I was of age, and exiled there until my father's death there, a year ago; always grinding in a mill I always hated; what is to be expected from *me* in middle life? Will, purpose, hope? All those lights were extinguished before I could sound the words." (p. 20)

His embarrassment at the opening phrase is a sign of his intelligence and self-awareness, for being able to say he has no will amounts to a denial of the truth of the statement. Arthur uses the past to justify his non-engagement in the present. He is responsible for projecting onto the world the indifference of his own distorting perception no less than the other characters in the novel. Thus the irony of his self-exploration is clear:

> "From the unhappy suppression of my youngest days, through the rigid and unloving home that followed them, through my

> departure, my long exile, my return, my mother's welcome, my intercourse with her since, down to the afternoon of this day with poor Flora," said Arthur Clennam, "what have I found!" (p. 165)

Naturally, nothing. When he does happen upon Amy he does not "find" her, does not see her, plays the rôle of father in order to protect himself against the challenges of love, of relating. In fact, he commits the sin of depersonalizing her by casting her in the rôle of heroine in a fantasy that reads like a Charlotte M. Yonge story of self-denial. He fictionalizes her.

> He heard the thrill in her voice, he saw her earnest face, he saw her clear true eyes, he saw the quickened bosom that would have joyfully thrown itself before him to receive a mortal wound directed at his breast, with the dying cry, "I love him!" and the remotest suspicion of the truth never dawned upon his mind. No. He saw the devoted little creature with her worn shoes, in her common dress, in her jail-home; a slender child in body, a strong heroine in soul; and the light of her domestic story made all else dark to him. (p. 382)

It is interesting that his one gesture of romantic love, after the disappointing renewal of acquaintance with Flora, is towards a girl who is unattainable, Pet; and Dickens gently emphasizes the self-delusory quality of this affair by reverting to the Nobody concept in a chapter called "Nobody's State of Mind." Clennam too has created a Nobody, who can not-act in his stead. Arthur is a good, gentle man who has found no meaning to his own existence and rationalizes his personal inadequacies by using his upbringing quite consciously to excuse himself. When Pancks, playing the rôle of moral inquisitor, asks Arthur what man was made for there is no answer forthcoming.

> "But I like business," said Pancks, getting on a little faster. "What's a man made for?"
>
> "For nothing else?" said Clennam.
>
> Pancks put the counter question, "What else?"
>
> It packed up, in the smallest compass, a weight that had rested on Clennam's life; and he made no answer. (p. 160)

The answer in the novel is love and life itself, joy and woe woven fine. Only after he has speculated and all but ruined his partner, and after he has found his way inside the prison, can Clennam lose the scales from his eyes and come alive to the truth and his own feelings. He has been an outsider and his entering the gaol is precisely similar to Jonah's entering the whale. First despair and then repentance and finally reconciliation to the limitations of being human make the "prison," earth, no prison at all.

> Duty on Earth, restitution on earth, action on earth; these first as the steep steps upward. Strait was the gate and narrow was the way; far straiter and narrower than the broad high road paved with vain professions and vain repetitions, motes from other men's eyes and liberal delivery of others to the judgment—all cheap materials costing absolutely nothing. (p. 319)

Yet Clennam's persistent search for a wrong from the past which he might right is itself a form of self-evasion, a vanity. The past can neither be eliminated nor used to excuse the present, which is why Arthur never learns the secret of his origins, because Amy rightly regards this as irrelevant and destroys the information. The past must be used for understanding both the self and the present and then incorporated into the capacity, the courage to be.

> "If, in the by-gone days when this was your home and when this was your dress, I had understood myself (I speak only of myself) better, and had read the secrets of my own breast more distinctly; . . ." (p. 760)

Clennam almost loses the best thing in his life and only Dorrit's speculation and the consequent loss of riches brings Amy and Arthur together.

Amy, Little Dorrit, is the only person in the novel actually born and raised in a prison. This is designed to suggest that she is different from others only in her total reconciliation to her human condition. For her, prison is home, a state of nature, and therefore no prison at all. Love and duty are enough to free her and she can pass in and out of the prison at will. Amy is the embodiment of love and devotion and compassion and represents Dickens' ultimate statement on Christianity in the humanist form which he endorsed. In *The Life of Our Lord* he interprets for his children the New Testament thus:

> "There is a child born to-day in the City of Bethlehem near here, who will grow up to be so good that God will love him as his own son; and he will teach men to love one another, and not to quarrel and hurt one another."[7]

When Little Dorrit preaches to Mrs. Clennam she says something very similar.

> "O, Mrs. Clennam, Mrs. Clennam," said Little Dorrit, "angry feelings and unforgiving deeds are no comfort and no guide to you and me. My life has been passed in this poor prison, and my teaching has been very defective; but, let me implore you to remember later and better days. Be guided only by the healer of the sick, the raiser of the dead, the friend of all who were afflicted and forlorn, the patient Master who shed tears of compassion for our infirmities." (p. 792)

Love and compassion in present social action and growing naturally out of an unshakeable integrity and wholeness are the clues to Amy's personality. Where others have moral games she has no games at all. She is simply herself at home in the world, unthreatened and therefore unprotected by forms. The contrasted responses to Pet's illness at St. Bernard might stand as illustration for the two modes of being revealed in the novel.

> "Pray let me call my maid," cried the taller of the young ladies.
>
> "Pray let me put this water to her lips," said the shorter, who had not spoken yet. (p. 436)

It is hardly surprising that nobody notices Little Dorrit, that she is left behind at the prison, that she troubles Mrs. General and the family, that she cannot learn the forms and system which she does not need. She does not fit into an alienated world.

> ". . . our tastes are evidently not her tastes. Which," said Mr. Dorrit, summing up with judicial gravity, "is to say, in other words, that there is something wrong in—ha—Amy." (p. 474)

Pushed much further this difference between Amy and her world would make her an enemy of the state or a candidate for a mental institution where she might be normalized. The two titles from which Dickens chose, while they are antithetical, do in fact stand equally well for the novel. On the one hand there is *Little Dorrit,* Amy, integrity, love, humility, acceptance, and on the other is "Nobody's Fault," alienation, rejection, pride and illusion and all the imprisoning systems and projections and forms which they create.

The novel begins with the image of Babel and ends with the

image of Adam and Eve, reconciled by their human love to their humanity and its new-found limitations composed of both joy and woe, and following the fall from riches—"going, going, gone." Just as poverty and riches are central to the ironic exploration of states of mind, of perceiving in the novel, even more significant is the use of light and shade. The opening chapter is called "Sun and Shadow" and reveals a world in which the sun, symbol of divine, "irrefragable law" is an enemy. The people of this world are like Mrs. Clennam, who is cut off from the seasons, of which she is an integral part, and thus crippled by choice.

> "All seasons are alike to me," she returned, with a grim kind of luxuriousness. "I know nothing of summer and winter, shut up here. The Lord has been pleased to put me beyond all that." With her cold grey eyes and her cold grey hair, and her immovable face, as stiff as the folds of her stony head-dress,—her being beyond the reach of the seasons, seemed but a fit sequence to her being beyond the reach of all changing emotions. (p. 34)

The Babelites of Marseilles, the port through which those scattered upon the face of all the earth pass without communication, seek the shade for protection. Yet this is the same sun and shadow of the novel's last paragraph.

> They went quietly down into the roaring streets, inseparable and blessed; and as they passed along in sunshine and shade, the noisy and the eager, and the arrogant and the froward and the vain, fretted, and chafed, and made their usual uproar. (p. 826)

So thoroughgoing is the imagery of sun, shadow, light, dark, joy, woe, cosmic law and human alienation, that Dickens can slip in the phrase "as certainly as the sun belongs to this system," (p. 489) when describing Rigaud's swagger as belonging to him. Evil has its own irrefragable laws as part of the whole. So much for any theory that serial publication weakens artistic control. Like everything else which the novel explores, sun and shade reflect the mind of the perceiver. Shadow may be light and sunshine may be blinding or punishing. When Amy returns to Arthur the prison shadow becomes for him too a light, "As they sat side by side, in the shadow of the wall, the shadow fell like light upon him." (p.

758) The sights of the city may be transformed by love to a vision of Jerusalem and Christ's example is fulfilled in human perception.

> As they crossed the bridge, the clear steeples of the many churches looked as if they had advanced out of the murk that usually enshrouded them and come much nearer. The smoke that rose into the sky had lost its dingy hue and taken a brightness upon it. The beauties of the sunset had not faded from the long light films of cloud that lay at peace in the horizon. From a radiant centre over the whole length and breadth of the tranquil firmament, great shoots of light streamed among the early stars, like signs of the blessed later covenant of peace and hope that changed the crown of thorns into a glory. (p. 793)

Amy brings sunshine with her as she brings the neglected and rejected with her into the prison, her home, "Little Dorrit, simply dressed as usual, and having no one with her but Maggy, came into the prison with the sunshine." (p. 824) When Arthur and Amy are united in love, the sun and the shadow and the image of Christ melt into an epiphany. "And they were married, with the sun shining on them through the painted figure of Our Saviour on the window." (p. 825) The image of the sun, which is the same sun as in the first chapter, linked to the married couple at the altar by the passage of its light through the "window" of Christ is as contracted and complete an image of the entire concept of spiritual quest as any symbolist could wish. We have seen Paradise lost and regained from the first chapter to the last. Yet the terms here are all existential, as Dickens comes to be increasingly persistent in the presentation of marriage as the metaphor of human fulfillment. The man and woman, joined in love, understanding and self-knowledge, provide in their union in Dickens' later novels the sense of an almost classical resolution, a ritual redemption as the divine takes human form, as harmony is achieved in a wedding of minds and hearts. The painted image of Christ *becomes* the living A.D., taking to herself the saved Arthur Clennam, who has indeed found his Holy Grail, and the whole is illuminated by the sun, the eye of Heaven, the master symbol of Divine System and "irrefragable law."

I have tried to show how Dickens has pursued to a new level of profundity his quest for the sources of evil and aberration and for moral response. Returning to the great Biblical archetypes of racial alienation, he examines the natural responses to life and to being human that lead to the endless impostures that compose most social activity. To be human is first to be born, the evidence of our separateness and the source of our alienation, and then to die, the evidence that we are not gods and the source of compassion and brotherhood. We are all in the same whale. The prison into which Little Dorrit is born is transformed into a home by her love, duty and humility. Hers is the only magic that can transform our presence on Earth from grim captivity to welcome lodging. Until we perceive this choice we multiply our prisons. Not only is there no Nobody, but there is not, could we but see it, even the Fault. This is Dickens' vision, who would conclude with Blake that

> It is right it should be so:
> Man was made for Joy and Woe:
> And when this we rightly know
> Thro' the world we safely go.[8]

[1]"Songs of Experience: Introduction," stanzas 3 & 4; "Earth's Answer," stanzas 1 & 2.

[2]*Charles Dickens: LITTLE DORRIT* (Studies in English Literature, 29), (London: E. Arnold, 1967).

[3]"Introduction," *Little Dorrit* (London: Oxford Univ. Press, 1953), p. xv.

[4]I have elsewhere pointed out many of the influences of Dickens on William Faulkner ("Dickens and Faulkner: The Uses of Influence," *Dalhousie Review* 49 (Spring 1969): 69-79.) While working on this book I have seen many more. One of the most interesting is the creation of a Christian, Stoical figure like Dilsey who clearly recalls Cavalletto (as well as Amy) by knowing a time that is God's time and not accurately measured by clocks.

> On the wall above a cupboard, invisible save at night, by lamp light and even then evincing an enigmatic profundity because it had but one hand, a cabinet clock ticked, then with a preliminary sound as if it had cleared its throat, struck five times.
>
> "Eight o'clock," Dilsey said. She ceased and tilted her head upward, listening.
>
> (*The Sound and the Fury*. New York: Modern Library, 1946, p. 290)

[5]Quoted in John Butt and Kathleen Tillotson, *Dickens at Work*, p. 229.

[6]*Dickens at Work,* p. 230. [Footnote 1. To Mrs. Watson, 10 Nov. 1855. (*The Dickensian*, June 1942, p. 166.) Mrs. Watson was one of the few to whom he had confided the original title.]

[7]Charles Dickens, *The Life of Our Lord* (London: Associated Newspapers, 1934), p. 14.

[8]William Blake, "Auguries of Innocence," *Poems from the Pickering MS*, lines 51-54.

"THE RESURRECTION AND THE LIFE" A TALE OF TWO CITIES

Hate is not the opposite of love; apathy is.

ROLLO MAY

•

God Appears & God is Light
To those poor Souls who dwell in Night,
But does a Human Form Display
To those who Dwell in Realms of day.

WILLIAM BLAKE

•

And I brought you into a plentiful country, to eat the fruit thereof and the goodness thereof; but when ye entered, ye defiled my land, and made mine heritage an abomination.

JEREMIAH 2:7

•

I am the Resurrection and the Life, saith the Lord: he that believeth in me, though he were dead, yet shall he live: . . . the glorious sun, rising, seemed to strike those words, that burden of the night, straight and warm to his heart in its long bright rays.

A TALE OF TWO CITIES

•

The growing intensity of Dickens' attempt to force art into the shape of an apprehensible vision of redemption and of human existential possibility for meaning is clearly discernible in *A Tale of Two Cities*. Here history is rendered into myth, psychology is given profoundly moral implications and theology is converted by metaphor into humanism. The effort leads Dickens close to the centre of Christian orthodoxy. At the end of *Little Dorrit* we see the sun, symbol of divine universal order, shining through the image of Christ, link between God and man, upon the married couple, redeemed by a love for each other made possible through self-awareness and reconcilement with their human situation on earth. In *A Tale of Two Cities* it is as though such a vision were not enough for Dickens. He seems to wish for an even greater integration of the Divine and the Human, to want to wrench the materials of art into a reality of salvation, a realization through the fact of fiction of the fullest human possibilities. The use of historical materials and the urgency of the author's moral purpose produce problems of disunity and artificiality that recall the almost discursive and allegorical quality of *Hard Times*.

The desire to analyze and integrate the damned and the redeemed in metaphor is the cause of the doubleness which is at the centre of this novel. For convenience one might think of the whole novel as springing from this passage:

> Now, from the days when it was always summer in Eden, to these days when it is mostly winter in fallen latitudes, the world of a man has invariably gone one way—Charles Darnay's way—the way of the love of a woman. (p. 123)

We are led to realize, if we follow the implications of this and trace similar overtones in the novel, that Dickens is interpreting the myth of the Fall in humanistic terms. The two cities of the novel are certainly Paris and London but just as certainly are they the cities of the mind, Babylon and Jerusalem, the city of man and the city of God. The problem of the radical visionary, the artist who refuses to shelter in theology, is to find a metaphor which will accomplish the translation of the one into the other. The Babel of *Little Dorrit* has become the world as Babylon. Let us examine how Dickens sees the modern Babylon. It is, of course, a world of false Gods. The aristocrats in the first place are themselves absolute demonic gods and have been "reading the Lord's Prayer backwards for a great number of years." (p. 223) Reading the Lord's Prayer in this way is a characteristic of the Devil's party, the totally alienated. They are false gods as represented by the Marquis St. Evrémond, whose callous brutality is able to snuff out life easily, but unable to bring back life as an ironic allusion to the resurrection theme suggests.

"He has paid all, Monseigneur. He is dead."
"Well! He is quiet. Can I restore him to you?" (p. 110)

This attitude of absolutely inhuman indifference and murderous *laissez-faire* is shared equally by Charles' father, Marquis Two, twin brother to the Marquis who is murdered in his bed.

> "As I turned my eyes to the elder brother, I saw him looking at this handsome boy whose life was ebbing out, as if he were a wounded bird, or hare, or rabbit; not at all as if he were a fellow creature." (p. 307)

We come to the Republic and we find again that it replaces the God who could demand of Abraham the sacrifice of Isaac.

> "If the Republic should demand of you the sacrifice of your child herself, you would have no duty but to sacrifice her." (p. 301)

The destroying guillotine has replaced the salving cross and all things in God's order have become inverted.

> It superseded the Cross. Models of it were worn on breasts from which the Cross was discarded, and it was bowed down to and believed in where the Cross was denied. (p. 260)

We are reminded of Milton's poem in a passage on the Carmagnole which suggests the poet's description of the fallen Angels cast into Hell yet retaining traces of an earlier state.

> It was so emphatically a fallen sport—a something, once innocent, delivered over to all devilry—a healthy pastime changed into a means of angering the blood, bewildering the senses, and steeling the heart. Such grace as was visible in it, made it the uglier, showing how warped and perverted all things good by nature were become. The maidenly bosom bared to this, the pretty almost-child's head thus distracted, the delicate foot mincing in this slough of blood and dirt, were types of the disjointed time. (p. 265)

The Saints that have attained Divine Grace through the full achievement of their humanity now are reduced to ignominy as in Saint Antoine where "cold, dirt, sickness, ignorance, and want, were the lords in waiting on the saintly presence," (p. 28) and the churches themselves are now "churches that are not my father's house but dens of thieves." (p. 353) Indeed Christianity itself participates fully in the inversion of Jerusalem into Babylon as in this image of France.

> Under the guidance of her Christian pastors, she entertained herself, besides, with such humane achievements as sentencing a youth to have his hands cut off, his tongue torn out with pincers, and his body burned alive, because he had not kneeled down in the rain to do honour to a dirty procession of monks which passed within his view, at a distance of some fifty or sixty yards. (p. 2)

But England is no different. Not only is life itself of no account but the human form itself is bereft of its sacred dignity.

> "Ah!" returned the man, with a relish; "he'll be drawn on a hurdle to be half hanged, and then he'll be taken down and sliced before his own face, and then his inside will be taken out and burnt while he looks on, and then his head will be chopped off, and he'll be cut into quarters. That's the sentence."
>
> "If he's found Guilty, you mean to say?" Jerry added, by way of proviso.
>
> "Oh! they'll find him guilty," said the other. "Don't you be afraid of that." (p. 57)

What we find running through this novel is a portrait, Breughel-like, of a society gone wild, mad, chaotic in which all the humane values of Christian civilization have been inverted.

> . . . musketeers went into St. Giles's, to search for contraband goods, and the mob fired on the musketeers, and the musketeers fired on the mob, and nobody thought any of these occurrences much out of the common way. (p. 3)

This then is the Fallen City that pervades the novel like a living presence; but somehow at the same time, in a kind of simultaneous double-image, there is another city present to our awareness, a city in the making but always unrealized, offered to our apprehension as a visionary conception. It is like the other city that London is in Wordsworth's "Sonnet on Westminster Bridge," the sleeping city that will come awake and yet retain its purity and beauty and tranquility only when the human imagination can transcend the human sense of alienation and see the Divine order of which it is part. Wordsworth expresses for me best, what I see as Dickens' moral aspiration. For those who can attain to this vision by dint of continuous striving for understanding through the exercise of thought and feeling,

. . . the highest bliss
That can be known is theirs, the consciousness
Of whom they are habitually infused
Through every image, and through every thought,
And all impressions; hence religion, faith
And endless occupation for the soul
Whether discursive or intuitive;
Hence sovereignty within and peace at will
Emotion which best foresight need not fear
Most worthy then of trust when most intense.
Hence cheerfulness in every act of life
Hence truth in moral judgements and delight
That fails not in the external universe.[1]

What Wordsworth describes is in Dickens a form of Redemption, and to suggest that Sidney Carton attains it is to reveal the distance in *A Tale of Two Cities* between Dickens' intention and his achievement. Obviously Wordsworth describes a life-time process and Dickens is forced to fall back on a Scrooge-like conversion. When we come to the last complete novel we shall see how close Dickens comes to the convincing presentation of such a redemptive understanding-in-process. In Carton we see the completed image of one who has achieved "sovereignty within and peace at will" and "cheerfulness in every act of life" and "truth in moral judgements." It is through Carton that our first glimpse of the other city, the potential Jerusalem, is first attained, quite early in the novel.

> Waste forces within him, and a desert all around, this man stood still on his way across a silent terrace, and saw for a moment, lying in the wilderness before him, a mirage of honourable ambition, self-denial, and perseverance. In the fair city of this vision, there were airy galleries from which the loves and graces looked upon him, gardens in which the fruits of life hung ripening, waters of Hope that sparked in his sight. A moment, and it was gone. (p. 85)

Here the two images, the Garden and the desert, are brought together in a single act of imagination. It is a vision anticipating the final prophecy, the final affirmation of the redemptive faith kept alive as long as one man can sustain it.

> "I see a beautiful city and a brilliant people rising from this abyss, and, in their struggles to be truly free, in their triumphs and defeats, through long long years to come, I see the evil of

> this time and of the previous time of which this is the natural birth, gradually making expiation for itself and wearing out." (p. 357)

If there are four cities, not two, in the novel's title and theme, there is also a pun in the "Tale" of this novel, for there is evidence in the text to suggest this. When the gaoler Barsad comes to bring Darnay away, the following dialogue takes place:

> "Don't fear me. I will be true to the death."
>
> "You must be, Mr. Carton, if the tale of fifty-two is to be right." (p. 335)

Now Dickens knows that the word "tale" for tally or reckoning is archaic in his day and he can afford to offer it as a normal usage because this is an historical novel. The richness of the irony in this scene is achieved then by the reverse pun of the title, for the "tale of fifty-two" is another way of describing the book itself which is a tale (story) or tale (reckoning) made "right" both numerically and morally by Carton's sacrificial death. So in *A Tale of Two Cities* we have reference to a moral tally or assessment of two images of human existence, the relative moral nature of the cities of Heaven and Hell. We appear then to have at least two tales of four cities.

The overall effect of the double moral vision embodied in the myth of two cities is achieved through a complex series of interwoven duplicities. There is, as we have said, the sense of alternate, parallel but antithetical cases on a grand, even universal scale.

> . . . two immense processions, one ever tending westward with the sun, the other ever tending eastward from the sun, both ever tending to the plains beyond the range of red and purple where the sun goes down! (p. 147)

Beyond this there are all the more obvious human doubles in the novel. Darnay thinks of the past and present as inseparable when embodied in the two brothers, his uncle and father.

> "Why need I speak of my father's time, when it is equally yours? Can I separate my father's twin-brother, joint inheritor, and next successor, from himself?" (p. 117)

Here doubleness is used deliberately to suggest the sameness of recurring facsimiles of rapacious and brutal inhumanity. In a land governed by such rulers Christ appears as a kind of skeletal figure, "a new large figure of Our Saviour . . . dreadfully spare and thin." (p. 110) Darnay has his own double in the figure of Carton, a likeness which saves his life in the second major insertion of the resurrection theme.

> "What a change you have made in yourself! A good reason for taking to a man, that he shows you what you have fallen away from, and what you might have been! Change places with him, and would you have been looked at by those blue eyes as he was, and commiserated by that agitated face as he was? Come on, and have it out in plain words! You hate the fellow." (p. 79)

To understand fully the resurrection theme in the novel one must turn to Jerry Cruncher, for he holds the key to the mystery that links the themes of doubleness and life and death. Cruncher is much linked with Christianity and it is clear that we are meant to understand him as a parody of Christ, a parody adapted to Dickens' savage presentation of a Christian world that has sold itself to false gods and to Satan. Thus it is that in a world built on Christian language but without the faith and vision, without belief in Divine order and moral salvation, the great Christian myth is reduced to figure of speech and the metaphysical mysteries are reduced to blasphemous literalities. Thus it is that Jerry Cruncher is one of that band of "tradesmen" known as "Resurrection-men," body-snatchers who raise the dead by robbing graves to supply the schools of anatomy. Jerry Cruncher's initials are those of Jesus Christ, but even more amusing is his ignorance of the origin of the myth of Christ's presence in his world signified by A.D.

> (Mr. Cruncher himself always spoke of the year of our Lord as Anna Dominoes: apparently under the impression that the Christian era dated from the invention of a popular game, by a lady who had bestowed her name upon it.) (p. 51)

Has Christianity become merely a "popular game"? Jerry's links with Christianity are emphasized by his wife's adverse and perverse "flopping" and the details of his christening, for

> His surname was Cruncher, and on the youthful occasion of his renouncing by proxy the works of darkness, in the easterly parish church of Houndsditch, he had received the added appellation of Jerry. (p. 51)

Now though his name is Jerry he was baptized Jeremiah, who, we remember, was the prophet foretelling and warning of the destruction of Jerusalem, one of our two Cities, because the people had departed from the ways of God and as a consequence would be held captive in Babylon. It is worthy of note in passing, how Dickens brilliantly impregnates his novel with apparently casual support for his moral themes; thus for instance the watchman of the novel's opening, referring to his horses, "could with a clear conscience have taken his oath on the two Testaments that they were not fit for the journey." (p. 5) The genius of Dickens thus makes Jerry Cruncher the link between the non-Christianity of the world portrayed and the theme of death and resurrection.

Dickens has by this time arrived at the stage of his moral quest when he must form something akin to a religious answer yet translate that answer into human terms, into a vision of possibility for existential faith and action that will work towards social alteration now. He must then force death and resurrection into a myth of the loving life. Survival is one form of defeating death. Regeneration and survival in the loving memory of those who live and come after, is another. Dr. Manette is recalled from a living burial and death to life. To him Darnay can say,

> "I know perfectly well that if you had been restored to her from the world beyond this life, you could hardly be invested, in her sight, with a more sacred character than that in which you are always with her." (p. 126)

Darnay is twice saved from death by his double.

> "Do you feel, yet, that you belong to this terrestrial scheme again, Mr. Darnay?"
>
> "I am frightfully confused regarding time and place; but I am so far mended as to feel that."
>
> "It must be an immense satisfaction!"
>
> He said it bitterly, . . . (p. 77)

Carton is brought to life from a living moral death by his love for Lucie, the guiding light that her name suggests. She says to him, " 'can I not save you, Mr. Carton? Can I not recall you . . . ?' " (p. 144) Roger Cly is believed dead and is alive, having escaped the tomb. But it is in Carton that Dickens seeks to embody the full force of his translation of the Christian metaphysic into humanistic terms. To allay any misunderstanding that might accuse his hero of a death-wish he has Carton plead with Manette to win Darnay a reprieve.

> "But try! Of little worth as life is when we misuse it, it is worth that effort. It would cost nothing to lay down if it were not." (p. 319)

Faced with the failure of this venture Carton must commit himself to an act that will reprieve his own moral failure in the past, that will render his existence into meaning and give his life point. It is interesting to note the echo from *Macbeth* that occurs in his contemplation of an eternal cycle of pointless slaughter that he must break with his sacrifice.

> In a city dominated by the axe, alone at night, with natural sorrow rising in him for the sixty-three who had been that day put to death, and for to-morrow's victims then awaiting their doom in the prisons, and still of to-morrow's and to-morrow's, . . . (p. 298)

If Jerry Cruncher is the Christ-parody, Carton is the Christ-human. When Lucie asked him earlier "Is it not . . . a pity to live no better life?" he answered "God knows it is a shame" and this is to be read quite literally. Now he must eradicate the shame. We are never allowed to forget that all the consequences of his act are realized in this world. Dickens will allow himself no theological wish-fulfillment. For himself Carton can say, " 'I see that I hold a sanctuary in their hearts, and in the hearts of their descendants, generations hence.' " (p. 358) More than that, he even achieves at last a kind of marriage, a theme Dickens will not allow to be absent in any of his novels. In the love and trust he finds in the condemned girl's dependence on his strength, he realizes finally the compassion, the human link through the sympathy of his own heart. "As the last thing on earth that his heart was to warm and soften to, it warmed and softened to this pitiable girl." (p. 337) Thus the New Testament words are given new meaning by Dickens in Carton's existential decision. " 'I am the resurrection and the life, saith the Lord: he that believeth in me, though he were dead, yet shall he live.' " (p. 298) It is Carton who at one moment, on the new cross which is the guillotine, transforms the city from Fallen into Redeemed, turns the guillotine into the instrument of salvation and looks through "the little window" into an endless union of Grace.

> They said of him, about the city that night, that it was the peacefullest man's face ever beheld there. Many added that he looked sublime and prophetic. (p. 357)

There are many features of *A Tale of Two Cities* to recall us to *Barnaby Rudge*. The relation of St. Evrémonde to his nephew is akin to Chester's to his son. The mob that accompanies the funeral of Cly might easily have come from the earlier novel, the period is the same, the same Guards disperse the same riots ready to erupt at any time and on any pretext. The same causes produce these social symptoms.

> Crush humanity out of shape once more, under similar hammers, and it will twist itself into the same tortured forms. Sow the same seed of rapacious licence and oppression over again, and it will surely yield the same fruit according to its kind. (p. 353)

What has been added to the subject, in addition to the elliptical style and the elaborate metaphors and the extraordinary conservation, is the perspective of a visionary artist. Here again, as in *Little Dorrit,* we are conscious of Dickens writing his tale against a background of irrefragable laws. Produce a certain cause, violate a certain order, and inevitable consequences follow, as suggested by Dickens' view of a Stoic Nature serving Divine ends: "the great magician who majestically works out the appointed order of the Creator, never reverses his transformations." (p. 353) Dickens' remaining problem is to translate these convictions into recognizable individual cases free from melodrama. How can a man be seen to arrange his life so as to come to a redemptive understanding of himself and to the consequent acceptance of his, and therefore everyone's, humanity? Dickens must return to the first person and to the ordinary young man who must learn what he is before he can realize what he might be. The moral surgery has not yet been radical enough. The path between the radical process and the moral vision has still to be further cleared.

[1]William Wordsworth, *The Prelude,* Bk. 4, lines 107-19.

"YOU MAKE YOUR OWN SNARES"
GREAT EXPECTATIONS

Oh! who is he that hath his whole life long
Preserved, enlarged this freedom in himself?
For this alone is genuine Liberty.

WILLIAM WORDSWORTH

•

The human race began to wither, for the healthy built
Secluded places, fearing the joys of Love,
And the diseased only propagated.

WILLIAM BLAKE

•

"Have you seen anything of London, yet?"

"Why, yes, Sir," said Joe, "me and Wopsle went off straight to look at the Blacking Ware'us. But we didn't find that it come up to its likeness in the red bills at the shop doors: . . ."

GREAT EXPECTATIONS

•

Just as *A Tale of Two Cities* brings into focus what was blurred or merely latent in *Barnaby Rudge,* so *Great Expectations* brings to fulfillment the moral implications of *David Copperfield* by the attainment of total control over the first-person narrative, an experiment begun in the earlier novel. The semi-private joke quoted above in reference to the "Blacking Ware'us" experience shows how far Dickens has come in understanding and mastering the past in his own case, how he is now able to confront and accept with good humour the most painful of personal experience which no longer has power over him, no longer "comes up to its likeness" as earlier "advertized." The novel suggests to us how firmly he has come to grasp the universal necessity of such self-awareness and the significance of honesty and self-knowledge for the moral life. Many elements of earlier novels are brought together and integrated in *Great Expectations*. Mrs. Clennam now becomes Miss Havisham, a much more significant and powerful agent and symbol. The doubling technique of *A Tale of Two Cities* is given a less obtrusive but no less vital role in *Great Expectations,* for part of Pip's moral quest is the confrontation of the most undesirable elements in himself embodied obliquely in others.[1] A number of critics have drawn attention to the opening images of *Great Expectations* and have pointed out the ironies of the title.[2] It still seems necessary, however, to come to grips with the profundity and universality of the opening. What Dickens does with his contemporary social class idiom, the phrase "great expectations," is to probe its moral implications ironically until he comes to the confrontation, to the encounter with the expectations of living, of life itself. The fact of Being-In-The-World carries with it the two polarized and inescapable possibilities that we have been examining: withdrawal and its thousand faces, and acceptance, the hero's quest.

At the novel's opening we are presented in the first instance with the image of birth, with the fact of simply being. It is as though Dickens has sought a metaphor for the suddenly finding oneself here, in the Now, stripped of all confusing qualifications, attachments and dependencies. Pip is an "infant," "a bundle of shivers," and once more we see the human being alone, surrounded by the bare essential facts of the earth, that is by the churchyard (death and the human search for consolation), the past (in the graves of his unknown relatives), and the non-human, the sea and the wind and the land. No scene that I know of in English literature conveys more clearly the weight of the most ancient questions, "who am I?" "why am I here?" The miserable Pip, whose very name is embryonic, then encounters "society" in the form of Magwitch. This transition is not gradual but instantaneous. That is to say that it too becomes one of the simultaneous facts of discovering that one is here. Pip is wrenched into the human community and meets in Magwitch all the concentrated implications of human inter-relatedness. Magwitch introduces Pip, by this encounter, to authority, to the presentness of the past, to crime and punishment, and to Pip's own feelings of fear and pity and the resulting loss of freedom which is the consequence of all of these. "Mag" means, among other things, to steal, and this stealing witch, this sorcerer, has it in his power to transform Pip's life. Pip is later to call Miss Havisham his "fairy godmother" but the real magician of this parable fairy-tale in nineteenth-century dress is the convict, Magwitch. Faced with choices, burdened by fear and obligation, what else is Pip undergoing but the Fall? First Birth, then Fall and finally Redemption through understanding and love: this is the story of *Great Expectations*. Even the hint of the redemption to come is contained in this first chapter, for the boy has the capacity to feel compassion for the man, the compassion that is later to reassert itself when Pip returns to the best impulses of childhood. What is Magwitch but another, larger, "bundle of shivers"? Pip returns home, the home to which he will return again at the end of the novel, to steal the food and file that the convict has demanded. In doing so he forges the irrevocable link that becomes the central fact of his story, and not only his but everyman's story, for it is the link of suffering and sin and need, as well as the link of love. The leg-iron worn by the prisoner haunts Pip forever and it is on this rich symbol of the common bondage of our human weakness that Dickens rests one half of his novel. The other half is focused on the file that Magwitch carries to his dying day, the file that suggests the redemption of sympathy and finally love, the file that severs the imprisoning chain, the file that the convict carries as others might carry a cross. What we have then, as suggested by the opening chapter, is not just the expectations that are social, not simply the irony of disappointment in position and wealth contrasted with the values of moral expectations, but something more profound: the expectations of life realized in understanding and meaning. Pip's progress is simply a thoroughly worked out "Parish Boy's Progress" towards the finding of a home in the world. Like David, Pip progresses towards the hearth. The fires of forge and hearth take on traditional meaning. The very word "forge" carries the weight of the novel's meaning. The irony of *Great Expectations* is that they are indeed great when most modest. Pip's desire to eradicate Magwitch from his past is part of Dickens' satire of the wish to be off this planet, to be in effect not human at all. Pip sees Magwitch as a dog.

> I had often watched a large dog of ours eating his food; and I now noticed a decided similarity between the dog's way of eating, and the man's. The man took strong sharp sudden bites, just like the dog. He swallowed, or rather snapped up, every mouthful, too soon and too fast; and he looked sideways here and there while he ate, as if he thought there was danger in every direction of somebody's coming to take the pie away. He was altogether too unsettled in his mind over it, to appreciate it comfortably, I thought, or to have anybody to dine with him, without making a chop with his jaws at the visitor. In all of which particulars he was very like the dog. (p. 16)

Later in the novel we find the comparison once again presenting itself to Pip's mind.

> He ate in a ravenous way that was very disagreeable, and all his actions were uncouth, noisy, and greedy. Some of his teeth had failed him since I saw him eat on the marshes, and as he turned his food in his mouth, and turned his head sideways to bring his strongest fangs to bear upon it, he looked terribly like a hungry old dog. (p. 312)

Pip has himself been compared by Pumblechook to a pig. He can escape this same alienated view of others only when he comes to see Magwitch as a man. Pip is first a pig, then a "finch" and finally a man when he sees his benefactor as a fellow man.

The birth imagery of the opening chapter is the making of a new person in another sense also. As Robert Partlow points out, the story of Pip must be remembered all the time as a story told by a middle-aged Pip.[3] The "infant" of the beginning is then actually created by the man of the conclusion. What we have is not simply Dickens' existential parable, but a work of art that paradigmatically illustrates itself, revealing that the existential fact is inextricably linked to the confrontation with one's own life. Living must be made into an art that renders the abstract into the concrete and art in turn illustrates the ideal process. The truth is made by the honest ordering of experience. Pip is made by Pip in the telling. By using the first person Dickens eliminates himself and this makes clear his moral-psychological conviction that the remaking of oneself by the confrontation with the past and one's own nature is essential to being fully alive and aware in the present.

The question of time is indeed central to the novel and to the moral issue of being in the present. Miss Havisham, who has stopped all the clocks at twenty to nine, has tried to opt out of time. By refusing to attempt any coordination with time's passage she becomes its victim twice, for she not only decays like everything and everyone else, but loses the present also by punishing herself in a form of extended petulance. Ironically, her refusal to live in the present makes her part of a continuous past. She is not merely symbolized by the monstrous vermin-ridden fungus that was once a wedding cake.

> The most prominent object was a long table with a tablecloth spread on it, as if a feast had been in preparation when the house and the clocks all stopped together. An épergne or centrepiece of some kind was in the middle of this cloth; it was so heavily overhung with cobwebs that its form was quite undistinguishable; and, as I looked along the yellow expanse out of which I remember its seeming to grow, like a black fungus, I saw speckled-legged spiders with blotchy bodies running home to it, and running out from it, as if some circumstance of the greatest public importance had just transpired in the spider community. (p. 78)

She is the wedding cake, and sees herself as an uneaten wedding feast, still-to-be-consumed.

> "Matthew will come and see me at last," said Miss Havisham, sternly, "when I am laid on that table. That will be his place—there," striking the table with her stick, "at my head! And yours will be there! And your husband's there! And Sarah Pocket's there! And Georgiana's there! Now you all know where to take your stations when you come to feast upon me." (pp. 81-82)

The wax-work (echoes of Jarley), the skeleton, the living embodiment of Death itself that Pip recalls and sees, are all embodied here in a figure who cannot do what Dickens' entire novel conspires to present as vitally necessary, that is, absorb and reconcile the past by compassionately accepting it into the present. Not to do so is not only to destroy oneself and others, it is to violate a Divine order.

> . . . in shutting out the light of day, she had shut out infinitely more; that, in seclusion, she had secluded herself from a thousand natural and healing influences; that her mind, brooding solitary, had grown diseased, as all minds do and must and will that reverse the appointed order of their Maker, I knew equally well. (pp. 377-78)

Nor is Miss Havisham merely an image of one who makes a tyrant of time by insisting on her victimization. She is also an explanation of how such horrors come to be. Here once again Dickens' sure grasp of the psychological origin of moral aberration is revealed. Miss Havisham was a "spoilt child," she was "too haughty and too much in love, to be advised by any one." (p. 171) What is she as an old woman but a "spoilt child?" It seems that this pride has made her the centre of her own world. The jilting damages her self-image and rather than accept the truth about herself, about her hurt pride, about her misplaced love, and about the falsity of the world's appearances, she sets out to punish mankind for not conforming to her wishes. Part of her punishment of the world is to hurt herself, as the child will bite itself when it cannot bite authority. Another part is to rear a girl-child to be an avenging woman. The chain of destruction and suffering is thus lengthened and strengthened. Miss Havisham has been and presumably is in love with herself, which accounts for the central presence of the Narcissus image of the mirror. "But prominent in [the room] was a draped table with a gilded looking-glass, . . ." (p. 52) Like Satan also then, who loves himself to the exclusion of God, she brings death into the world, hers is a killing instinct. She becomes for Pip the image of the dead past, as though his parents were to be resurrected, say by Jerry Cruncher, into the present.

> Once, I had been taken to see some ghastly waxwork at the Fair, representing I know not what impossible personage lying in state. Once, I had been taken to one of our old marsh churches to see a skeleton in the ashes of a rich dress, that had been dug out of a vault under the church pavement. (p. 53)

Magwitch and Miss Havisham, the father and surrogate mother of Estella and the "adoptive" parents of Pip, become the principal vehicles of the past in the lives of the children, a past that continually works its influences in the present. The past cannot be rejected, for when it is, as we have seen, it comes to dominate the present. Magwitch also succumbs to this error, nursing his revenge and, like Miss Havisham, working his retribution through an attempt to shape the future by creating an agent, an instrument of reprisal, in Pip. The obsessive involvement with the past focuses all action on an illusory future fulfillment and thus destroys the present.

Pip and Estella are thus parallel cases. Yet their stories are only exaggerations of a phenomenon that Dickens has shown throughout his work to be natural, one of the conditions of being born. The adult world will try to shape the future and rectify the past through its children. Children will be the instruments adults use to perpetuate themselves and in the case where the image to be perpetuated is a monstrous self-delusion, the child may be similarly distorted. Children may even come to look like their elders.

> In some of her looks and gestures there was that tinge of resemblance to Miss Havisham which may often be noticed to have been acquired by children, from grown persons with whom they have been much associated and secluded, . . . (p. 224)

Estella tells Miss Havisham that the latter's success in destroying all capacity for affection has been eminently successful. Pumblechook and his patronage are present in the novel to emphasize further this desire of adults to use children for entirely selfish reasons. This is why on two occasions at least the narrator recalls with resentment the ruffling of his hair by arrogant adults.

> And then he would rumple my hair the wrong way—which from my earliest remembrance, as already hinted, I have in my soul denied the right of any fellow-creature to do— (p. 90)

Mrs. Gargery also regards Pip and his bringing up by hand as a means for puffing her own reputation as a self-sacrificing figure and as an excuse for her wilful bad-temper and sadism. Only Joe and Herbert and Biddy and perhaps Wemmick seem interested in Pip as a separate and loveable entity. Estella not only is conscious of her powerlessness to shape her own destiny, she even seems to embrace, albeit bitterly, her passivity, so well-trained has she been.

> "Oh, you must take the purse! We have no choice, you and I, but to obey our instructions. We are not free to follow our own devices, you and I." (p. 251)

Pip, too, as he becomes aware of his situation, increasingly sees himself and Estella as made by somebody else and without freedom to decide. It is as though he were always forced to react rather than act. To Estella he says, " 'You speak of yourself as if you were some one else.' " (p. 252) He imagines himself in reversed rôles with Frankenstein, so that he is not only the man pursued by the monster, he *is* the monster, the creature of someone else's imagination at the same time.

> The imaginary student pursued by the misshapen creature he had impiously made, was not more wretched than I, pursued by the creature who had made me, and recoiling from him with a stronger repulsion, the more he admired me and the fonder he was of me. (p. 320)

Dickens' brilliant application of Mary Shelley's plot to his own metaphor is worth analyzing. Pip, unlike the student, is pursued not out of hostility on the part of the "monster" Magwitch but out of love and admiration. As Magwitch's "creature," Pip thus becomes the monster and the pursued, which is an ironic comment on his monstrous pride and ingratitude. Since, however, he regards Magwitch as a monster pursuing him we must be conscious of the parallel we noticed before in the animal imagery, that is, that Pip is a monster as long as Magwitch is a monster. When Pip's perception is altered *he* is altered. Pip and Estella are merely then magnified versions of us all, men and women, enlarged that we may see the power of the past which becomes a force over us by our being born. It cannot be rejected or forgotten or pushed away, for of necessity we shall lose the fight to eliminate it and it will overwhelm us just as it overwhelmed Mr. Dorrit, who wanted to sweep it all away and just as it tyrannizes Miss Havisham.

The answer to this question is not new to the readers of these chapters. More and more insistently Dickens points to a rigorous self-examining honesty as the beginning of self-acceptance and thence the love and compassion which alone redeem. The file is a stronger link than the leg-iron. *Great Expectations* is for this reason in the first person; this is why the adult Pip must tell the story. In no prior novel has Dickens presented the story of a man's examination of himself with such systematic thoroughness. For instance, Pip is able to say that he knew his love for Estella to be a folly.

> I asked myself the question whether I did not surely know that if Estella were beside me at that moment instead of Biddy, she would make me miserable? I was obliged to admit that I did know it for a certainty, and I said to myself, "Pip, what a fool you are!" (p. 123)

The loneliness that commences with Satis House is not lessened but increased by the infatuation with Estella. She and her name are contrasted thematically as a coldness opposed to the warmth of the forge and the hearth. Her name is in the background when Pip looks at the remoteness of the stars in which there is no comfort.

> And then I looked at the stars, and considered how awful it would be for a man to turn his face up to them as he froze to death, and see no help or pity in all the glittering multitude. (p. 46)

Biddy on the other hand knows Pip better than he knows himself, as Agnes knew David, and as the narrator recognizes. What was painful enough when it happened takes on a great deal of humour, as does most of the novel, in the ironic but compassionate recollection. The adult Pip looks back at himself over the vastest distances and yet with intimate and poignant sympathy.

> "Hear me out—but if I were to remove Joe into a higher sphere, as I shall hope to remove him when I fully come into my property, they would hardly do him justice."
>
> "And don't you think he knows that?" asked Biddy.
>
> It was such a provoking question (for it had never in the most distant manner occurred to me), that I said, snappishly, "Biddy, what do you mean?" (p. 141)

It cannot all be remembered. Some mysteries remain. The degree to which inherited human nature itself is responsible cannot be separated from the influences that surround the child. In describing his conduct resulting from cowardice the "I" tells us,

> I had had no intercourse with the world at that time, and I imitated none of its many inhabitants who act in this manner. Quite an untaught genius, I made the discovery of the line of action for myself. (p. 37)

What remains after all is not finally attributing blame. The truth itself and the full recognition of the resulting state of mind are now paramount.

> How much of my ungracious condition of mind may have been my own fault, how much Miss Havisham's, how much my sister's, is now of no moment to me or to any one. The change was made in me; the thing was done. Well or ill done, excusably or inexcusably, it was done. (p. 100)

The "ungracious" is used advisedly, religiously. Pip describes the early state of his religious and spiritual awareness as a comic literal-mindedness.

> My construction even of their simple meaning was not very correct, for I read "wife of the Above" as a complimentary reference to my father's exaltation to a better world; and if any one of my deceased relations had been referred to as "Below," I have no doubt I should have formed the worst opinions of that member of the family. Neither were my notions of the theological positions to which my Catechism bound me, at all accurate; for I have a lively remembrance that I supposed my declaration that I was to "walk in the same all the days of my life," laid me under an obligation always to go through the village from our house in one particular direction, and never to vary it by turning down by the wheel wright's or up by the mill. (p. 39)

This ironic rendering of Heaven and Hell and the Catechism is not satire only of Pip but also of the conventional theology. Pip is not, in the course of the novel, to learn merely the usual meaning of these phrases but is to learn Dickens' humanizing rendering of them. "To walk in the same" is to love and honour Joe as he does when "I had a new sensation of feeling conscious that I was looking up to Joe in my heart," (p. 45) and it is to forgive his sister and to understand himself.

In confessing his attitude to Joe, Pip tells the truth relentlessly. There is no need for the critic to become exercised at Pip's snobbishness. Pip himself suffers at that very knowledge. "Let me confess *exactly*, with what feelings I looked forward to Joe's coming." (p. 206, my italics) The whole novel is an effort at "exactly." Pip knows that he has been guilty of rationalization and self-delusion,

> Their influence on my own character I disguised from my recognition as much as possible, but I knew very well that it was not all good. (p. 258)

yet he is tougher with himself than most people can be. Dickens, however, will permit redemption at no lower price. By the time we near the conclusion we see Pip making links between relationships and joining people in his mind without regard to category in a way that would have been impossible earlier. "I only saw in him a much better man than I had been to Joe." (p. 423) Finally Pip realizes that in the world he has judged, whatever shape it had has probably been given to it by himself, just as others in the novel have made their worlds into reflections of themselves.

> We owed so much to Herbert's ever cheerful industry and readiness, that I often wondered how I had conceived that old idea of his inaptitude, until I was one day enlightened by the reflection, that perhaps the inaptitude had never been in him at all, but had been in me. (p. 456)

In spite of all her evil, Miss Havisham is right in denying that she has ultimately had power to determine the lives of others.

> "I did. Why, they would have it so! So would you. What has been my history, that I should be at the pains of entreating either them or you not to have it so! You make your own snares. *I* never made them." (p. 341)

This is the painful truth. Not only does the past and its adult authorities and its ghosts try to shape us; it challenges us to free ourselves by forgiving it and absorbing it so that the suffering from this confrontation may be used in softening our response to ourselves and others. The future then is more free in proportion as we are reconciled to our past and alive to the possibilities of the present.

This is as far as Dickens can go in the use of this technique. The story of Magwitch, the secret benefactor, has one other parallel in the novel than that of Estella's being raised in "comfort" by Miss Havisham. Pip is the secret benefactor of Herbert, and it is worth examining the detailed account given as to why he should wish to play this rôle.

> I told him how we had first met, and how we had fought. I glanced at Herbert's home, and at his character, and at his having no means but such as he was dependent on his father for: those, uncertain and unpunctual. I alluded to the advantages I had derived in my first rawness and ignorance from his society, and I confessed that I feared I had but ill repaid them, and that he might have done better without me and my expectations. Keeping Miss Havisham in the background at a great distance, I still hinted at the possibility of my having competed with him in his prospects, and at the certainty of his possessing a generous soul, and being far above any mean distrusts, retaliations, or designs. For all these reasons (I told

> Wemmick), and because he was my young companion and friend, and I had a great affection for him, I wished my own good fortune to reflect some rays upon him, . . . (p. 281)

What we are given is a precise account of the circumstances and the motivation under which it is morally permissible to play at benefactor. Pip here engages in a simple act of generosity from love and remains secret only because the gift would not otherwise be accepted. There is no thought of making Herbert into anything, of using him for any personal scheme of one's own distorted vision. Gradually, with the commencement of this act, Pip comes to see more and more clearly where his actual satisfactions lie. "I had always wanted to be a gentleman, and had often and often speculated on what I would do, if I were one." (p. 140) Now that the die is cast Pip feels lonelier and more isolated than ever.

> . . . I drew away from the window, and sat down in my one chair by the bedside, feeling it very sorrowful and strange that this first night of my bright fortunes should be the loneliest I had ever known. (p. 137)

What Pip must strive for is a return, in a way, to childhood. One of his models is Wemmick, who never ceases to be a loving child to the aged P. Wemmick illustrates for us Dickens' sophisticated awareness and presentation of the two worlds that man somehow must live in at the same time. Let me quote a recent critic to show how easy it is to distort Dickens' purposes:

> Wemmick is a mechanical character because an inhuman dichotomy is the key, symbolic reality of his nature. He is a schematic and limited but poetic, embodiment of the utterly alienated man of modern capitalist civilization. . . . Walled impenetrably in the private world of the Englishman's castle, Wemmick can gratify normal human impulses in his bizarrely tender relationship with the Aged P; but in the world of business he is a sinister scavenger, willing to take his last possession from a man who stands condemned to death.[4]

Nothing could be further from the truth, from the spirit of Dickens' creation. Wemmick is one of Dickens' most attractive characters and it is natural that he and Pip should become friends out of mutual respect. There *are* Newgate, crime, sin, murder and the whole bag of human tricks, and Wemmick has managed to keep alive his own humanity and compassion in all of this. He is not a social worker or a revolutionary. He is a lawyer's clerk, a professional, and he does a professional job. That he is at home in Newgate is one of his human achievements, for what is this meant to signify if not an ironic contrast to Pip's proud superiority and squeamishness at the thought of his link with convicts and prison? Wemmick is at home in the two worlds that represent the two sides of human nature and he keeps them separate to avoid confusing them and in order to survive. Jaggers' washing of his hands has a similar force. Wemmick's success is a testimonial to his devotion. As for his taking "portable property" from the condemned, what is this but Dickens' way of demonstrating the man's grasp of reality, his rejection of false sentiment, his comic reconciliation with the fact of death and his amused affection for the dead rogues he has known? It is life Wemmick is interested in. Not only is he not alienated, he is one of the most integrated characters in the fiction. Would the critic have a surgeon return home from the hospital and practice on his family, or regard them as anesthetized, or conversely would he have him weep at every case brought to the operating room? Should an undertaker regard his children as corpses? That Wemmick has enough love and respect to honour his aged P. and enough courage to marry after all his Newgate work is an astonishing feat of his humanity. So much that Pip can say,

> I could not help wishing more than once that evening that Mr. Jaggers had had an Aged in Gerrard-street, or a Stinger, or a Something, or a Somebody, to unbend his brows a little. (p. 277)

Wemmick is very conscious of time, and is deliberately contrasted to Miss Havisham when he regularly fires a small cannon to mark the hours. Comic though he is, Wemmick holds for us the key to understanding what is necessary for Pip, whose reconciliation with his own humanity depends upon his uses of suffering, his acknowledgement of the bond that joins him with others, so that he may acquire the compassion that redeems, even while it grows from the pain of being in the world.

[1]See Julian Moynahan ("The Hero's Guilt: The Case of *Great Expectations*," *Essays in Criticism* 10(Jan. 1960):60-79) who refers to these figures, especially Orlick and Drummle, as "functional equivalents." There is so

much excellent criticism of *Great Expectations* that one could hardly acknowledge it all. The critic who would say something new must necessarily face the preliminary task of integrating much of what has already been written.

[2]See, for instance, Dorothy Van Ghent ("On *Great Expectations*," *The English Novel: Form and Function* (New York: Rinehart, 1953), pp. 125-38) and J. Hillis Miller (*Charles Dickens: The World of His Novels,* pp. 249-78.) Monroe Engel (*The Maturity of Dickens*, pp. 156-68) explains at length the presence of two echoes from *Paradise Lost,* in terms of expectations and the encounter with the fallen world.

[3]See "The Moving I: A Study of the Point of View in *Great Expectations,*" *College English* 23(Nov. 1961):122-31.

[4]Grahame Smith, *Dickens, Money, and Society* (Berkeley: Univ. of California Press, 1968), pp. 206-7.

"A MATTER OF FEELING"
OUR MUTUAL FRIEND

Surely there is enough reality to go round? Let us say: inside me is real, and inside *them* is real. It is real outside me and I am inside reality, and reality is inside myself. So where is unreality? Unreality does not exist, and does not *deserve* to exist.

RONALD D. LAING

•

Jesus answered and said unto him, Verily, verily, I say unto thee, Except a man be born again, he cannot see the kingdom of God.

Nicodemus saith unto him, How can a man be born when he is old? can he enter the second time into his mother's womb, and be born?

Jesus answered, Verily, verily, I say unto thee, Except a man be born of water and of the Spirit, he cannot enter into the kingdom of God.

ST. JOHN 3:3-5

•

Golden lads and girls all must,
As chimney sweepers, come to dust.

SHAKESPEARE

•

. . . an artist (of whatever denomination) may perhaps be trusted to know what he is about in his vocation, if they will concede him a little patience, . . . the whole pattern . . . is always before the eyes of the story-weaver at his loom.

OUR MUTUAL FRIEND

•

If Dickens had known for certain that *Our Mutual Friend* was to be his last completed novel he could not have more systematically collected all his major themes and metaphors and more precisely focused all his moral conclusions than he did. The poorhouse, the horrors of degrading indignity in the system of public "charity" from which Betty Higden runs, is here again presented so that the author seems to come full circle in his career. The drowning of *David Copperfield* is now made central and explicit; the Thames and all its associations of pollution and primeval slime and the moral identity of the protagonist are continued from *Great Expectations*; the doubling technique, presented in *A Tale of Two Cities* in Carton and Darnay, is here pursued as far as it can be; the Society of Mrs. General and Mr. Dorrit is found again in Veneering and Podsnap. The Bishop and Bar of the Merdle dinners now become at Veneering's,

> a Member, an Engineer, a payer-off of the National Debt, a poem on Shakespeare, a Grievance, and a Public Office, who all seemed to be utter strangers to Veneering. (p. 7)

Charlie Hexam is an unredeemed Pip and all the idle young men of all the novels are consummated in Eugene Wrayburn; even Fagin himself, the most singular of all the early characters, is resurrected in patriarch's clothing. But what is stunning upon discovery is the unity, the cohesion, the compounding of all these into a single, concentrated, moral theme. The novel is so taut that wherever one enters it one seems to be at the centre, for the centre is everywhere, for instance at the beginning.

Nicodemus was the Pharisee who came to Christ in the night and who asked the question about rebirth and was given the answer that heads this chapter. It was Nicodemus who brought the myrrh with which Christ was buried. Death by water and resurrection by water open the novel. "The Cup and the Lip," the first book, asks us to understand that there is "many a slip betwixt," but what has this to do with the novel's subject? Everything indeed, for this implied cup is the cup of life and between it and those who would drink at it lies the delicate moral balance that Dickens explores. If there is any doubt about this, Mr. Boffin's comment should dispel it.

"When the old man does right the poor boy after all, the poor

> boy gets no good of it. He gets made away with, at the moment when he's lifting (as one may say) the cup and sarser to his lips." (p. 89)

In *A Tale of Two Cities* we find a man redeeming his life but able to do so only by giving it up. *Our Mutual Friend* demonstrates how unsatisfactory Dickens found this. Now he must force the metaphor into conveying the sense of a death and a rebirth, not in the namesake of future generations, not in the memory of the loving survivors, but in the live, reborn man himself, in the act of living, in the realization of human communion. Dickens must kill John Harmon and resurrect him in the here and now at the same time. Consider for a moment the extraordinary nature of the plot that must be devised to bear the weight of this moral symbolism. The Hexams fish up a dead body in the Thames and John Harmon is, as far as this world goes, a murdered man with a reward posted for his killer. In reality the dead man is one George Radfoot, John Harmon's double. But the surviving double is a changed man and therefore in one real sense not John Harmon at all. Both men were thrown into the river and given up for dead, one returned and one did not. The one who returned comes back as John Rokesmith. John Harmon is thus dead and resurrected. He returns to his own name publicly only very late in the novel when he has, in his own mind, merited his original presence in the world. This is how Dickens presents his version of "except a man be born again, he cannot see the Kingdom of God" and "except a man be born of water and of the Spirit, he cannot enter into the Kingdom of God." The Kingdom of God is here the Grace of love that produces total loss of Ego and total commitment to another, the love of Bella and the love of the Boffins, which having been earned and returned, Rokesmith can once again be Harmon. This is how Dickens insists on rendering the death and resurrection stories of the Bible, in his novel.

> ". . . Pharaoh's multitude, that were drowned in the Red Sea, ain't more beyond restoring to life. If Lazarus was only half as far gone, that was the greatest of all the miracles." (p. 19)

Yet even then, at the very end, it is not the same John Harmon, but a man who gives the name Harmon a new meaning, a harmony without irony, just as Harmony Jail has been made into Boffin's Bower. Not only is this pattern of moral regeneration pursued throughout the novel in many characters, but the psychological processes by which this is possible are presented with more thoroughness and clarity and precision than anywhere else in Dickens' work.

Can a man take up Christ's challenge and remake himself? Can he be the parents of his own rebirth? One of the principal difficulties in his way is the presence and power of the past, especially as embodied in parents. We have seen Dickens struggling all along with the problem, in Clara Copperfield, in Mr. Dombey, in Miss Havisham, and now we see many instances of it in *Our Mutual Friend.* The most straightforward statement of Dickens' understanding in this regard is seen in his elaborate description of Pleasant Riderhood, where he confesses his inability to formulate a theory as to how environment and heredity conspire to produce a given character. His common sense tells him that no one can measure these influences.

> As some dogs have it in the blood, or are trained, to worry certain creatures to a certain point, so—not to make the comparison disrespectfully—Pleasant Riderhood had it in the blood, or had been trained, to regard seamen, within certain limits, as her prey. Show her a man in a blue jacket, and, figuratively speaking, she pinned him instantly. Yet, all things considered, she was not of an evil mind or an unkindly disposition. For observe how many things were to be considered according to her own unfortunate experience. Show Pleasant Riderhood a Wedding in the street, and she only saw two people taking out a regular license to quarrel and fight. Show her a Christening, and she saw a little heathen personage having a quite superfluous name bestowed upon it, inasmuch as it would be commonly addressed by some abusive epithet; which little personage was not in the least wanted by anybody, and would be shoved and banged out of everybody's way, until it should grow big enough to shove and bang. Show her a Funeral, and she saw an unremunerative ceremony in the nature of a black masquerade, conferring a temporary gentility on the performers, at an immense expense, and representing the only formal party ever given by the deceased. Show her a live father, and she saw but a duplicate of her own father, who from her infancy had been taken with fits and starts of discharging his duty to her, which duty was always incorporated in the form of a fist or a leathern strap, and being discharged hurt her. All things considered, therefore, Pleasant Riderhood was not so very, very bad. (p. 351)

Old Mr. Harmon not only mistreated his children but everybody else also, and his perverse, sadistic intention of influencing the future is shown both in his preoccupation with wills, a central symbol for what we are discussing, and in his selection of Bella as a kind of helpless inheritor. He notices Bella when she is being willful, spoilt and vicious, and it is this that appeals to him. He becomes, in spite of being dead, a brooding presence in the novel. Bella herself somehow reflects through the genius of her creator both the gentle loving propensity of her Pa and the willful, ambitious, complaining pretension of her Ma. That she gradually becomes entirely like the one and totally unlike the other is made clear by her husband's conviction at the end of the novel.

> Yet John Harmon enjoyed it all merrily, and told his wife, when he and she were alone, that her natural ways had never seemed so dearly natural as beside this foil, and that although he did not dispute her being her father's daughter, he should ever remain steadfast in the faith that she could not be her mother's. (pp. 807-8)

Georgiana Podsnap is another victim of parents and like Paul Dombey is not herself but "the young person," archetypalized by her father and her "rocking horse" mother. She is the frighteningly accurate portrait of that kind of Victorian English womanhood sheltered and protected and harassed out of existence or into madness or melancholia. Eugene Wrayburn is victim to "MRF" and knows enough of psychology from his own experience as a child to be able to portray Lizzie accurately to herself in her thoughts of her father, for she, too, is in need of liberation from misplaced guilt and loyalty that can become for the child a form of self-deceit. If the parent uses the child, the child also uses the parent, as Arthur Clennam for instance uses the past, as self-excuse. The true loyalty is to be oneself. Lizzie asks how her pride, her false pride as it is called, can cause her to do wrong to the memory of her father.

> "How to your father? Can you ask! By perpetuating the consequences of his ignorant and blind obstinacy. By determining that the deprivation to which he condemned you, and which he forced upon you, shall always rest upon his head." (p. 236)

It is a profound piece of psychoanalysis and reveals that Wrayburn can put "in its true light" the character of another, even though he cannot so readily alter his own.

The difficulty then is to discover oneself, examine with a scrupulous honesty one's relation to the past, to one's parents, to one's earlier self, and in so doing re-cast oneself in the role of ego-free, game-free, being. The capacity to do this remains a mystery. There is, of course, no quick course of instruction to ensure a success-or-your-money-refunded result. But Dickens knows that models of the process in literature are themselves a form of spiritual exercise. He cannot pinpoint the moment of conversion, indeed he wishes to move far beyond the conversion resorted to in Scrooge. His object is to show how the process, for it is now process more than conclusion, appears. The process in question involves a lifetime of experience and an infinity of genres that come to bear at every moment of time, but this does not stop Dickens from reaching for the images of moral redemption. The symbolic climax for Wrayburn is a battering on the head. Nothing less can break through his reserve. It is done most complexly in Bella and her struggle and it is deliberately not done in many other characters to illustrate the contrast of the redeemed and the unregenerate.

One chapter suffices to present in its most concentrated form Dickens' account of the actual process of self-examination and self-discovery. John Harmon has been murdered and reappears as Julius Handford.

> "A body missing?" asked Gaffer Hexam, stopping short; "or a body found? Which?"
>
> "I am lost!" replied the man, in a hurried and an eager manner. (p. 23)

From being "lost," Handford, after seeing himself dead in the police-station morgue, becomes Rokesmith, who tells Boffin, " 'I may say that I have now to begin life.' " (p. 97) The process of discovering everything that it is possible to know begins as the secretary:

> If, in his limited sphere, he sought power, it was the power of knowledge; the power derivable from a perfect comprehension of his business. (p. 193)

With the assistance of his falling in love voluntarily with the girl designed for him to marry without reference to his inclination, he is able to embark on the journey for himself, the quest which, during the walking vigil of one night, puts his past into perspective and his future on a moral basis—the effect is similar to Hamlet's sea-journey for the Prince. At first, as always, the searcher tends to proceed round well-worn tracks and end where he began. The process of self-evasion produces a captivity so that the world itself becomes in its circularity without end, a prison.

> "This is like what I have read in narratives of escape from prison," said he, "where the little track of the fugitives in the night always seems to take the shape of the great round world on which they wander; as if it were a secret law." (p. 365)

This echo of *Little Dorrit* is not an oddity in *Our Mutual Friend* and Dickens remains fully conscious of the relation of freedom and self-realization and of imprisonment and self-evasion. We are told that "Mr. Podsnap's world was not a very large world, morally; no, nor even geographically:" (p. 128) and when the compulsion and demonic passion of Headstone have reached their tormenting climax and the only points on his compass are the river-bank scene of his crime, the school with its accusatory pupils and the lockhouse on the weir, we are told that "To these limits had his world shrunk." (p. 796) It is a deliberate repetition of "the world has narrowed to these dimensions" in *Little Dorrit*. Finding himself going around and around the truth, finding the past too painful and frightening to face, and the future too challenging to endure, Rokesmith sets himself a psychological test.

> "But this is the fanciful side of the situation. It has a real side, so difficult that, though I think of it every day, I never thoroughly think it out. Now, let me determine to think it out as I walk home. I know I evade it, as many men—perhaps most men—do evade thinking their way through their greatest perplexity. I will try to pin myself to mine. Don't evade it, John Harmon; don't evade it; think it out!" (p. 366)

It is, as Dickens knows, the hardest task of all; none the less so for being abbreviated here. The chapter is called "A Solo and a Duett" and obviously refers to the man's dialogue first with himself and then with Bella, but the play on words, characteristic of this whole novel, here reaches a kind of high metaphysical wit. John Harmon was two, himself and George Radfoot, the double. Both were "drowned" but one came back to life.

> "This is still correct? Still correct, with the exception that I cannot possibly express it to myself without using the word I. But it was not I. There was no such thing as I, within my knowledge." (p. 369)

There follows a kind of birth struggle and suddenly John Harmon, freed of a "something," survives alone.

> " 'This is John Harmon drowning! John Harmon, struggle for your life. John Harmon, call on Heaven and save yourself!' I think I cried it out aloud in a great agony, and then a heavy horrid unintelligible something vanished, and it was I who was struggling there alone in the water." (p. 370)

In some way John has been two and is now one, "solo," and by being one is able now to be two, "duett." Both forms of being are song or "harmony" like his name, and the analogy is precise, for only by being in harmony with himself can he be whole enough to win the love of Bella, indeed convert Bella and with her make the marriage duett that is Dickens' redemptive fulfillment. To achieve a true union requires whole individuals first, unconstrained by external pressures for union. To be this one whole man, the purpose of the quest, requires forgiveness of the past. John Harmon returned from exile angry, hurt and afraid and engaging in a scheme to exchange himself for another in a deceit, the aim of which is to guarantee the present.

> "When I came back to England, attracted to the country with which I had none but most miserable associations, by the accounts of my fine inheritance that found me abroad, I came back, shrinking from my father's money, shrinking from my father's memory, mistrustful of being forced on a mercenary wife, mistrustful of my father's intention in thrusting that marriage on me, mistrustful that I was already growing avaricious, mistrustful that I was slackening in gratitude to the two dear noble honest friends who had made the only sunlight of my childish life or that of my heart-broken sister. I came back timid, *divided in my mind*, afraid of myself and everybody here, knowing of nothing but wretchedness that my father's wealth had ever brought about. Now stop, and so far think it out, John Harmon. Is that so? That is exactly so." (pp. 366-67, my italics)

Thus it is clear that Harmon must come to regard himself as responsible for the events that lead to the present and hold himself morally responsible for the future.

> "Now, is it all thought out? All to this time? Nothing omitted? No, nothing. But beyond this time? To think it out through the future is a harder though a much shorter task than to think it out through the past. John Harmon is dead. Should John Harmon come to life?"
>
> "If yes, why? If no, why?" (p. 372)

But if John Harmon's case is the most precise, the neatest instance of self-confrontation in Dickens, Bella Wilfer's is surely the most convincing and the most winning. It is hard to find a more attractive and completely believable woman in English literature. It is what Dickens has always worked towards and never before achieved. Bella is Dora and Agnes in one, she is Biddy and Estella joined, she is Amy and Fanny Dorrit brought into synthesis. Bella is never completely unpleasant and so the alterations in her are not surprising. She is capable of openness and generosity instinctively.

> With the natural tendency of youth to yield to candour and sweet temper, Miss Bella was so touched by the simplicity of this address that she frankly returned Mrs. Boffin's kiss. (p. 109)

Rokesmith's intervention in her life is timely. Having become himself he may now become her mentor.

> "No, I do not doubt it. I deserve the reproach, which is very just indeed. I beg your pardon, Mr. Rokesmith."
>
> "I should beg you not to do so, but that it shows you to such admirable advantage," he replied, with earnestness. "Forgive me; I could not help saying that." (p. 309)

By encouraging the best in her, by giving her time to do all by herself and not forcing any issue, Rokesmith becomes a silent guide. But it is Boffin, the Nicodemus who does good by stealth, the Noddy who acts a part, who performs the real therapy. Boffin makes a mirror of himself to be held up to Bella, which says, not you are the fairest of them all but you are in a fair way to becoming the ugliest. The now irresistibly attractive, self-possessed Bella presents Boffin as

> ". . . saying in your own mind, 'This shallow creature would never work the truth out of her own weak soul, if she had a hundred years to do it in; but a glaring instance kept before her may open even her eyes and set her thinking.' That was what you said to yourself; was it, sir?" (p. 775)

Bella's real sense of change comes at the time of Betty Higden's burial. Confronted with the awful reality of death and the moral preciousness of time, and with the image of Lizzie's devotion and goodness before her, Bella begins to feel her own inadequacies.

> "I shall be happy, Mr. Rokesmith," returned Bella, "to be of the least use; for I feel, after the serious scene of to-day, that I am useless enough in this world." (p. 520)

Rokesmith challenges her to an attempt at self-exploration.

> "Oh, don't speak of *me*," said Bella, giving herself an impatient little slap with her glove. "You don't know me as well as—"
>
> "As you know yourself?" suggested the Secretary, finding that she stopped. "*Do* you know yourself?" (p. 521)

After her conversation with Lizzie, Bella is able to say,

> "Can you believe, Mr. Rokesmith," said Bella, "that I feel as if whole years had passed since I went into Lizzie Hexam's cottage?" (p. 530)

Just as John Harmon has great difficulty fitting the changes of personality to the events of time, so Bella feels as if she has aged years in a few minutes. It can be accounted for only by fundamental alterations in the sense of self, so that one looks back at oneself as at a stranger. The process of seeing the past truthfully is not one to be discarded at any time. Bella is right in resisting, however kindly the intention, her father's desire to present her past in the most favourable light through the prejudice of his love.

> "A vexatious—"
>
> "No, you weren't," said Pa.
>
> "A vexatious (do you hear, sir?), a vexatious, capricious, thankless, troublesome Animal; but I hope you'll do better in the time to come, and I bless you and forgive you!" Here, she quite forgot that it was Pa's turn to make the responses, and clung to his neck. (p. 663)

Her famous plea to her husband not to love her, as it were, for granted, on trust, but to withhold his judgement of her until her strength and fidelity and reliance are proved, has a splendid dignity and yet a poignant ring to it.

> "Stop, sir! No, John dear! Seriously! Please not yet awhile! I want to be something so much worthier than the doll in the doll's house." (p. 679)

Thus Bella and John, by mutual assistance, form their duett, their beautiful marriage, not in the garden or the country cottage of so many novels, but in the city itself.

Not only these two but Wrayburn also undergo this process of self-recognition and regeneration, though his beating and recovery recall the baptismal sicknesses that accompany so many conversions from Oliver's to Pip's. Wrayburn, however, partakes of this novel's much more careful treatment of psychological process. First he confesses he does not know himself, "Upon my soul, don't know. I know less about myself than about most people in the world, and I don't know," (p. 285) though one cannot help feeling that his effort to do so is but half-hearted.

Wrayburn is after all the last of the feckless idle young men, like Harthouse in *Hard Times,* whom Shaw calls,

> . . . an Idler, and therefore a man bound to find some trick of thought and speech that reduces the world to a thing as empty and purposeless and hopeless as himself.[1]

We recognize here one of the most persistent of all the characters in Dickens, and the list of such rakes would be a long one, up to and including part of Pip. Wrayburn is not a simple figure, however; he is a man in conflict.

> He looked at her with a real sentiment of remorseful tenderness and pity. It was not strong enough to impel him to sacrifice himself and spare her, but it was a strong emotion. (p. 692)

As the novel progresses we find him actively beginning to dislike himself.

> ". . . for I am wearily out of sorts with one Wrayburn who cuts a sorry figure, and I would far rather be out of sorts with somebody else." (p. 697)

What changes him is his presence on the brink of death, his dying as his old self and returning as new, thus bearing out the theme of the novel. Once again the Hamlet change is referred to as Wrayburn suggests that he is not mad but sane now, whole indeed. " 'I can say to you of the healthful music of my pulse what Hamlet said of his.' " (p. 812) The change in him reminds us, in the following description, of Esther's affliction and the beauty her husband still sees in her, as Wrayburn appears "irradiated" to those who love him, Lightwood and Lizzie.

> The glow that shone upon him as he spoke the words so irradiated his features, that he looked, for the time, as though he had never been mutilated. (p. 813)

It is Lizzie who has resurrected him, saving him first from the river and then by her love holding him in this world by making this world a place of meaning and purpose.

> "Lizzie," said Eugene, after a silence: "when you see me wandering away from this refuge that I have so ill deserved, speak to me by my name, and I think I shall come back."
>
> "Yes, dear Eugene."
>
> "There!" he exclaimed, smiling. "I should have gone then but for that!" (p. 753)

The identity quest is finally underlined by this focus on the name, the intimacy of the Christian name taking its significance from Lizzie's recognition.

Nothing in the novel is more pervasive than this play on the idea of the mysteries of life and death. Much is made of Rogue's drowning. He is all but given up for dead and later suggests that others had no right to revive him. Contrast this with Wrayburn, who is explicitly described in terms of death by water.

> This frequent rising of a drowning man from the deep, to sink again, was dreadful to the beholders. But gradually the change stole upon him that it became dreadful to himself. His desire to impart something that was on his mind, his unspeakable yearning to have speech with his friend and make a communication to him, so troubled him when he recovered consciousness, that its term was thereby shortened. As the man rising from the deep would disappear the sooner for fighting with the water, so he in his desperate struggle went down again. (p. 740)

Dickens is at his most philosophical as he speculates on where, to what limbo, a man who is suspended between life and death resorts.

> If you are not gone for good, Mr. Riderhood, it would be something to know where you are hiding at present. This flabby lump of mortality that we work so hard at with such patient perseverance, yields no sign of you. If you are gone for good, Rogue, it is very solemn, and if you are coming back, it is hardly less so. Nay, in the suspense and mystery of the latter question, involving that of where you may be now, there is a solemnity even added to that of death, making us who are in

> attendance alike afraid to look on you and to look off you, and making those below start at the least sound of a creaking plank in the floor. (p. 444)

There is much awe in Dickens' treatment of the mystery of life itself. The men who attend Rogue become poignantly absorbed in the struggle for his recovery as they identify with the life-spark itself, the magic energy they preciously share.

> All the best means are at once in action, and everybody present lends a hand, and a heart and soul. No one has the least regard for the man: with them all, he has been an object of avoidance, suspicion, and aversion; but the spark of life within him is curiously separable from himself now, and they have a deep interest in it, probably because it *is* life, and they are living and must die. (p. 443)

On his recovery one of the men expresses the hope that Riderhood will use his priceless gift, as Harmon and Wrayburn use it, to better purpose, since its price ought now to be dear. " 'It's to be hoped he'll make a better use of his life,' says Bob Glamour, 'than I expect he will.' " (p. 446) This is not to be and Rogue immediately resumes his brutalized and sadistic existence. Just as he underlines and contrasts to the water-rebirth theme, of which his is the antithesis, so he also has his double in Bradley Headstone. With consummate brilliance Dickens creates his double, not by facial or physical appearance, for his last wish is to stretch our credulity now. He does it by the clothing assumed deliberately for the purpose.

> Truly, Bradley Headstone had taken careful note of the honest man's dress in the course of that night-walk they had had together. He must have committed it to memory, and slowly got it by heart. It was exactly reproduced in the dress he now wore. And whereas, in his own schoolmaster clothes, he usually looked as if they were the clothes of some other man, he now looked, in the clothes of some other man, or men, as if they were his own. (p. 631)

Headstone, as Rogue notes, has a name which suggests the graveyard. It is in a graveyard that he confronts Lizzie and smashes his hand on the wall in one of the most powerful and penetrating psychological scenes in fiction, as he turns his frustration and insecurity first onto Lizzie and then onto Wrayburn. Headstone must project his self-loathing in order to live with himself, and in his dialogue with the lawyers he reveals his guilt and self-doubt so clearly that Eugene can say, " 'A curious monamaniac,' . . . . 'The man seems to believe that everybody was acquainted with his mother!' " (p. 294) So obsessed with a necessary hatred does he become that he must in fact work to keep his murderous impulse alive. Dickens understands this state of mind with an uncanny perception.

> The state of the man was murderous, and he knew it. More; he irritated it, with a kind of perverse pleasure akin to that which a sick man sometimes has in irritating a wound upon his body. Tied up all day with his disciplined show upon him, subdued to the performance of his routine of educational tricks, encircled by a gabbling crowd, he broke loose at night like an ill-tamed wild animal. Under his daily restraint, it was his compensation, not his trouble, to give a glance towards his state at night, and to the freedom of its being indulged. If great criminals told the truth—which, being great criminals, they do not—they would very rarely tell of their struggles against the crime. Their struggles are towards it. They buffet with opposing waves to gain the bloody shore, not to recede from it. This man perfectly comprehended that he hated his rival with his strongest and worst forces, and that if he tracked him to Lizzie Hexam, his so doing would never serve himself with her, or serve her. All his pains were taken, to the end that he might incense himself with the sight of the detested figure in her company and favour, in her place of concealment. (p. 546)

The man can justify himself, so deep is his self-dislike, only by this cultivated intensity of projecting his suffering, entirely self-made, upon Wrayburn. It is a toss-up between self-destruction and murder, and either way it is a deep death wish and might be a case history from Karl Menninger.

> It was fierce, and full of purpose; but the purpose might have been as much against himself as against another. If he had stepped back for a spring, taken a leap, and thrown himself in, it would have been no surprising sequel to the look. Perhaps his troubled soul, set upon some violence, did hover for the moment between that violence and another. (p. 636)

The schoolmaster's name not only suggests death by an incapacity for love, but there is also the quality of death, of impenetrability in his unchangeable, unconvertible, non-regenerative mind, which remains fixed in its obsessions. What hurts Headstone is not the loss of love but the blow to his shaky pride, built not on self-respect but on self-contempt. He is rejected by the girl he would raise up. Headstone and Riderhood then are parallel cases and become one figure, almost literally in their final scene where the lock-keeper follows the teacher's every step. They are the precisely inverted use of John Harmon. He started out as two and in his double's death found his own redemption; in the water alone he becomes the I, having thrown away the worst part of himself, so to speak. The teacher and Riderhood, by contrast, start as two, grow closer together until they are linked in a watery grave at the weir, the teacher having embraced the monstrous side of his destructive nature embodied in Rogue.

> Riderhood went over into the smooth pit backward, and Bradley Headstone upon him. When the two were found, lying under the ooze and scum behind one of the rotting gates, Riderhood's hold had relaxed, probably in falling, and his eyes were staring upward. But he was girdled still with Bradley's iron ring, and the rivets of the iron ring held tight. (p. 802)

It is obvious that class plays a major part in the novel and affects the lives of most of its characters. Bradley is driven by his desire to climb and Charley becomes infected with this obsession. Podsnap refuses to recognize that any world other than his own exists and the Veneerings have wrenched themselves into a new class. Eugene is almost destroyed by his belief in a class-barrier between himself and Lizzie, and I cannot resist noting that his name invites us to think of breeding and inheritance. Bella is made unhappy by her desire to be a lady. Boffin parodies all this by his rôle of miser-guarding-newly-gained-riches. It is Dickens' intention to point to the concept of class as a killing mode of perception. That such a view partializes, fragments its subscribers is made perfectly clear. To see oneself in terms of class is to close off one's imagination, producing a false and diminishing view of one's own humanity and subsequently distorting the humanity of others. Georgiana, in such a system, is cruelly squeezed into a concept and becomes "the young person"; Twemlow becomes one more piece of furniture in a Veneering world of things, where all reality is reduced to furnishing; Headstone becomes a predatory killer. Nowhere in Dickens is class explored, or perhaps even seen, as such a totally pervasive, destructive concept as it is in *Our Mutual Friend*. Concluding his novel with a disarmingly simple redefinition of "gentleman," Dickens is, in fact, aspiring to put all social value on a profoundly new moral footing. " 'I beg to say that when I use the word gentleman, I use it in the sense in which the degree may be attained by any man.' " (pp. 819-20) The speaker is Twemlow, but the meaning is clearly his creator's, who intends not only a new concept of the word but a literal rendering of it. To say that any man can be a gentleman is tantamount to saying that any man can achieve moral redemption, for it is obvious that in a narrow social sense not just any man can be a gentleman in 1865. The point is that there is no significance to any status except in moral terms.

Behind all this action in the novel is the figure of the Golden Dustman, Nicodemus Boffin. It is tempting to move from the water imagery to a discussion of death, money and feces in a kind of Freudian analysis, but it is hardly helpful and less than necessary. Dust clearly is linked with old Harmon and the legacy and with death in terms of dead values and anti-life pursuits. A man can redeem his own life by self-knowledge and love. So too can dusty death, ill-gotten wealth and social power be redeemed by moral conviction and love.

> These two ignorant and unpolished people had guided themselves so far on in their journey of life, by a religious sense of duty and desire to do right. Ten thousand weaknesses and absurdities might have been detected in the breasts of both; ten thousand vanities additional, possibly, in the breast of the women. But the hard wrathful and sordid nature that had wrung as much work out of them as could be got in their best days, for as little money as could be paid to hurry on their worst, had never been so warped but that it knew their moral straightness and respected it. In its own despite, in a constant conflict with itself and them, it had done so. *And this is the eternal law*. For, Evil often stops short at itself and dies with the doer of it! but Good, never. (p. 101, my italics)

This is an allusion to and inversion of Anthony's oration over Caesar. The Boffin story puts into perspective the themes of ethical, social and moral values by which life may be lived. Boffin works in and with dust and knows its limitations.

> "My dear Mr. Boffin, everything wears to rags," said Mortimer, with a light laugh.

> "I won't go so far as to say everything," returned Mr. Boffin, on whom his manner seemed to grate, "because there's some things that I never found among the dust." (p. 91)

Love is not found in the dust, nor is life, but dust may be made into gold and then, with a kind of moral alchemy, made into the golden heart. Boffin is the alchemist and in passing through his hands the dust is converted. Boffin is a kind of Prospero with his stick for a wand, making the world accord to his larger vision of possibility, practicing psychotherapy instead of older magic, and finally, after bringing about the proper marriage, relinquishing his power to its rightful possessors who shall inherit the earth. There is a kind of joyous exuberance in Dickens' portrayal of Boffin's pretense, a relish that the author shares with his character, and he plants plentiful and ironic clues to enable us to penetrate the game, as when he says to Harmon, " 'You wouldn't like it if it was your money.' " Boffin's pleasure in the rôle is easily understood and shared and both the reader and the character can take a cathartic pleasure in it through their absolute security as to his character. Indeed it is because of Boffin's dependability that he can act the part so perfectly and never be tainted by the rôle, for he is rôle-free, the totally liberated man.

> A kind of illegibility, though a different kind, stole over Mr. Boffin's face. Its old simplicity of expression got masked by a certain craftiness that assimilated even his good-humour to itself. His very smile was cunning, as if he had been studying smiles among the portraits of his misers. Saving an occasional burst of impatience, or coarse assertion of his mastery, his good humour remained to him, but it had now a sordid alloy of distrust; and though his eyes should twinkle and all his face should laugh, he would sit holding himself in his own arms, as if he had an inclination to hoard himself up, and must always grudgingly stand on the defensive. (p. 472)

Dickens knows acting and he knows how rôles function on and off the stage. So here again we have an echo of earlier material from *Nicholas Nickleby*. Nothing could be more surprising than to find the most recent criticism complaining that Boffin turns out not to be like Dancer and Elwes and the other marvellous misers, who were never real anyway, after all.

One of the biggest disappointments in literature occurs in *Our Mutual Friend* at the moment when we discover that

> Boffin's moral degeneration has been nothing but a well-intentioned sham.[2]

Only a complete misunderstanding of the moral force of this comedy could ask for Dickens to be Hardy. Dickens never fooled us for a minute. We know him and Boffin too well for that and it was never his intention. Boffin and his creator take a proper delight in the "Mew-mew, Quack-quack, Bow-wow-wow" of Boffin excelling himself in his part and doing so well that even Harmon, in on the game all along, looks at him as though he is slightly mad. This is just as priceless as Wegg's declining and falling and finally asserting that Boffin has corrupted his mind by forcing him to read so much about misers. The reader who cannot still roar with delight at all this had best turn his attention to somebody other than the "inimitable." I cannot escape the Prospero feeling about Boffin or the idea that Dickens is sprinkling jokes about himself and his art when he presents us Wegg's private, as opposed to public, readings.

> "You see," returned Mr. Boffin, with a confidential sense of dignity, "as to my literary man's duties, they're clear. Professionally he declines and falls, and as a friend he drops into poetry." (p. 98)

It is tempting to regard this "literary man," writing at the end of his career, as Dickens himself, declining and falling in sad earnest, but nevertheless dropping into sublimest "poetry."

To go on writing of *Our Mutual Friend* is to indulge oneself in the endless riches of the novel, almost to write it out again in pleasure and admiration. In addition to all the themes explored above, one might show how these personal stories are related to the general social picture, how politics and institutional responses are derided in contrast to the charity of the loving heart. We might notice how thoroughly the themes are all underlined and kept ever-present by innumerable, apparently casual references. Wegg comments on John Harmon:

> "A double look, you mean, sir," rejoins Wegg, playing bitterly upon the word. "That's *his* look. Any amount of singular look for me, but not a double look!" (p. 306)

This remark needs no explanation, save that now we see the richness of irony in the speaker's respect for the "singular." Jenny

Wren's frustration with "Mr. Dolls," her father, when she says, "'I'd give the dustman five shillings to carry you off in the dust cart,'" (p. 532) brings before us half the novel. Even more superb is Mr. Venus' key passage when, summing up and synthesizing the book's whole object, he replies to

> "Never say die, sir! A man of your mark!"
>
> "It's not so much saying it that I object to," returned Mr. Venus, "as doing it. And having got to do it whether or no, I can't afford to waste my time on groping for nothing in cinders." (p. 478)

Even more surprising is the continual play upon the word "will." We have seen how Dickens confronts the problem of past and present and nothing suggests this problem more clearly than the use of the will. Bella revives the whole issue of John Harmon's attempt to escape his father's will, an attempt rendered successful by his acquiring the love of Bella and thus substituting her "will" for his father's written command:

> "My dear Bella," replied the cherub, still pathetically scared, "and my dear John Rokesmith, if you will allow me so to call you—"
>
> "Yes, do, Pa, do!" urged Bella. "*I* allow you, and my will is his law. Isn't it—dear John Rokesmith?" (p. 607)

The opening of Chapter 16 of the last book of *Our Mutual Friend* suggests the making of arrangements akin to the making of a will. That wills should be made and carried out by live testators is the entire point of this novel, which begins and ends with death and wills. John Harmon's quest is for freedom, just as Bella's desire to be liberated from the "doll's house" is really a wish to be free to form herself, make her own choices, and be able to love by her own will, rather than by somebody else's. Lizzie enrages Headstone by not acceding to his "will." Wegg's disappointment derives from dependence on somebody else's "will." Eugene is hampered by his father's "will." The power of "wills" is a metaphoric pun central to all the events of the novel, and, along with the power of the concept of class, leads us to the conclusion that the entire force of the novel is directed to imaging forth the necessity for moral liberation. Dickens has tried to compress into this work the whole vision of radical redemption through means that are sometimes fortuitous and sometimes psychological but always obtainable. It is a moral vision based on faith that there is meaning, that the world can be seen to make sense and human beings can attain accord with it.

> And oh, there are days in this life, worth life and worth death. And oh, what a bright old song it is, that oh, 'tis love, 'tis love, 'tis love, that makes the world go round! (p. 671)

Love is the key that actually keeps the spheres in their places and man in his sphere and reconciled to a world where life and death are among those laws of being to which he thankfully submits. One must aim to have

> "A heart well worth winning, and well won. A heart that, once won, goes through fire and water for the winner, and never changes, and is never daunted." (p. 529)

When one has such a heart it may be given and will in turn receive the same gift. It has all come to this.

The afterword to *Our Mutual Friend* conveys even more strongly the sense of the "great inimitable" bidding a final farewell to his beloved and loving readers. When he rescues Bella Wilfer and her friends from the train it is, as he says, with a consciousness of the death that he has narrowly escaped and with a profound awareness, as he conveys it in this novel, of the kinds of resurrection possible for us and worth working for.

> On Friday the Ninth of June in the present year, Mr. and Mrs. Boffin (in their manuscript dress of receiving Mr. and Mrs. Lammle at breakfast) were on the South-Eastern Railway with me, in a terribly destructive accident. When I had done what I could to help others, I climbed back into my carriage—nearly turned over a viaduct, and caught aslant upon the turn—to extricate the worthy couple. They were much soiled, but otherwise unhurt. The same happy result attended Miss Bella Wilfer on her wedding day, and Mr. Riderhood inspecting Bradley Headstone's red neckerchief as he lay asleep. I remember with devout thankfulness that I can never be much nearer parting company with my readers for ever than I was then, until there shall be written against my life, the two words with which I have this day closed this book: —THE END. (p. 822)

[1]George Bernard Shaw, "*Hard Times*," *The Dickens Critics*, p. 134.

[2]Smith, *Dickens, Money, and Society*, p. 182.

CONCLUSION

For Mercy has a human heart,
Pity a human face,
And Love, the human form divine,
And Peace, the human dress.

And all must love the human form,
In heathen, turk, or jew;
Where Mercy, Love, and Pity dwell
There God is dwelling too.

WILLIAM BLAKE

•

And so the deep enthusiastic joy,
The rapture of the Hallelujah sent
From all that breathes and is, was chasten'd, stemm'd
And balanced by a Reason which indeed
Is reason; duty and pathetic truth;
And God and Man divided, as they ought,
Between them the great system of the world
Where Man is sphered, and which God animates.

WILLIAM WORDSWORTH

•

In one of the most sensitive and intelligent books on Dickens, when he begins to discuss "The Social and Political Issues," Monroe Engel says,

> In Dickens' novels, characters are cast in detailed and purposeful social situations, and an evaluated social world is created. Yet even those critics who agree roughly that this is so, and agree further on the stature of these novels, disagree markedly as to Dickens' own politics and view of society—disagree in fundamental respects, that is, on what disposition of mind lies behind and shapes these novels.[1]

I have tried to add one more dimension to our estimate of "the disposition of mind" that produced this fiction. An appreciation of the richness of Dickens' imagination and the power of his perception seems hardly necessary or justifiable, though it is impossible to read Dickens and not experience again, as though for the first time, that sense of wonder and awe that occurs in the presence of great art. Nor is it necessary to list the talents and techniques that have so amply been exposed by the thousands of critical items that have accumulated over the years. I am struck rather by the impression of coherence that it is possible to feel in a survey of the Dickens canon. The mind that looks at man and informs the pages of the fourteen novels from *Pickwick* to *Our Mutual Friend*, is relentlessly insistent on the framework in which it comprehends its world. It is a visionary mind, able to grasp, by the power of its imagination, the possibility of some altered state of society and some better set of values than those which it encounters. Dickens is a moralist, supported by a religious faith. The tradition of his English Christianity is powerful in giving shape to his vision. As a humanist, however, Dickens absorbs and reshapes his religious awareness into something quite different from an orthodox theology or a codified ritual practice. It is a religious impulse that tries to distill the humanistic spirit of Christianity and breathe it into the yearning of the fiction for a more humane world. Christ becomes for Dickens the perfect man. As the fiction proceeds one gains the impression of deeper and deeper compassion for man and his inability to be perfect. Death becomes, for the older Dickens, the inescapable condition regardless of the quality of the individual life. Thus it is that the gradual shift occurs from a mere goodness of heart and generosity of impulse as the celebrated virtue to a more profound compassion, an identification with the mortality of other human beings. Social goodness and charity are not enough, not even when they finally become the goodness and charity of the individual heart. The heart must be disciplined as well as charitable. The movement is from images of goodness, from Cheeryble philanthropy, to a disciplined self-knowledge and understanding. Indeed, Dickens comes to question whether real goodness, the redemption of the individual first and his compassion for others thereafter, is possible without the quest for the truth about oneself and unless the truth about oneself encompasses the recognition that one must die. The hardest realities must be faced as fully as is humanly possible. Dickens' work appears to become increasingly existential, increasingly profound, more and more penetrating until we reach the metaphysical speculation of *Our Mutual Friend.* Thus it is that the humanistic and Christian quality of all his work becomes ever more Stoical. Acceptance of and reconciliation with the world and with death come to be seen as preconditions for redemption and social change. No theoretical system or panacea will make life meaningful. Only this profound self-searching will produce the *ataraxia,* the peace of mind and the freedom to love from which all good and right action stems. Dickens sees this as a truth, but it is another thing to show how it may be realized. So it is that we find the increasing emphasis on and exploration of human psychology in the novels. Without benefit of theology there is dependence on psychology, which must indeed become central to modern religion. The mentors in Dickens are not priests, who come off rather badly, imprisoned in their formulae and rhetoric. Nor is there the new priest, the psychoanalyst, to whom Miss Wade or Bradley Headstone might turn in their desperation. Mostly there is experience itself and man alone facing it. The women, like Florence and Agnes, who point "upwards," are mysteries and we regard those who can depend upon them as simply fortunate. Yet when we arrive at Rokesmith and Boffin we come upon a process as old as the quest for truth itself, clothed in modern psychoanalytic garb, but with a moral base.

In the case of Dr. Manette, who, as might be expected, has a great deal of insight into his own psychic disorder, Dickens reveals how deeply interested and profoundly aware he is of the systems of rationalization, evasion, substitution, projection and their therapy. Miss Pross and Mr. Lorry discuss the case prior to the latter undertaking some treatment.

> "It's a dreadful remembrance. Besides that, his loss of himself grew out of it. Not knowing how he lost himself, or how he recovered himself, he may never feel certain of not losing himself again. That alone wouldn't make the subject pleasant, I should think."
>
> It was a profounder remark than Mr. Lorry had looked for. "True," said he, "and fearful to reflect upon. Yet, a doubt lurks in my mind, Miss Pross, whether it is good for Doctor Manette to have that suppression always shut up within him." (*Tale of Two Cities*, p. 192)

The reader will remember that Manette reverts to withdrawal and plays the rôle of mechanic shoe-maker when pressure, or reversion to his past, occur. His evasion of the truth is connected with the difficulty of eradicating the impulse to avenge his wrongs. The passage in which the case is discussed is a piece of modern clinical description, astounding, given the date of the novel. " 'Be explicit,' said the Doctor. 'Spare no detail.' " (*Tale of Two Cities,* p. 190) The good doctor realizes fully that in some cases the truth cannot be told.

> "You have no idea how such an apprehension weighs on the sufferer's mind, and how difficult—how almost impossible—it is, for him to force himself to utter a word upon the topic that oppresses him."
>
> "Would he," asked Mr. Lorry, "be sensibly relieved if he could prevail upon himself to impart that secret brooding to any one, when it is on him?"
>
> "I think so. But it is, as I have told you, next to impossible. I even believe it—in some cases—to be quite impossible." (*Tale of Two Cities,* 92)

There is much more to the same effect. As one looks at Dombey's struggle with himself and Miss Wade's neurosis and Rosa Dartle's bitterness and all the other cases of aberration, until one arrives at Headstone on the one hand and Bella on the other, one realizes just how central the subjects of psychological exploration and its moral relevance are in the fiction and how thoroughly they have been integrated into Dickens' work and his view of the human situation.

This is only one side of the picture. Dickens knows that the strength and courage to be, the impulse to undertake a quest for meaning at all, must derive from something outside of man. Therefore, we find God in every novel. The critics have wanted to regard this religious presence as sentiment or cliché or concession to social taste, but it is much more than that. A faith in universal order and in the possibility of the meaningful life, a profound belief in the dignity and supreme value of man, derives from an individual's sense of place in a grand design. Given this faith, the process of living may become dynamic and purposeful. One cannot dig for treasure unless one grants that it may be there. It cannot on the other hand be found without digging. When the individual arrives at the truth about himself and at a reconciliation with his being human, when he is capable of realizing the love and compassion that may consequently occur, then he also can discover a truth and order and compassion in the world and its design. Inner harmony accords at last with a harmony that has been present all along. Dickens' vision of a better world is not a vision of another world but of this one seen and celebrated. Dickens might be the meek man addressing Podsnap.

> He was not aware (the meek man submitted of himself) that he was driving at any ization. He had no favourite ization that he knew of. (*Our Mutual Friend,* pp. 140-41)

He may be Mr. Boffin hiding behind the smiling alligator.

> The yard or two of smile on the part of the alligator might have been invested with the meaning, "All about this was quite familiar knowledge down in the depths of the slime, ages ago." (*Our Mutual Friend*, p. 583)

Most assuredly he is Mr. Riah when he reveals a perspective that is larger than usual, by showing us the necessity of a divinely ordered time and space superior to any improvements we could devise in a Satanic wish to make new worlds in our own images.

> "You had better change Is into Was and Was into Is, and keep them so."
>
> "Would that suit your case? Would you not be always in pain then?" asked the old man tenderly. (*Our Mutual Friend,* p. 435)

Riah, from the wisdom of ancient suffering, knows that any world we, like Satan, would make in our arrogance, would be infinitely more painful than the one designed for us. We, as readers, are tempted to say to Dickens what Jenny says to her mentor and father-surrogate.

> "Right!" exclaimed Miss Wren with another chop. "You have changed me wiser, godmother.—" (*Our Mutual Friend,* p. 435)

[1]Engel, *The Maturity of Dickens,* p. 33.